365 Daily
Affirmations
to Attract the
*Life You Want*

AFFIRMATIONS FOR

# manifestation

**candice nikeia**

ADAMS MEDIA
NEW YORK LONDON TORONTO SYDNEY NEW DELHI

**A**adamsmedia

Adams Media
An Imprint of Simon & Schuster, Inc.
100 Technology Center Drive
Stoughton, Massachusetts 02072

Copyright © 2024
by Simon & Schuster, Inc.

First Adams Media hardcover edition
January 2024

ADAMS MEDIA and colophon
are registered trademarks of
Simon & Schuster, Inc.

Simon & Schuster: Celebrating
100 Years of Publishing in 2024

For information about special
discounts for bulk purchases, please
contact Simon & Schuster Special
Sales at 1-866-506-1949 or
business@simonandschuster.com.

The Simon & Schuster Speakers
Bureau can bring authors to your
live event. For more information or
to book an event, contact the
Simon & Schuster Speakers Bureau
at 1-866-248-3049 or visit our
website at www.simonspeakers.com.

Interior design by Julia Jacintho

Manufactured in the
United States of America

10 9 8 7 6 5 4 3 2 1

Library of Congress Cataloging-in-
Publication Data has been applied for.

ISBN 978-1-5072-2150-1
ISBN 978-1-5072-2151-8 (ebook)

To my family, Bruce, Cathy, and
Cortland, for teaching me the power
I have within the words I speak.

# Contents

# Introduction

Today is the day to start shifting your mindset.
Today is the day to draw on your positive energy.
Today is the day you start changing your life.

---

With *Affirmations for Manifestation*, you have the ability to transform your future and manifest your deepest desires—all with the power of daily affirmations. Affirmations are spiritual and inspirational statements designed to help you bring forth the life of your dreams. Each lovingly crafted sentence helps you tap into your inner self, alter your perception of the world around you, and change negative habits and quirks. When you manifest your highest vibrations through affirmations in your daily life, they can help you create abundance, love, and achievement.

*Affirmations for Manifestation* is a powerful tool for personal growth and self-discovery—use it to express trust, gratitude, and confidence in what the Universe has for you. Throughout the first part of the book, you'll learn how manifestation helps you overcome the roadblocks holding you back from your best life, why manifestation and affirmations are key to self-transformation, how to get the most out of this daily spiritual practice, and more.

Explore Part Two to find 365 daily affirmations that cover finding career and financial abundance, cultivating relationships, nurturing your health and wellness, embracing self-love, unlocking your spirituality, and so much more. Each transformative affirmation will help you revolutionize your mindset and create positive change toward your goals.

Each day, approach your manifestation practice with an open mind and heart, and remember to fully embrace the power of affirmations to help you actualize the goals that are core to your being. Every morning, read out loud an affirmation that speaks to you, feeling every word with excitement and gratitude, and freely share your affirmations with others. Not every day's affirmation will align with your manifestation goals for the day, so feel free to flip forward or back to find the affirmation that works best for you. Mark up, sticky note, or dog-ear pages that resonate with you for easy access when you need them. Allow this book to be your "go-to" when you're in need of manifesting change for despair or grief, but also as you experience excitement and celebration.

So, take a deep breath, let go of your doubts and fears, and trust the power of affirmations to help you manifest the life you desire. Let this book be the help you need to reach all your goals. Remember: You are a powerful creator, and nothing can stop you from achieving your greatest desires! With this cleansing and empowering feeling of motivation, let's dive into your manifestation journey.

# PART ONE

---

# Introducing Affirmations for Manifestation

Unleash the limitless potential in your life. Whether you're chasing career dreams, craving amazing relationships, or vibing with the Universe, get ready to transform your world. Tap into your inner spirit, where true magic happens, and watch your desires come to life. It's time to spice it up with affirmations: positive, goal-oriented statements that help achieve manifestation. Dive into the power of manifesting and how affirmations can make your wildest dreams a reality.

Welcome to the exciting realm of *Affirmations for Manifestation*. This amazing guide will show you how to alter your daily routine with affirmations and support your unique journey toward becoming your highest, most incredible self. You are now entering a transformative adventure in the world of manifesting, affirmations, and the incredible ways they intertwine. Let the magic begin!

## What Is Manifestation?

If you're seeking a way to align your desired reality with your day-to-day, step into the realm of manifestation! Manifestation is a daily spiritual practice that lovingly combines focusing on positive thoughts, vibrations, and goals; offering those intentions to the Universe; and having higher powers bring your desires into existence. But it's not enough to just wait for the Universe to take care of your dreams for you; it's up to you to commit to accepting and making positive changes. Plus, to fully absorb the magic of this practice, reflect on these important steps for manifesting:

- *Know what you want.* To transform your reality, encourage clarity in your mind. Dreaming of a new career path? Picture daily life following your passions.
- *Release negativity.* Positivity is vital in transforming your life. Trust that the Universe is working for the highest good of everyone, and kick any limiting beliefs to the curb. Remember: You are a powerful, authentic spiritual being.

- *Embrace your role as cocreator of your destiny.* While the Universe is certainly full of power, your action toward your goals uplifts your spirit and sense of resolve.
- *Be flexible with your expectations.* Sometimes your highest good looks different from what you had planned. Going into things with flexible expectations helps you adapt to wherever you end up, even if it's a totally new experience.

When you're clear about your desired reality, stay positive, act, and embrace flexibility, you're on the road to successful manifestation.

## How Affirmations Help You Manifest Your Dream Life

Affirmations are empowering, mindful statements that fuel your mind with positivity and unleash a cascade of change, directing you toward your dream life. Most effective when used daily, these uplifting, spoken sentences alter the way you think about yourself and invite an influx of positivity into your inner world—which makes them a powerful manifestation tool that can help you will your desires into existence! When you use affirmations to support the magic of manifestation, you amplify the vibrations of your goals while transforming your innermost self into its highest version. For example, when trying to manifest confidence in the workplace, affirming you are confident and professional begins to change your mindset.

Your daily affirmations broadcast a signal to the Universe, ensuring the higher power understands your intent and helps you actualize the highest outcomes. By repeating your affirmations, you'll uncover personal truths, rid yourself of bad habits, and manifest your dreams. As you delve into the realm of affirmation as a tool for manifesting, you'll discover their profound impact on your mindset, confidence, and overall well-being. Your words have boundless potential in the pursuit of your goals.

# Receive Life-Changing Benefits by Manifesting Through Affirmations

Tap into the positive vibes from the Universe to allow for some truly amazing things to happen! When you infuse your day with manifestation magic, your thoughts, feelings, and even reality itself will take an uplifting and cleansing breath. Brace yourself for an upgrade in your mental, emotional, and physical well-being, thanks to the superpowers of optimistic and intentional speech.

## Cleanse Yourself of Stress and Anxiety

Stress can harsh the vibes of both your amazing body and mind. While a little stress can give your immune system a boost, long-term stress can bring about health issues like diabetes and depression. Fortunately, daily affirmations combat stress and anxiety. Manifestation knocks out those daily pesky worries.

## Uplift Your Mood

The dynamic duo of manifestation and affirmations greatly uplifts your mood. If you've been feeling down for an extended period, these positive tools can help counteract harmful negative self-talk. Replace spiraling thoughts such as "I'll never achieve anything" with empowering statements like "I am enough."

## Celebrate Yourself by Working On Your Self-Image

Affirmations of self-love and manifesting confidence allow you to fully embrace and celebrate your amazing qualities and can help you find ways to rid yourself of unwanted habits and traits. When envious of a friend, practice gratitude by affirming your appreciation for the abundant blessings the Universe has bestowed upon you. Embrace the power to reveal new and improved sides of your being, leading to personal growth.

# Explore Your Dream Manifestation Categories

*Affirmations for Manifestation* has a year's worth of affirmations for you to speak aloud. As you delve into its pages, you'll discover that many manifestations can be grouped into a handful of categories. It's up to you to identify which of these topics align most closely with your current aspirations. Remember to explore categories you may want to manifest first as you embark on this exciting journey of self-discovery and intentional creation.

## Seek Career and Financial Abundance

If you want to turn your hobby into a career or seek a more stable income, manifesting success in business and financial abundance is a valuable goal. By aligning your intentions and actions, you can manifest the success and financial abundance you desire.

## Cultivate Relationships

Are you mustering the courage to manifest a romantic partner who sweeps you off your feet? Or perhaps you want to cultivate meaningful friendships? Relationships hold immense importance in our lives. Through the power of manifestation, speak your intentions into existence and attract the company of others.

## Nurture Your Health and Wellness

Before fostering meaningful connections and personal growth, you must focus inward and manifest physical, emotional, and mental health. Nurturing yourself in these areas sets the stage for receiving abundant blessings from the Universe. Through the practice of affirmations, you ensure that the Universe hears you.

### Embrace Your Awesomeness with Self-Love

Gazing into the mirror and declaring your love for yourself may feel vulnerable, but the rewards are immeasurable. Manifest a life where you exude genuine confidence and inner love, and witness how it empowers you to fearlessly pursue and achieve your dreams.

### Unlock Your Spirituality

Through the repetition of affirmations, you can manifest a profound connection with the Universe, unlocking a gateway to spiritual growth and enlightenment. As you delve deeper into the realm of manifestation, you may find yourself drawn to other spiritual practices such as meditation or yoga, opening yourself up to a world of spiritual serenity and inner wisdom.

# Maximize the High Vibrations of Your Manifestation Journey with Affirmations

With your new and deeper understanding of manifestation, you may now unlock the secrets of harmonizing affirmations with your journey. The affirmations in this book focus on the present, are specific, and are filled with positivity. To maximize their potential, speak them with conviction, repeat them often, adapt them, and practice gratitude.

### Make Your Affirmations Crystal Clear

When speaking affirmations, it is essential to be specific and crystal clear about your desired outcomes, allowing the Universe to easily receive your message. For instance, if you aim to enhance your physical health, use "I am strong and flexible." Less specific affirmations, such as "I am healthy," may result in fewer colds, weight loss, or improved sleep, which don't align with your intended manifestation goals.

## Empower Your Affirmations with Positive Vibes

Throughout this book, you'll encounter affirmations that are positive in nature. Rather than using phrases like "I am not a failure," the affirmations focus on empowering statements such as "I am successful." By consciously choosing positive phrasing, you won't focus on failure and instead will allow your mind to embrace the uplifting message of success.

## Enhance Your Conviction with Present Tense

The most impactful affirmations are crafted in the present tense, reflecting the belief that you have already achieved your desired goal. Present-tense affirmations enhance your conviction. However, you'll notice that the final sentence of each affirmation is written in future tense, which serves as a promise to continue your manifestation journey.

## Reinforce Your Goals Through Repetition

Throughout your time with this book, repeat your affirmations often. Consistency and confidence are key to harnessing their transformative power. When you discover a set of affirmations that deeply resonate with you, consider incorporating them into your daily routine. Whether it's reciting them once or ten times a day, the regular repetition of affirmations amplifies their impact.

## Project Your Intentions with Confidence

It's crucial to speak affirmations with authenticity and intention, projecting unwavering confidence. Believe wholeheartedly in yourself and the affirmations you declare. Remember, affirmations help cultivate a positive mindset, but they must be accompanied by purposeful action. Align your thoughts with your actions, merging the strength of your mindset with intentional steps toward your goals, and your possibilities are limitless.

### Practice Gratitude to Complement Your Manifestation

In addition to affirmations, cultivating a practice of gratitude is a vital component of your manifestation journey. Set aside a dedicated moment each day to deeply reflect. Appreciating family, nature, or simple pleasures allows you to receive abundant blessings from the Universe.

### Personalize Your Affirmation Journey

Navigate your affirmation journey your way! There may be days when you're drawn to past affirmations instead of following a linear progression. Make this book your ally by personalizing it to suit your needs. Dog-ear pages, highlight sentences that profoundly resonate with you, or adorn the pages with sticky notes containing your personal reflections. Consider exploring a new affirmation each day to spark fresh inspiration, or repeat your cherished favorites regularly. This book is your companion on this transformative journey, and its pages should mirror your individuality and aspirations.

# Open Your Mind to Manifesting

Venturing into the thrilling realm of manifestation through affirmations ignites a radiant fire within, revealing exhilarating possibilities. Each carefully chosen word resonating with your goals and values sets forth a transformative cascade. With dedicated and joyful practice, you rewrite the script of your subconscious mind and bring your deepest desires to life. As you conquer limiting beliefs, nurture unshakable confidence, and cultivate a tenacious mindset, you master your reality. These affirmations empower you to harness the extraordinary power of your thoughts and words, gifting you success, abundance, and self-discovery. Dive into a year-long journey and witness the magnificent tapestry of your dreams manifesting in awe-inspiring ways.

# PART TWO

---

# 365
# Affirmations
# for
# Manifestation

Now that you understand the power of manifesting through affirmations, you're ready for the next part of your affirmation journey. This section of the book is where you'll find the 365 powerful affirmations to transform your mind from the inside out. While speaking these affirmations, you will let go of negative thoughts, discard feelings of envy and disappointment, and learn to embrace an abundance mindset that will propel you to greater heights.

While on your manifestation journey, you will discover how affirmations can be a game changer for personal transformation. Negative self-talk and limiting beliefs can keep you from reaching your full potential, but replacing the negativity with these affirmations can help you rewrite your story. By accepting the meaning behind these positive affirmations, you'll start to see a real shift in your mindset and life.

Through these affirmations, you can break free from the scarcity mentality that holds you back and adopt a mindset of abundance. Make sure to repeat these affirmations to call in the abundance you deserve. Soon you'll reprogram your mind to attract more opportunities and success into your life. The result? A life full of possibilities, prosperity, and joy!

So, buckle up and get ready to continue to transform your life with these affirmations. With consistent practice and a positive attitude, you will be able to manifest your deepest desires and live a life beyond your wildest dreams.

# Engage In Daily Spiritual Practice

**I am committed to prioritizing my daily spiritual practice as a form of growth and self-nurturing.**

I commit to nourishing my mind, body, and soul with consistent spiritual rituals. My spiritual practice helps me stay centered and connected to my inner wisdom. I release any hesitancy or resistance toward dedicating time to my spiritual growth. I am at peace knowing that the Universe's wisdom and guidance are always available to me through my practice. I make time for my spiritual practice every day so that I can peacefully nurture my soul. I trust in the Universe and its support throughout my spiritual journey. My daily goal is to establish a profound connection with my higher self and the divine. My well-being is enhanced by this commitment. Ultimately, I trust that I can design a spiritual practice that caters to my growth and progress. I am thrilled to experiment with different daily spiritual methods and techniques that align with my growth. I open my heart to an unlimited and vast number of opportunities for my spiritual growth and advancement. My spiritual practice is an essential part of my daily routine, and I am dedicated to honoring this commitment. Today and going forward, I will make my daily spiritual practice a priority, and through this journey, I am embracing growth and connections to the Universe.

# DAY 2
# **Forgive Yourself and Others**

I am fully and deeply worthy of forgiveness, and I choose to forgive myself for past misunderstandings or wrongdoing.

Forgiveness is not about forgetting, but it is about releasing negative emotions and finding peace within. I am grateful for the opportunity to let go of past grievances and embrace joy and serenity in the present moment. I allow myself to take the time I need to heal and forgive, as it is a process that requires patience. With compassion and understanding, I forgive others for their past mistakes. I honor my healing journey, and I recognize that forgiveness requires self-compassion. I now free myself from negative emotions and promote healing by letting go of resentment and forgiving those who have hurt me. I am grateful to the Universe for allowing me to forgive and be forgiven. Forgiveness deepens my connections with others and offers a better understanding of the world. I learn from my mistakes with compassion and kindness. Grudges and bitterness are best left behind, and I choose to approach conflicts with a willingness and grace to resolve them. Through the act of forgiveness, I experience love, empathy, and positivity. With forgiveness as a core value, I cultivate a heart of compassion and understanding regardless of the circumstance. Daily, I will commit to practicing forgiveness to enhance my personal well-being and reach my highest potential.

# Accept Patience As a Way to Engage with the Present

*I am patient, trust the Universe's sense of time, and know that things unfold for me at the right moment and in the way they are meant to.*

I acknowledge that life moves forward in its own time and trying to rush things only causes frustration and disappointment. Instead, I accept the process and know that everything will happen as it should. Living in the present moment allows me to fully engage with the experiences of life. I recognize that developing patience requires practice and discipline. It is not an easy skill to master, but I am committed to cultivating it in all aspects of my life. Whether it is in my personal growth, relationships, or career, I commit to having patience. I am now letting go of the need for immediate results and allowing myself to enjoy the process as it guides me. I trust that the Universe is working in my favor and that my desired outcomes will manifest in due time. I am grateful for the gift of patience, as it allows me to experience life more fully, spread joy to those around me, and bring peace to my soul. Patience strengthens my relationships and deepens my connections. I choose to be patient with myself and others, knowing that it is essential for building a better future. Patience is a virtue that I am proud to embody, and I will be dedicated to nurturing it every day.

# DAY 4

## Empower Yourself Through Hardships

**I am an empowered person, capable of making positive changes and decisions for myself despite my challenges.**

I am thankful to the Universe for blessing me with my inner strength, but I acknowledge my power is also a result of my actions. The struggles I face are opportunities for me to showcase a growth-focused mindset and embrace new learning experiences. I can achieve anything when I believe in myself. When faced with unexpected obstacles, I respond with resilience and adaptability. I can bounce back from anything like a boss. I only focus on what I can control—my thoughts, feelings, and actions. I take bold steps toward my dreams, even when I feel scared or uncomfortable. My intuition and inner wisdom are my superpowers because they guide me toward making sound decisions and seeking help when needed. I possess the power to make changes to myself and my life when I need to. My unique contributions to the world make me irreplaceable and valuable. I am grateful for the strength, courage, and determination required to crush my goals and manifest my dreams into reality. I will work through my problems successfully and skillfully, radiating positivity and abundance in everything I do.

---
## DAY 5
---

# View Curiosity As
# a Vehicle for Growth

I am full of curiosity that fuels growth
in my knowledge, respect for others,
and understanding of the world.

---

My boundless curiosity and thirst for knowledge are the driving forces to move me forward on my journey. Every day, I am becoming smarter, wiser, and more open-minded. I am hungry for knowledge and eager to learn. I embrace new experiences and perspectives with a compassionate heart and mind. I love to ask questions and challenge my assumptions because I know it is essential to my personal growth and understanding of the world around me. I am curious about the world and open to new experiences that will change my life. Living with curiosity is vital to discovering my passions and purpose in life. I love that curiosity fuels my creativity and inspires me to think outside the box. The more I live life, the more I realize how much there is to discover, and that realization excites me and drives me to continue exploring. I remain curious about life, knowing that curiosity is essential for unlocking endless possibilities and opportunities for self-discovery. I am grateful for my insatiable curiosity and wonder for the world, and I embrace each day with enthusiasm and a strong desire to learn and grow. My curiosity is a gift that allows me to see the world with childlike wonder. I will continually allow my curiosity to fuel the journey toward enriching my life.

# Experience Joy
# Through Many Lenses

I am grateful for the abundant joy that flows into my heart every day, and I am committed to nurturing it within myself and those around me.

As I journey through life, I invite many sources of joy into my experience. My joy stems from spending time with my loved ones, being surrounded by nature's beauty, and engaging in activities that bring meaning to my life. I find joy in the simple pleasures of life, such as a warm cup of tea or a good book, and I savor each moment with gratitude. By embracing life's twists and turns, I am able to find joy in every experience. I know that joy is infectious, and I make a conscious effort to spread it to others by being kind, compassionate, and open to new experiences. Happiness is fleeting, but joy is a state of being that I have the ability to cultivate daily through positive thoughts and actions. Joy is an integral part of who I am, and I deserve to experience it. I know that by consciously choosing to invite joy into my life, I am creating a life filled with happiness, love, and positivity. I am surrounded by joyful people and experiences that lift me up and inspire me to spread happiness wherever I go. My life is joyful, and I will continue to radiate this positive energy out into the world, attracting abundance and love back to me in return.

# Fight Against Internal and External Discouragement

I am resilient in the face of discouraging thoughts, feelings, and words and have the capacity to think through and reason against these negative forces.

Although there may be times when I feel discouraged, I know that these feelings are only temporary because I will overcome them. I recognize my emotions and allow myself to process them, but I will not let them overwhelm me. I will hold my head up when facing discouragement, even when things are at their hardest. I can manage any obstacle that is put in front of me. I acknowledge that setbacks and failures are natural occurrences in life and that they offer opportunities for growth and learning. Therefore, I focus on the positives in my life and remind myself of my strengths and accomplishments. Even in the face of adversity, I am committed to staying motivated and persistent. I intentionally seek out people who support me and encourage me to keep going. My resilience and strength are unmatched, and discouragement will not prevent me from reaching my goals and living my best life. I am confident in my abilities and know that I can overcome any challenge that comes my way. Discouragement is a small bump in the road of my life's adventure, and I can't wait to see what exciting challenges life brings me next! I will prioritize fighting against the discouragement of my own thoughts as well as negative words from others and continue to grow.

# Let Go of Negativity

### I am brave for letting go of negativity and having optimism about the unknown.

I realize that clinging to past pains, grudges, and negative emotions only weighs me down. I relinquish any attachments to outcomes or expectations that do not align with my values and aspirations. I am like a bird, free to soar higher and higher as I let go of anything that weighs me down. I choose to go with the flow and release anything that tries to hold me back from my dreams. I let go of fear and doubt, recognizing that they only hinder my growth and prevent me from realizing my full potential. I forgive myself and others, realizing that forgiveness is a powerful tool for my development. I am choosing to live in the present moment and appreciate the opportunities it offers, rather than dwelling on the past or worrying about the future. I can do this—I can let go of what I need to release. I am surrendering to the natural flow of life, believing that I am precisely where I am supposed to be. By letting go, I am opening myself to new experiences, eager to embrace all the possibilities that come my way. I will continue to learn how to release things that no longer serve me and embrace the best version of myself.

# DAY 9

# Live with Serenity

I am serene, intentionally living life
with a sense of inner peace and calmness,
despite life's chaotic and unpredictable nature.

I welcome today with serenity throughout my mind, body, and spirit. I approach life with a centered mindset, and I am learning to not be troubled by things beyond my control. I ask the Universe to give me a sense of full serenity so that I may accept life as it is, knowing that everything is working in the way it needs to. By embracing calmness, I prioritize mindfulness and self-reflection and allow myself to be fully present and aware of my thoughts and emotions. Self-care and self-love are fundamental to me, and I recognize that they are essential for a peaceful and harmonious life. I create a peaceful and positive environment around me, surrounded by people and things that bring me joy. I am confident that I can handle—and not be stressed by—any challenge that comes my way, knowing that I am strong and capable. I am living in a state of serenity and peace, grateful for everything I have and content with where I am. My heartfelt serenity toward myself grants me the strength to face any challenges because I know they are opportunities for me to learn and grow. I will continue to face the obstacles in my path calmly and will encourage peace at the forefront of my thoughts.

# Resist the Urge to Give Up

I am a strong person with the power to fight
through points where I feel like giving up.

When I feel like giving up, I remind myself that I possess the tenacity to overcome any setback. When I choose to not give up, I exude so much magic! I can achieve anything when I believe in myself, regardless of how difficult it may seem. My goals and dreams are important to me, and I am committed to manifesting them into my reality. Regardless of any missteps, I am destined for great things. I understand that success does not come easy, but I believe that it is always worth the effort. I am determined to keep pushing forward but am wise enough to know when I need to step back and recharge. I am focusing on progress rather than perfection and taking one step at a time. I allow myself to make mistakes along the way, am compassionate to myself in response, and learn from these blunders. I believe I am deserving of success and happiness. When I struggle, I seek support from those around me, appreciating the fact that I do not have to face my challenges alone. I am grateful for the people in my life who encourage me and help me stay motivated. I am a resilient and strong individual, capable of overcoming anything. Giving up is not an option for me. In the future, I will continue to choose to persevere through my hardships and, ultimately, I know I will succeed.

# Respect Yourself
# and Those Around You

### I am a respectful person, acknowledging that every person (including me) has worth.

---

I strive to practice thinking respectfully daily, as living with respect is fundamental to cultivating healthy relationships. Whether it is toward myself or others, I believe that everyone deserves to be treated with dignity and compassion. I show respect to others regardless of their backgrounds or beliefs. When I treat myself with respect, I show others my value and how I desire to be treated. For me, respect means actively listening and communicating honestly with kindness and consideration. Everyone has a unique perspective, and I am excited to learn from others and expand my knowledge. I believe in respecting myself, both physically and emotionally, and do this by setting healthy boundaries and prioritizing self-care. When I honor and stand up for my values and beliefs, my relationships with others are influenced positively by my sense of self-respect and self-worth. Living with respect allows me to create a positive and uplifting environment for myself and others. Respect fosters trust, builds deeper connections, and promotes mutual understanding. I am grateful for opportunities to show respect every day and for the beautiful gifts respect brings to my life. It allows me to live an uplifting life full of peace and strong relationships. I will strive to practice respecting myself and those around me on a daily basis, especially when it's challenging.

# DAY 12

# Extend Acceptance to Every Part of Your Life

### I am an accepting person, I embrace challenging people and situations, and I love myself for who I am.

I believe acceptance is an integral part of my personal growth and overall well-being. Acceptance involves recognizing and embracing reality without any judgment or resistance. Whether it's dealing with people, situations, or circumstances, I'm committed to accepting them for who or what they are. I honor the importance of self-acceptance in my life. Instead of trying to change what I don't like about my life, I trust in the plans of the Universe. I accept myself as I am now and also work toward a better me. I recognize and acknowledge all aspects of myself, including my strengths and weaknesses. Even when I make mistakes and encounter challenges, I am compassionate and kind to myself. I focus on my strengths and embrace my uniqueness. I accept and love myself just as I am, flaws and all. I believe that acceptance doesn't mean complacency because it allows me to move forward with a clear sense of purpose. By living with acceptance, I can cultivate inner peace and happiness. Every day, I'm grateful for the opportunities to practice acceptance and trust that it will continue to bring positive change into my life. I affirm that acceptance is an essential part of my journey. I'm committed to practicing acceptance in every aspect of my life. With acceptance as my guiding principle, I'm confident that I will continue to experience a fulfilling and rewarding life.

# DAY 13
# **Prioritize Humor for Your Well-Being**

I am committed to prioritizing humor and laughter in my life as essential aspects of my overall well-being.

---

I recognize the power of laughter in reducing stress, improving my mood, and bringing joy to my life. I choose to embrace humor in every situation, find the lightness in life, and not take myself too seriously. I acknowledge my imperfections and quirks and willingly laugh at my own mistakes. When I surround myself with people who appreciate the value of humor and laughter, I create a positive and lighthearted environment in my daily life. Through movies, jokes, and playful activities, I actively seek out moments of humor and laughter, knowing that they bring happiness and positivity to my life. I am grateful for the moments of joy and laughter that brighten up my life and cultivate inner peace and fulfillment. It feels good to laugh and enjoy the moment, and I desire to share this positive feeling with everyone. Humor and laughter are integral parts of my well-being, and I am committed to cultivating them in all areas of my life. I am grateful for the blessings of laughter, and I make time for it every day. By prioritizing humor and laughter, I am confident that I can lead a happy and fulfilling life, free from stress and negativity. I will continue to embrace humor and laughter, and as a result, they will continue to bring positivity and happiness into my life daily.

# — DAY 14 —
# Offer Generosity and Kindness to Others

**I am a kindhearted and generous person who strives to embody these values in every aspect of my life.**

I understand that generosity goes beyond simply giving material possessions and encompasses giving my time, energy, and love to others. I am always on the lookout for ways to be generous and to positively impact the world around me. Whether it's through volunteering, lending a listening ear, or simply showing kindness to others, I know that even small acts of generosity can make a significant difference in people's lives. I recognize that giving generously helps others, and it leaves a meaningful legacy. I believe in the law of attraction, which states that whatever energy I give out will return to me. Therefore, I am committed to living a life of generosity and kindness, and I strive to inspire others to do the same. I trust that my acts of kindness and generosity will continue to create a ripple effect of positivity in the world. By embodying these values, I am creating a life that is filled with purpose and meaning. I am confident that my generosity and kindness will bring joy, happiness, and fulfillment not only into my own life but also into the lives of those around me. I will make positive changes to the world, and I will continue to embrace this beautiful journey with an unwavering commitment to generosity and kindness.

# Encourage Flexibility As a Mindset

I am flexible and make it a priority to
cultivate flexibility in all areas of my life.

Life is constantly evolving, and I understand that the ability to adapt and adjust is crucial for my success and happiness. I approach each situation with my flexible mindset and with my willingness to explore diverse perspectives. I love living a life open to change. I recognize that being flexible in life always offers me ways to grow and learn. I am not fixated on any particular outcome but rather concentrate on being present. I embrace fresh challenges and experiences with an open heart, knowing that I can change my mindset when things are hard. Regardless of the situation, I am willing to push my boundaries by taking risks and trying new things. I am a flexible and resilient being, and I welcome change and adapt easily to new situations. I am capable of gracefully navigating any circumstance. I have complete trust in my capacity to handle whatever life throws my way. My body and mind are flexible, and this allows me to move through life with ease and grace. I am committed to nurturing this valuable trait in myself, which will contribute to a more satisfying and successful life. By continuing to embody flexibility, I will create a life that is filled with opportunities for growth, learning, and personal development.

# DAY 16

# Use Perseverance to Fuel Motivation

**I am someone who perseveres through life's struggles, and I recognize this trait as one of my most valuable qualities.**

True success in life requires unwavering determination, hard work, and the willingness to overcome any obstacles. Rather than giving up when facing obstacles, I embrace them as opportunities to grow and learn and feel motivated. I focus on my goals, even when the road ahead may seem difficult or unclear. With perseverance, I can unlock my full potential and achieve my greatest dreams. I believe in myself and my abilities, and I know that when I work hard, I can achieve anything I set my mind to. Every setback is an opportunity, and I embrace these challenges to become stronger and more resilient. When the going gets tough, I dig deep and find the inner strength to keep pushing forward. I surround myself with positive and supportive people who believe in me and my dreams. Their encouragement fuels me, and I am grateful for their presence in my life. I trust in my abilities and know that through perseverance and hard work, I can accomplish anything I set my mind to. I know that my perseverance will continue to serve me well in all areas of my life, and I am committed to nurturing this quality within myself for a more fulfilling and successful future. I will challenge myself and my sense of determination to achieve my goals and create a life that is filled with purpose, meaning, and success.

# DAY 17
# Let Authenticity Guide You

I am unique and authentic, and I celebrate all my strengths, weaknesses, quirks, and experiences.

I refuse to conform to societal expectations or the opinions of others. I release any need to hide behind a mask built based on what others want from me. I am happiest when I am myself, even if it means standing out or being different. I choose to live my life in alignment with my own values and passions. Living authentically is key to me experiencing a purposeful life. I honor my values and beliefs, and I am proud to share them with the world. Without fear of judgment or rejection, I speak my truth with honesty and vulnerability. I understand that embracing my authenticity requires courage and self-discovery, and I am willing to take that journey. By being true to myself, I attract opportunities and connections that align with my true self. It brings me joy and fulfillment to be my true self. I trust in my identity and confidently express myself in all aspects of my life. I am grateful for all the unique qualities and experiences that have made me who I am. I embrace all my qualities with open arms. I affirm that I will continue to live as my authentic self, trusting in the journey of self-discovery and growth.

# — DAY 18 —

# Express Gratefulness
# for Life's Blessings

### I am so grateful for all the blessings, abundance, and experiences that have shaped my life.

I choose to focus on the good, no matter how small or seemingly insignificant. Gratitude is my state of mind, bringing joy and contentment that I cultivate daily. I am grateful to the Universe for every experience that has shaped me, the people who have been a part of my journey, and the opportunities that have come my way. I am even grateful for the hardest moments in my life because they have led me to where I am today. I appreciate the lessons that challenge me and the lessons I had to learn the difficult way. I express gratitude through my words and actions, by showing appreciation to others, and by giving back to those in need. Gratitude is a powerful force that brings positivity and light into my life. I am especially grateful for the quirks and imperfections in myself because they make me who I am. Gratitude is the transformative power I need every day. Gratitude is the quickest way to bring manifestations into my reality, and that's one of the reasons I live a life full of appreciation. Every day brings new opportunities for me to express gratitude for the simple pleasures of life, such as a beautiful sunset, a game of fetch with my dog, or a good book. Gratitude is an essential part of my life, and I will cultivate it daily for a more fulfilling and abundant existence.

# Exude Compassion to Yourself and Others

## I am compassionate and empathetic toward both myself and others.

I understand that everyone has their struggles, and I approach every person with kindness, understanding, and acceptance. I prioritize listening without judgment and offering support and comfort to those in need. Through practicing compassion, I connect with others on a deeper level and form authentic and meaningful relationships. I am patient and forgiving with myself, and I recognize the importance of self-compassion. I choose to focus on people's strengths and potential and to see the good in everyone. When faced with difficult situations, I choose to respond with compassion rather than reacting with anger. I believe that living with compassion can create a positive ripple effect, inspiring others to do the same and creating a more loving and supportive community. My life is full of compassion and empathy, and I am making a positive difference in the world by embodying these qualities. I radiate compassion toward myself and others because that type of love is the foundation for true connection and understanding. I am a shining example of compassion, and I inspire others to live with kindness and empathy toward themselves and others. Having compassion helps me recognize and appreciate that we are all doing our best with the tools we have. I will continue to be open and compassionate on a daily basis, offering an emotional "safe space" for myself and others.

# Choose Fun to Better Your Life

### I am someone who lives their life with joy and playfulness.

Instead of taking everything seriously, I approach each day with a spirit of fun and adventure. I view the world through a lens of light-heartedness, and I find humor and excitement in the little things. It gives me immense happiness to bring joy to others through my playful nature. I let go of worries and stress, and I allow myself to have fun in the present moment. Spontaneity and silliness come naturally to me, and I welcome unexpected experiences and surprises. Manifestation should be fun, so I use all elements of pleasure and entertainment to create the life of my dreams. I surround myself with people who share my playful spirit and who uplift me with their joyful energy. I am grateful for the simple pleasures in life, like singing, dancing, and spending time with loved ones. When I take the time to embrace a playful mindset, I cultivate a sense of optimism and positivity in my life. Joy and playfulness are important parts of me, and I commit to bringing them into every aspect of my life. I let go of any troublesome thoughts and instead embrace my playful side. Life is meant to be enjoyed, and I give thanks to the Universe for every moment of laughter and happiness that comes my way. I will choose to live my life daily in a way that honors fun through laughter, joy, and pleasure.

# Embrace Optimism Through Thoughts and Actions

**I am full of optimism and release all negative thoughts and emotions that do not serve me.**

I choose to live in the present and let go of any harmful past regrets that negatively affect my thoughts. I am deserving of love, respect, and abundance, and I surround myself with positivity and light. I am capable of overcoming any challenge or obstacle, and I am constantly growing and improving as a person. Negativity has no power over me. I am stronger than I think I am. I acknowledge and appreciate all the blessings in my life. I trust that the Universe always has my back. I am the creator of my thoughts and emotions and choose to fill them with optimism. I do my very best to not let my thoughts become negative. It's easy to dwell on the negative, but I find ways to focus my mind on the good things in my life. In moments of self-doubt, I remind myself that I am confident in my abilities and talents. By shedding pessimism, I have the power to create the life I desire. I focus on finding solutions instead of dwelling on problems. I let go of negative self-talk and replace it with words of encouragement and positivity. I am grateful for this moment I am in now and all the possibilities it holds. I will continue to honor the positive forces that allow light into my life, rejecting any negative energy that comes my way.

# DAY 22

# Develop Self-Awareness
# for Personal Growth

I am keenly self-aware, dedicated to
my personal growth and development.

I trust my intuition and inner wisdom to guide me toward my highest potential. I enjoy learning about myself, my likes and dislikes, and how my presence impacts others. Becoming more aware of myself has granted me full understanding of my wants and needs. I approach my thoughts, emotions, and actions with empathy, knowing that even when I am challenged, I'll learn about myself. As I constantly assess my life and perception of the world around me, I cast judgment aside, and I love others unconditionally. I view my mistakes as valuable lessons and opportunities for growth. I use my personal lessons to propel me forward in life. I release any self-limiting beliefs, and I embrace my full potential. I honor my worth and treat myself with genuine self-love. I am grateful for all the experiences, both positive and negative, that have shaped me into the person I am today. I welcome new experiences that are aligned with my growth. I have unwavering confidence in my ability to overcome obstacles, as I know I am up to the task. I am on track toward achieving my goals. I trust and believe that the Universe is conspiring in my favor. I will continue to develop self-awareness through reflecting on which actions build me and others up, forgoing those that are not beneficial.

# DAY 23

## Embrace Confidence for Self-Betterment

I am an unstoppable force, capable of
achieving any goal I set my mind to
and embracing a confident mindset.

---

I take pride in my abilities and know that success is within my reach. I choose to approach challenges with confidence, determination, and resilience, using each experience to expand and flourish. I am worthy of love, respect, and abundance, and I am committed to pursuing my dreams with unwavering confidence. I radiate self-assuredness and positivity, and as a result, I only attract the best life experiences. Through my journey, my confidence guides me to manifest wonderful companions, acquaintances, and friends. I trust my intuition and believe in my unique talents and skills. I let go of self-doubt and negative self-talk, as they do not serve me. I am grateful for all the experiences that have shaped me into the person I am today. My confidence and resilience are fueled through my gratitude. My positive energy attracts an overflow of abundance into my life. I am confident, capable, and empowered to create the life I desire with the highest form of joy and ease. Daily, I will embrace my inner confidence as a way to make permanent, healthy changes in my life.

# Observe Your Thoughts

I am a thoughtful person who embraces
a curious and compassionate mindset
and allows my thoughts to unfold.

My thoughts do not define me, as they are just thoughts. I choose to observe my thoughts without judgment or attachment, knowing some thoughts are out of my control. I choose to prioritize only the thoughts that serve my highest good and do not hurt others. My intuition guides me to recognize empowering and positive thoughts, releasing any negative self-talk or limiting beliefs. I observe uplifting affirmations that inspire me, keep me focused on my goals, and guide me to take control of my thoughts. I welcome new perspectives and ideas to expand my consciousness. I gain greater clarity and inner peace through the mindful observation of my thoughts. By observing my thoughts, I am able to detach from ones that don't serve me and focus on the ones that allow me to better the world around me. I am empowered to create the reality and dreams I desire through my thoughts. I recognize that my thoughts and beliefs shape my reality. I will continue to observe my healthy and happy mindset, and I will regularly affirm that it will bring peace into my life.

# Pursue Financial Abundance

**I am welcoming the abundance of the Universe and embodying financial prosperity in my life.**

I acknowledge that the Universe has an infinite supply of wealth and resources that are available to me. I release any limiting beliefs and negative emotions surrounding money. I cultivate a positive and abundant mindset. I am financially free, and abundance flows effortlessly in and through my life. I express gratitude for the money that flows into my life, and I use it to make positive changes in my own life and the lives of those around me. I trust my intuition and inner guidance to lead me toward financial opportunities that align with my values and purpose. My financial situation will reflect my positive mindset and unwavering belief in abundance; therefore, I commit to doing my best in believing and manifesting the abundance that is rightfully mine. I am deserving of financial success, and I take confident action toward achieving my goals. I trust in my ability to create multiple streams of income, and I invite in new and exciting opportunities for creating wealth. I am open to learning new skills and ideas that will enhance my income and wealth. I believe financial abundance is mine for the taking, so I will meet my monetary goals, and I will pursue opportunities to increase my wealth.

# Walk the Path of Enlightenment

I am open to receiving spiritual guidance
and wisdom from the Universe while
walking the path of enlightenment.

---

I trust that I am on a path toward greater spiritual awareness and enlightenment. I now release any limiting beliefs and negative emotions that hinder my progress toward a higher level of consciousness. I embrace a positive and expansive mindset. I trust my intuition and inner guidance to lead me toward my soul's purpose. I honor the interconnectedness of all beings and strive to live in harmony with the natural world and the Universe. I welcome new experiences and perspectives that challenge and broaden my spiritual beliefs. Things are always working out for me and leading to a higher state of being. As I become more enlightened, I allow myself to evolve as a spiritual being. Through meditation, self-reflection, and mindfulness, I cultivate a deep understanding of myself and the world around me. I am thankful for the opportunities and the ability to connect with my authentic self and the divine. I am spiritually awakened and empowered. As time passes, my journey toward greater spiritual enlightenment will continue to unfold with ease and grace.

# Strive for and Honor Friendships

I am full of warmth, acceptance, and respect—
qualities that make me an excellent friend
and attract friends of a similar caliber.

---

I am grateful for each of my friends; they bring me perspective and joy. I am manifesting friends I can count on. I am always attracting wonderful people into my life. My friendships require healthy boundaries and clear communication. Maintaining boundaries with grace and respect will protect me as well as those around me. Creating purposeful connections with my friends will result in stronger and more fulfilling friendships. My values and goals align with the potential for new friendships. People desire to be friends to me. I am a magnet for amazing friendships. Since I emit constant positivity, kindness, and authenticity, I attract like-minded people who appreciate and respect me for who I am. My friends are self-motivated and constantly inspire me to improve. By releasing negative emotions and beliefs from my past, I welcome positive and meaningful relationships. I am a loyal, supportive, and caring friend. Having these traits attracts positivity and kindness into my life. Despite all the challenges in my life, I know that my relationships will thrive and bring me a great deal of joy and fulfillment. The people who surround me are wonderful, and I'm looking forward to building a lifetime of memories with them. Every day, I will follow my intuition to connect with others who inspire and support me in positive and uplifting ways.

# DAY 28

# Value Contentment
# and Inner Peace

I am overflowing with contentment
and peace in this very moment.

---

Instead of focusing on any lingering feelings of inadequacy or scarcity, I focus on the abundance and blessings that surround me. My life experiences, both good and bad, have shaped me into the content person I am now. I am satisfied in the way I approach achieving my goals and dreams. My life is perfect as it is, and I am grateful for everything I have. I am open to receiving all the resources and opportunities that come my way, knowing that the Universe helps me achieve my goals. Whenever I feel lack or dissatisfaction, I release it and embrace the abundance of joy around me. It is my choice to stay present, content, and mindful so that I can fully enjoy the beauty and wonder of life as it unfolds before me. In my journey toward greater inner peace and fulfillment, I trust that the Universe will continue to support me, allowing me to live free from worries about basic needs and wants. I am grateful for all that I have and all that is yet to come. I will continue to be content with the blessings the Universe provides and will work toward finding inner peace.

# Rely On Inner Strength

**I am strong and resilient, and these traits allow me to overcome any obstacle that crosses my path.**

When I encounter tough times, I rely on my inner fortitude and let go of any negativity that may impede my progress. My thoughts and words carry a great deal of power, and I choose to use them in positive ways to empower myself and other people. I take decisive action toward my goals with confidence and perseverance, and this is what makes me courageous and tenacious. My inner strength is constantly developing, and I am open to learning from my mistakes and experiences. Strength comes from within, and I use my strength to empower myself and others around me. I am utilizing my natural talents and tenacity to create positive change in the world. Honoring my strengths and weaknesses is one of my core values. I am a survivor, and deep down I know I have the strength to overcome any adversity. It is my inherent strength that empowers me, and I trust that it will guide me toward success and fulfillment in the future. I am grateful for the strength I possess, and I know I can conquer any challenge with ease. In the future, I will remain confident in my strength, knowing it will allow me to create the life I desire.

# Replace Loneliness with Compassion and Connection

**I am never truly alone due to the love and support of my friends and family, even when they aren't physically present.**

When I feel loneliness creeping in, I choose to shift my focus toward self-love, connection, and fulfillment. I understand that loneliness is a transient feeling and trust that I have the power to overcome it. I release negative beliefs and emotions that might contribute to my feelings of loneliness and choose to cultivate a positive and compassionate mindset. To combat loneliness, I prioritize my physical, emotional, and mental well-being and am mindful of the importance of self-care. I am open to new experiences and connections, extending kindness and empathy to those around me. My solitude allows me to reflect, grow, and express myself creatively. I trust that the Universe will bring meaningful, deep relationships and experiences into my life. I am valued and loved, and I choose to radiate optimism and kindness, attracting positive and uplifting people into my life. I believe that the Universe has my best interests at heart, and I am confident that my life will continue to be filled with joy and love from those closest to me. The Universe has a plan for me, and I am confident that the right people and experiences will come into my life at the right time. Each day, I will replace any trace of loneliness in my daily life with my compassion and connection with others.

# Embrace Fear As a Catalyst for Change

*I am a brave and courageous individual,
capable of overcoming or utilizing any
fear that may come my way.*

Although fear is a natural human emotion, I do not allow it to control me. Instead, I confront my fears with unwavering determination and a steadfast spirit. I recognize that my fears can be catalysts for growth and change, and I choose to embrace them as opportunities for transformation. I release any negative thoughts and beliefs that hold me back and focus on the endless opportunities that await me on the other side of fear. I cultivate self-love, confidence, and resilience in times when I am scared of what the future brings. My positive and optimistic approach to challenges allows me to conquer any fear. I trust my inner strength and resilience to address fear and self-doubt. With each step toward embracing my fears, I become stronger and more empowered. Fear may be present, but I am more powerful than it, and I have the courage to face it head-on. I will continue to live my life with bravery and determination, knowing that I have the ability to overcome any obstacle or challenge that comes along.

# Regulate Your Nervous System

I am a centered person with a strong, resourceful body that serves and protects my nervous system.

When my nervous system becomes overwhelmed, I choose to take intentional steps to calm myself. With slow, deep breaths and present-moment awareness, I release any anxiety and remind myself of my inherent strength and resilience. I trust my body's innate ability to regulate my nervous system, and I am calm, centered, and grounded. I let go of negative thoughts and emotions, and I intentionally cultivate a sense of peace and serenity within me. I visualize a tranquil and harmonious inner world and immerse myself in that feeling of calmness and relaxation. To calm my nerves and create a sense of peace and tranquility, I practice deep breathing and mindfulness. I trust my ability to manage stress and anxiety, and I prioritize self-care activities such as meditation, yoga, and spending time in nature to promote the well-being of my nervous system. I allow myself to take breaks and rest to recharge my body and mind. I release tension from my body, allowing it to relax and find a natural state of balance and harmony within itself. As days move on, I will continue to flow with the rhythm of life and check in with my nervous system as I cultivate calmness and relaxation.

## — DAY 33 —
# Experience and Treat Sadness

**I am a complex, intelligent, and creative individual who is more than their current unhappiness.**

When I feel deep sadness, I remember I must be kind and gentle with myself. Instead of berating myself for my emotions, I commit to trying to approach them with compassion and understanding. It is okay for me to be sad; I give myself space to feel every emotion I have. Plus, my sadness won't last forever—with each day there is always hope for healing and growth. To take care of myself during this difficult time, I focus on activities that bring me joy and peace, like going for walks in nature or listening to my favorite music. If I need support, I spend quality time with loved ones who nurture and uplift me. And yes, sometimes, I need to allow myself to cry and release my emotions. During the tough times, I challenge negative thoughts and self-talk. It's so easy to get stuck in a cycle of negativity and hopelessness when I'm feeling sad, but I try to remind myself that things will always get better. I believe that even in my sadness I can still manifest my desires with ease because the Universe honors every emotion I have. My emotions are a part of the natural ebb and flow of my life. Sometimes I feel joy, and sometimes I feel sadness. By continuing to treat myself with kindness and compassion, I will heal and grow in ways I never thought possible.

# Recognize Subtle and Substantial Blessings

**I am filled with gratitude due to the many blessings in my life, knowing I am fortunate to have all that I do.**

From the air I breathe to the sun that shines on my face, I am thankful for every little thing that makes my life so rich and fulfilling. I know that even the difficult times I face are blessings in disguise, helping me grow stronger and more resilient. When I look around me, I see so many amazing things to be grateful for. I am surrounded by friends and loved ones who support me and are always there to lift me up when I'm feeling down. I have a roof over my head, food on the table, and my happiness, which are the greatest blessings of all. Whenever I feel like life is throwing me in an unwanted or unclear direction, I remind myself of all the Universe has blessed me with. With a grateful heart, I bring miracles into my life, and I live each day with a sense of joy and purpose. I strongly believe that no matter what life sends my way, I will always be thankful for the blessings that surround me. Through my gratitude, I will continue to attract even more blessings, and I know that my life will always be filled with joy and abundance.

# Revel In Feeling Wonderful

### I am truly feeling wonderful and ready to take on life with good vibrations today.

I know that what I think and feel affects my reality, so I try to focus on the good things and let go of the bad. It may not always be easy, but I believe that every effort toward positive vibes counts. I find joy in the simple things, like having a roof over my head, a warm cup of coffee, or a loving friend. To revel in my truest happiness, I must take care of all aspects of my health: physical, mental, and emotional. I freely take breaks from social media or work, and I use that time to do something that brings me peace and happiness, like reading a good book or taking a long walk in nature. Embracing what feels good, I surround myself with people who uplift and inspire me, and I let go of anyone who brings negativity or drama into my life. Life is too short to waste it on toxic relationships. I believe in myself and my abilities, and I don't let any limiting beliefs hold me back. Each day is a new opportunity for growth and learning, and I make the most of it. Life is a precious gift, and I am so grateful for every moment of it. I will continue to live each day with purpose and intention, feeling wonderful and grateful for all that life has to offer.

# Trust In Timing

**I am trusting that life is unfolding with the most perfect timing, and I am excited to see what's in store for me.**

---

I practice gratitude and acceptance, knowing that everything happens for a reason when it's supposed to. Even when things don't go as I have planned, I know there's a lesson to be learned and I'll come out stronger. My journey is unique and created just for me, and I embrace every experience as an opportunity for growth and learning. I have faith that my dreams are coming true, and I'm patient as they manifest in their own time. Trusting in the timing of my life allows me to live with ease. I willingly put my life and the timing of my desires into the control of the Universe. Instead of stressing about the future or dwelling on the past, I focus on the present moment and savor it. By living in the now, I see the beauty in the small things, like the warmth of the sun on my skin or the sound of rain falling. I know that my path is unfolding perfectly, and I'm excited to see what's next. The Universe has a plan for me, and I trust that it's even better than what I could have imagined for myself. So, I will continually embrace every moment with an open heart and mind and be open to all the possibilities life has to offer.

# Say No and Prioritize You

**I am capable of showing myself love and respect by setting boundaries that prioritize my mental and physical health.**

---

If something doesn't align with my values or serve my highest good, I won't hesitate to say no. Trusting my gut and communicating my needs clearly and honestly is key to my well-being. I know that taking care of myself isn't selfish; it's necessary. Saying no doesn't mean I'm a bad person—it simply means I'm putting myself first. When I stand up for myself, I create a positive and centered sense of self. This paves the way for healthy relationships built on mutual respect and understanding. When I value my own needs, I attract people who honor my boundaries and support my growth. Saying no sets the tone for positive and fulfilling relationships with myself and others. I'm aware that setting boundaries can be challenging, but I'm willing to put in the effort for my own happiness. By doing so, I open up a world of possibilities for growth, transformation, and abundance. Prioritizing myself allows me to live an authentic and meaningful life that aligns with my values and purpose. I honor myself by saying no when necessary, trusting my instincts, and creating a life that reflects my priorities and values. Because I will continue to put myself first, I will be able to live a life that is fulfilling, purposeful, and true to who I am.

## DAY 38

# Embody Determination to Achieve Your Dreams

**I am fiercely determined to make my dreams come true, regardless of the effort it will take to get there.**

---

I refuse to let anything get in my way or lower my energy. I know that success takes hard work, tenacity, and dedication. I'm up for the challenges that may arise, and I'll do whatever it takes to make my dreams a reality. I know that I have the power to create the life I want, and I won't settle for anything less. When obstacles come, I face them with a positive, determined attitude and see them as opportunities to learn something new. I'm like a phoenix, rising from the ashes of setbacks with a renewed mindset and determined energy. I'm deeply committed to my vision for the future, and I won't stop until I achieve it. I know that the road ahead won't be easy, but I'm willing to put in the time, effort, and work required to succeed. Each step forward, no matter how small, is a victory worth celebrating. My determination is unbreakable, and I'm confident that with the Universe on my side, I can conquer anything. I trust in my innate potential and abilities to guide me toward a life that is meaningful. By staying true to my commitments, I will be ready to take on the challenges of the world today and make my dreams come true.

# Experience Loss As Part of the Human Condition

### I am strong and caring, and by experiencing my unique journey with grief, I embrace the human condition.

When I experience loss, I take a step back and show myself love. Dealing with grief may not be easy, but I know that it's undeniably part of life. I let myself feel every emotion that comes with loss. I prioritize self-care during tough times, as it is a crucial part of my healing process. I show my strength by asking for help from my loved ones and professionals. My journey to healing after loss will look different from someone else's, and that's okay. I go through my journey at my own pace with self-kindness. I reflect on the love, connection, positive memories, and lessons that I've learned from who or what I've lost. With time and grace, I let go of the pain that comes with this loss. I hold on to hope and trust that joy and happiness will return to me eventually. I am grateful for the simple, positive presences and events in my life. When I acknowledge my grief and work through pain, I'm truly becoming stronger and more resilient. I also know that I'm not alone in the experience of loss and grief. I extend compassion to others dealing with their own losses. I love supporting others and creating a space for healing, to share comfort and peace. I will continually give myself patience and space to experience grief, while allowing myself to grow and learn from it.

# Face Depression with Patience and Understanding

**I am kind and compassionate to myself when I experience feelings of sadness or depression.**

I know it's not easy, but I extend the grace that I would give to a loved one going through a difficult period. Depression is a common experience, and I take solace in the fact that I'm not alone in this struggle. I allow myself to feel all emotions that come with depression, knowing that it's all part of the healing process. At the same time, I take action to seek help and support from trusted friends, family, or a therapist when I need it. It takes courage and strength to admit when we need assistance. My mental health is my top priority, and I do activities that center me, such as spending time in nature, reading a good book, practicing yoga or meditation, or simply taking a long, hot bath. I set achievable goals and celebrate every accomplishment along the way. Recovery is a journey, not a destination, and every step forward is worth celebrating. Ultimately, healing takes time, and there will be setbacks and challenges along the way. But I can overcome this struggle with the help of others and my own inner strength. I'm worthy of happiness and fulfillment, and I'm capable of living a meaningful and purposeful life, even in the midst of difficulty. I'm proud that I prioritize my mental health and well-being. I still have a long road ahead, but I will face whatever comes my way with resilience, courage, and self-compassion.

# Be Excited about Life's Endless Possibilities

**I am full of an enthusiastic energy as I think about all the amazing things waiting for me in this life.**

The sheer force of my excitement is like a jolt of lightning, sparking me into action and propelling me toward my dreams and aspirations. I always look for new opportunities to explore and learn from. Focusing on the good gives me the courage to take risks and follow my passions. I trust that when I take leaps of faith, they guide me toward an authentic life full of endless possibilities. Life is abundant, and I'm not selfish—I celebrate all the wonderful, hardworking people in the world achieving their goals. Challenges may come, obstructing the easiest paths to success, but I see them as opportunities to positively transform. I'm ready to face anything that comes my way with determination because I know the rewards are plentiful and mine for the taking. I'm not afraid of a little hard work or a few setbacks—they're all important parts of the journey toward greatness. My life is overflowing with excitement, joy, and gratitude, and I am embracing all of it. I achieve true fulfillment and deep meaning in my life when I cherish these amazing feelings. Life has incredible possibilities in store for me, and I will look forward to them with enthusiasm and a deep sense of joy!

# Listen to the Universe's Promises

*I am immensely humbled by the power of
the Universe's love and abundance, which flows
through my life today and every day.*

I trust in the Universe's promises with all my heart and soul and know that everything will work out in the end. Even when I can't see a way forward, the mystic power of the Universe guides me. Waiting for the Universe's timing can sometimes be hard, but I've learned to trust that everything will happen when it's supposed to. I don't always understand why things happen the way they do, but I know that the Universe has a plan to bring about the best possible outcome for me. The Universe will do more for me than I can comprehend, and that excites me. In every situation, I choose to look for blessings and to focus on the good things in my life. The power of the Universe is at work even when things seem dark or difficult, willing my best interests to come to light. I feel a sense of peace and joy when I trust in the Universe's plan, and I know I can handle whatever comes my way. I am grateful for the Universe's sustenance, and I trust that I can face any challenge, overcome any obstacle, and live a life of hope, joy, and serenity. I will continue to place my faith in the higher power of the Universe, while working hard and staying positive, to ensure my success.

# Show Appreciation

I am showing my appreciation for my past,
finding peace in the present, and
creating a vision for tomorrow.

Life is a gift, and I choose to unwrap it with a grateful heart! I choose to practice gratitude outwardly and openly, as it is the greatest of virtues. Focusing on the positive brings joy and contentment to me and others. I appreciate my body because it has helped me in so many ways in life, so I treat it with love and care. I check in with myself, demonstrating self-love, and prioritize my self-care. Relationships are like sunshine in my life, and I cherish love and support from those who freely give it. There is so much for me to show appreciation for. I appreciate even the small things in life, thanking each one. I choose to live every moment displaying my grateful heart! I display my appreciation for the people who bring happiness into my life. I am grateful to have a thankful heart that blossoms in my soul and outwardly into the Universe. I will continue to appreciate all the people and things in my life and acknowledge that my willingness to express gratitude can change someone's day.

# Celebrate Your Unique and Exceptional Talent

### I am uniquely talented and possess an endless number of skills that can change the world for the better.

My brain is a powerhouse of creative ideas, always coming up with new and unconventional solutions. When faced with tough situations, I can cut through the confusion with lightning-fast thinking and razor-sharp analysis. No detail is too small to escape my eagle eyes; I make sure everything I do is top-notch. Leading comes naturally to me, and I inspire others to be their best selves by setting a high bar for myself. My talents are as diverse as they come, so I'm always eager to take on new challenges and learn new things. Each roadblock I encounter is another opportunity to flex my creative muscles and teaches me something valuable. I know that I've got what it takes to achieve my dreams and make a real impact in the world. I'm proud of my talents and the hard work that's brought me to where I am today. But I never rest on my laurels; I'm always looking for the next big thing to tackle. With each new challenge, I will continue to celebrate my talent as the strong, capable person I am becoming.

# Face Challenges Head-On

**I am a fearless soul who takes on new challenges and dives headfirst into the unknown.**

---

I believe in confronting my fears while standing up to the difficulties that come my way. Even when the odds seem stacked against me, I possess a deep well of tenacity and confidence that keeps me going. I trust my instincts to guide me toward the best outcomes, regardless of initial challenges in my way. Taking risks is part of who I am, and I welcome any new opportunities along my journey. I'm not afraid of failure because I understand that failure is a part of the life process and is a chance to learn and improve myself. I am not defined by what I am going through. This challenge will pass me by in time, leading me closer to my goals. I am unyielding in my determination, no matter how difficult the journey may be. For me, my courage is a source of pride, and every day I strive to become an even more unshakable version of myself. Challenges may come, but I am always going to remain confident in my own abilities and trust that I have what it takes to succeed. I will face challenges head-on every day, acknowledging that I am a force to be reckoned with, and bring a sense of excitement and purpose to every obstacle.

# — DAY 46 —

# Mold Your Life As You See Fit

I am the ultimate creator of my own life, empowered
to shape my destiny in whatever way I see fit.

My past and present circumstances don't define me, but they
provide me with valuable lessons that can help me make positive
changes in the future. Setting and achieving goals will take effort,
perseverance, and maybe even some sacrifices, but I am committed to taking the reins and making my dreams come true. My journey involves a great deal of discipline, and I am willing to develop
this skill in order to succeed. There will be obstacles along the way,
but I'm resilient and determined to overcome them with optimism
and courage. I take full responsibility for my actions because they
have the power to shape my destiny. The things that are beyond
my control are less important to me, so I focus on what I can control. Surrounding myself with positivity and support is absolutely
vital, and I'm incredibly grateful for the encouragement and guidance of the people who love, uplift, and believe in me. The life I
want is within my reach, and I am confident and will work hard to
reach my potential. In pursuit of my goals, I am willing to be patient
and persistent regardless of how long and winding the road to my
desires may be. The only person who can determine my destiny is
me, and I will continue to make my life the best it can be every day.

# DAY 47

## Appreciate Your Family

I am appreciative of my biological or
chosen family and know that they are
a large reason I am who I am today.

---

Family is everything to me. They're my rock, my world, my support, and my cheerleaders. I feel incredibly lucky to have them by my side through thick and thin. I appreciate all the sacrifices my family has made for me, even in the hardest of times. Their support has taught me resilience, and they've given me the courage to tackle life's challenges. I communicate with my family openly and honestly, and our relationships are strengthened by this honesty. I trust and respect my family members, and they trust and respect me in return. I am a valuable member of my family, and I contribute to our collective well-being and happiness. My family brings me joy and fulfillment, and I prioritize spending quality time with them and showing them my love. Family is more than just blood relatives; it's the people I choose. This chosen family brings so much joy and fulfillment to my life, and I cherish them. I believe that a strong family foundation is essential for a happy and meaningful life, and I will build that in my family, whether passed down to my own children or shared within my chosen family. I will continue to be grateful for my family's love, guidance, and support, and I'm committed to fostering strong relationships with them.

# Achieve a Balanced Selflessness

I am selfless and kind, and I find joy in giving to others.
I choose to approach life with a selfless attitude.

When possible, I prioritize the needs of others above my own. My selfless actions have the power to make a positive impact. I am committed to contributing to my community and to touching the lives of those around me in meaningful ways. However, I understand that selflessness does not mean neglecting my own needs or well-being. I am not being selfish by providing self-care. When I am capable, I strive to be a beacon of selflessness, always mindful of the impact my words and actions have on others. It is important to find a balance between caring for others and taking care of myself. I am committed to practicing self-care and self-compassion while also being selfless. I recognize that by taking care of me, I am better equipped to serve others with a joyful and generous heart. I am deserving of kindness, compassion, and understanding, and throughout my life I extend these same qualities to others. I hope to inspire others to see the value in themselves, and through my actions, I will demonstrate how to approach life with an open mind, a spirit of generosity, and a selfless heart. I will affirm my self-worth daily and will live a life characterized by selflessness and empathy.

# — DAY 49 —
## Live Aligned

I am living a life that's in tune with my heart's deepest desires, and it feels incredible.

As I align with the positive energy of the Universe, I effortlessly attract abundance and excitement into my life. I am in perfect alignment with my higher self, and I trust that everything I desire is making its way to me at the right time. I am grateful for every experience in my journey that has brought me to this point. I focus on thoughts that feel good and bring me into alignment with my true desires, knowing that the Universe is always conspiring in my favor. Abundance flows freely into my life, and I know that I am worthy of success, happiness, and prosperity. I trust the path that the Universe is guiding me toward, and every moment brings me into closer alignment with my true purpose. My alignment with the Universe brings me a sense of inner peace and contentment, allowing me to effortlessly manifest my dreams into reality. I release all negative thoughts and beliefs that do not serve me, instead choosing to focus on the abundance and possibilities that surround me. Today and every day, I will affirm my alignment with my true purpose and trust in the Universe to guide me toward a fulfilling and meaningful life.

# Appreciate Miracles Big and Small

I am in awe of the everyday miracles that the
Universe is constantly revealing to me in my life.

I see evidence of the Universe's love and support all around me, in the beauty of nature, in the kind words of strangers, and in the synchronicities that guide me toward my dreams. I am open and receptive to the small wonders and blessings that show up in my life today. I choose to focus on the positive aspects of my life, knowing that what I focus on expands. I am grateful for the blessings that I have, and I choose to see every situation as an opportunity to grow and learn. Even in the midst of challenges, there are miracles waiting for me. The Universe always provides exactly what I need in the perfect moment. My life is filled with love, joy, and prosperity. I choose to surround myself with positive energy, and I attract only the best into my life. I am grateful for the opportunity to experience magical moments. I am open to receiving all the miracles that the Universe has in store for me. I am amazed by the beauty and wonder that surrounds me every day. I will continue to be grateful for the abundance of blessings in my life, and I choose to live each day with joy, appreciation, and wonder in my heart.

# Embrace Mindful Contentment

I am living a satisfying and exciting life, and
happiness naturally flows from my contentment.

As I look around me, I can't help but feel a deep sense of contentment and satisfaction. I realize and appreciate all that I already have in my life, and I am content with it. I know that every moment presents an opportunity for personal growth and enlightenment, and I am open to everything the Universe has to offer. My heart is overflowing with gratitude for the countless opportunities and love that come my way. I am rich in support, joy, and happiness. Through my content mindset, I embrace intentional optimism and let go of any limiting beliefs that are holding me back. I am surrounded by positive energy and encouragement from those around me. I am content with where I am, but I am always so excited for where I am going. I embrace the present moment and find joy and bliss in everything around me. I am grateful for my journey and the abundance of opportunities it brings for personal transformation and self-discovery. I am now pursuing my dreams, while also being thankful and content with the present moment. As time goes on, I will remain content to explore the mystery and magic of life while I am directed by the Universe toward the path of my highest good.

# Manifest Your Dream Career

*I am destined for a career that fulfills my deepest desires and brings me joy beyond my wildest dreams.*

The Universe is bringing me abundant employment opportunities that perfectly align with my passions, skills, and values. I am confident in my abilities and know that I am uniquely qualified for a perfect job that is waiting for me. My talents and viewpoints are assets that make me an attractive candidate to potential employers. I focus on my strengths and nurture a mindset of self-improvement. My happiness is not dependent on success, but on doing what I love. I have the ability to thrive in the workplace and/or start my own business. My possibilities are limitless, and I'm excited about the future and what is available to me. I visualize myself thriving in my chosen field, reaching new heights of success and fulfillment. My unwavering belief in myself and my abilities attracts the perfect job and career to me. As I move forward on my journey, I trust that my dream career will unfold at the most perfect time. I am grateful for everything and everyone leading me toward this ultimate goal. I trust myself, and I have the courage to follow my heart toward a fulfilling career. I am a powerful manifester, and my dream career is already manifesting into my reality. Every day, I will continue to affirm my faith in my career journey and the infinite possibilities that await me.

# DAY 53

## Use Your Thoughts to Affect Reality

**I am profoundly aware of the immense power that my thoughts and beliefs hold in shaping my reality.**

My thoughts create my reality, and when I change my thoughts, I can change my life. I choose to focus on positivity, abundance, and gratitude. This optimism will attract even more positivity and abundance into my life. My thoughts have the power to create my world, and I intentionally channel energy toward the things that I truly desire. My life is constantly changing in response to my thoughts, emotions, and experiences, and I hold the power to rewire my thoughts for success. I am more than my thoughts: I am the observer of my thoughts. I choose to observe my thoughts to utilize them in a way that serves me. At this moment, I am thankful for all the blessings in my life that were created through my positive mindset. My musings have a powerful effect on my body; therefore, I commit to optimism to improve my overall health. I live with intention and purpose, understanding that my thoughts and actions contribute to my wonderful life. I have the power to manifest my desires through the power of my thoughts. When I focus on what I desire and believe it to be true and possible for me, I am able to attract my wants into my life. Every single day, I will renew my faith in the unlimited potential of my thoughts and the boundless possibilities that exist all around me.

# — DAY 54 —

# Focus On Your Wants and Self

I am a caring and focused individual, and I dedicate time and space to focus on my growth and my wants.

Focusing on my desires aligns me with the power of the Universe and allows that power to flow through me. I trust in the abundance of the Universe and receive all the blessings that come my way. I am a deliberate creator, knowing that my thoughts and emotions shape the reality I want. I am worthy of love, success, and happiness, and with these positive feelings on my side, I can achieve my wildest dreams. I am in tune with my inner being, and I use my emotions to lead me to my highest good. I acknowledge my growth and progress, and I celebrate my successes with self-care. I release any limiting beliefs and doubts that may hold me back and embrace the possibilities before me. I take care of myself and prioritize my well-being, knowing that it is essential for me to show up fully in all areas of my life. I honor my boundaries and communicate my needs effectively. I am my own best friend and ally, and I treat myself with love and kindness. As I move forward on my journey of growth and expansion, I will continue to trust in myself and the Universe, knowing that all my dreams are within my reach.

# Assume the Best to Transform Your Life

### I am choosing to assume only the best for my life.

I know that my thoughts and assumptions shape my reality, so I choose to think positively and expect the best outcomes in every situation. When I assume only the best, I attract positive energy and opportunities into my life. My life is full of abundance and joy, and I am grateful for every moment. I understand that my assumptions create my reality, so I choose to make positive assumptions about myself and my life. I assume that everything is working out in my favor, and I trust the Universe to bring me the best outcomes. My assumptions have the power to change my life, and I choose to make them work in my favor. My thoughts and emotions are aligned with my highest vision for my life, and I am attracting positive experiences and people into my orbit. I am becoming the best version of myself, and I am excited to see where my journey takes me. I release all doubts and fears about the future and assume that everything is working out in my favor. I am excited for the abundance and joy that is coming my way, and I am grateful for all the blessings in my life. Going forward, I will choose to assume only the best, and I am excited to see where this positive mindset takes me.

# DAY 56
# Utilize Affirmations for Manifesting

I am a powerful being, capable of creating positive change in my life, and I use affirmations as a tool to reprogram my subconscious mind and manifest the life I desire.

As I repeat affirmations to myself, I feel their power and truth flow through me. I believe that I radiate love and light wherever I go. I trust in myself and in the Universe to provide for me in abundance. What I affirm, I believe, and what I believe, I become. I know that everything I need is already within me. I am very much ready to receive all the blessings that the Universe has in store for me. My thoughts and actions create my reality. Stating affirmations is like sowing seeds in the soil. At first, they take time to sprout and germinate, developing roots, and eventually they blossom into stunning flowers. I am now planting seeds of affirmation so they can help me grow into my most optimal self. Affirmations inspire me, uplift me, and help me become the best version of myself. I am constantly evolving and developing, and I freely welcome the lessons that each new experience brings. I love that affirmations assist me in building a positive frame of mind that helps me accomplish anything I set my sights on. Daily, I will continue to commit to using truthful and positive affirmations and create my desired reality.

# Embark On a Journey

**I am ready to embark on a life-changing
journey of unforeseen obstacles,
allowing me to realize my highest good.**

As I step forward on my journey toward my true destiny, I am filled with eagerness and anticipation. I know that the Universe has a divine plan for me, and I trust in its infinite wisdom to help me along the way. I will follow my intuition and take the path that resonates most with my inner being. Even if it may feel unconventional or challenging, I choose to focus on the positive aspects of my journey. I understand that the path to my destiny may be accompanied by setbacks, but I am resilient enough to overcome them. I abandon the familiar and any fears because I know what lies ahead is full of prosperity. I am surrounded by an abundant and supportive Universe that is always providing me with the resources and guidance I need to succeed. I do not take for granted all the blessings in my life, though I am also excited for what is to come. I am ready to seize this adventure because when I take the first step, the rest will fall into place. I am fueled by the priceless growth and learning that come with embarking on a new journey. As I embark on a quest to find my destiny, I will put gratitude at the front of my mind and continue to take steps toward achieving my wildest dreams.

# Listen to Your Intuition

**I am confident in my intuition—it helps me navigate life's challenges and make choices that align with my purpose and values.**

Whenever I face a decision, I trust in the wisdom and insight of my inner voice. I take the time to tune into the sensations in my body and listen to my gut feelings. I know that my intuition is based on deeper wisdom and understanding beyond my comprehension. I am committed to strengthening my connection to my intuition through meditation and self-reflection. By honoring my intuition and making choices that feel right for me, I am creating a fulfilling and purposeful life. My intuition is the whisper to my soul, it is the compass of my life. I am grateful for my intuition because it is a powerful force within me that is capable of guiding me to my highest good. My intuition is a spiritual power that points the way throughout my journey. I believe my intuition knows what my conscious mind has yet to discover. My intuition helps me tap into the wisdom of my subconscious mind. I love that my intuition bridges the gap between my conscious and unconscious mind. Every day, I will get better at listening to my intuition, building a clearer understanding of the unseen.

# Leave Guilt Behind

**I am now letting go of any guilt or shame
that has been weighing me down.**

I am speaking to myself with positive words and acknowledging my mistakes because they are a part of my journey toward transformation. I am learning to be self-aware and gentle with myself. Guilt does not serve me, and I choose to instead focus on my positive intentions and actions. I am grateful for the lessons that my mistakes have taught me. I choose to honor my experiences and incorporate them into what is in store for me. I am committed to treating myself with kindness and compassion regardless of my past decisions. I release all feelings of guilt and embrace my inherent worthiness and deservingness. I am eager to see where my journey will take me. I am worthy of forgiveness and acknowledge and let go of any perceived mistakes or shortcomings. I believe that everything happens for a reason and that even my mistakes have led me to become the person I am today. My bad days do not define me, and my future is full of new promises. I am grateful for every chance to learn, grow, and develop my future self. I will relinquish guilt as I allow my past mistakes to guide me toward positive changes, focus on applying the lessons I've learned, and acknowledge my worth.

# Release Your Ego

## I am letting go of harmful emotions, items, and values that fuel my inflated ego.

When I accept my faults, I am able to move forward with greater clarity and purpose. I choose to release my need for control and domination over my life. I have insecurities and fears, but I harness a sense of compassion and courage for myself. I release my attachment to material possessions and external validation that enhance my ego. I am learning to abandon the need to constantly compare myself to others, and instead I focus on being the best version of myself. My ego is the enemy of my progress and the single biggest obstruction to my spiritual growth. Therefore, I'm fully committed to doing whatever it takes to release it. My ego is not a friend, and I only invite love, kindness, and grace to live within me. My ego is a false sense of self, but I am now shedding it to discover my true self. As I grow out of my ego and into my true humility, I begin to understand what true self-love is. The journey toward self-awareness and growth is a lifelong process. Every day, I will choose to release my ego, live in alignment with my values, and value the person I am becoming.

# Commit to Fostering Connections

**I am fully committed to fostering healthy and meaningful connections with others.**

Every time I interact with someone, I make it a priority to connect with them on a deep level, approaching each encounter with empathy, compassion, and vulnerability. I know that these qualities are the foundation of any authentic connection. I understand that each person has a unique perspective shaped by their experiences and beliefs, so I always strive to engage with and understand their point of view. Even in times when we don't see eye to eye, I believe that we can still create a safe space for each other to feel seen, heard, and valued. Life can be tough, and we all face struggles and challenges, but I am here to share love and connect with everyone. I am committed to supporting others through those difficult times. I am aware that vulnerability is essential for creating deep connections, so I show up as my true, authentic self. I encourage others to reveal their true selves as much as possible. I am always able to cultivate a profound sense of belonging with myself and the people around me when I focus on true connection. I'm so grateful for these meaningful relationships that will continue to bring me a sense of purpose and fulfillment with each passing day.

# DAY 62
## Ask For Help

I am unafraid of asking for assistance
from others, whether for a quick favor or
for aid with a deeply personal hardship.

I reaffirm to myself daily that asking for help is not a sign of weakness but rather a powerful act of self-care. I prioritize my well-being by seeking support when I need it. I've learned to recognize when I need help without being too hard on myself or feeling ashamed. Instead, I remind myself of the people who provide me with the help I need, as well as those I've helped along the way. I embrace my vulnerability and show humility when I ask for support. Whether I ask for help from religious or spiritual leaders, counselors or therapists, energy healers or practitioners, meditation or mindfulness teachers, support groups, or friends and family, I am ready to get the help I need. I know that seeking support is a positive and necessary step in my personal growth. I create a safe and supportive environment that encourages me to prioritize my self-care. When solo self-care is no longer sufficient, I am fully committed to taking care of myself by seeking help when I need it. When I get the help I need, I am strengthening my resilience and ability to thrive. Ultimately, asking for help is a powerful way to show that I am in control of my life. Daily, I will affirm that I am not afraid to take the steps needed to grow from the inside out and ask for help when I need it.

# Grow from Heartbreak

**I am a resilient, loving person who will grow and prosper from these current feelings of heartbreak.**

Sometimes my heart hurts, and that's okay. Sometimes I get disappointed and feel let down, but it's a beautiful part of my journey. I know that heartbreak is a part of life, and it's natural to feel sad and vulnerable. But I also know that these feelings won't last forever, and I can find strength to overcome them. I trust that the pain I feel now will lead me to growth and greater happiness in the future. Even though it's hard, I embrace the lessons that come with heartbreak and believe I will find a healthier and more fulfilling friendship or relationship in the future. It's okay to take my time and heal at my own pace. I won't rush myself through this process or try to ignore my emotions. Instead, I'll give myself the space and support I need to work through my feelings and come out stronger on the other side. I am deserving of love and respect, and I won't settle for anything less than what I deserve. Even though heartbreak may make me doubt my worth, I know that I am valuable and deserving of a healthy and loving relationship. Even though heartbreak can be all-consuming, I won't let it define my entire life. Instead, I will look for the good in each day and trust that happiness and love are still within reach.

# Welcome a Romantic Relationship

I am manifesting a loving, fulfilling relationship
that cultivates mutual respect, trust, and love.

My heart is prepared to receive love. I believe that the Universe is conspiring in my favor to connect me with the perfect partner. My positive energy, unwavering faith, and unyielding determination will help me attract a deep, meaningful connection. The partner that I seek is also seeking me. I bring valuable qualities to any relationship, and I am committed to personal growth to create a healthy, harmonious, loving partnership. I release any past relationship blocks that are holding me back from finding the ideal person. I am grateful for the opportunity to experience love and am excited to meet my soulmate. I strongly believe our connection will be deep, meaningful, and lasting. I stay positive, patient, and confident, knowing that my perfect match is out there waiting for me. I firmly believe that my thoughts and words have power, and I choose to focus on love, gratitude, and abundance. I am fully worthy of love, and I only attract healthy, supportive relationships into my life. I trust my intuition and follow my heart to lead me toward the right person. Thank you, Universe, for bringing me the loving relationship that I desire and deserve. With each passing day, I will affirm that my soulmate is one step closer, and I am ready to welcome them with open arms.

# Find Self-Love

## I am learning to love myself fully despite what I have gone through in my past.

Self-love is fundamental to cultivating a healthy inner world because the most important relationship I will ever have is the one with myself. Although I know I'm not perfect, I still show grace and compassion to myself on my journey. I forgive myself for any past mistakes and give myself permission to make new ones. I see myself the same way the Universe sees me. I have a deep belief in my own potential to achieve my goals and dreams. I respect the unique qualities and perspectives of those around me and embrace them to better myself. I am dedicated to creating an inner world where love, kindness, and compassion take precedence. As I go through my days, I remain grounded in my self-worth and my commitment to love. I consciously focus on the positives in my life and release any negative energy and self-doubt that may arise. I am grateful for all the blessings in my life, fully confident I deserve them, and anticipate what the Universe plans to bring my way next. I am confident in my ability to love myself and others and be loved, and I trust that the Universe will reveal the relationships and experiences that align with my highest good. Each day, I will continue to be amazed by the endless possibilities that exist for me and the boundless potential for self-love and growth.

# Make Responsible Choices

**I am responsible for my choices and am confident in my ability to make the right choices for myself.**

I trust my intuition. Every choice I make is an opportunity for growth and learning, regardless of the outcome. I am capable of making choices that align with my values and bring me closer to my goals. I have the power to choose my thoughts, feelings, and reactions to any situation. I choose to approach decision-making with a clear and open mind, free from fear and self-doubt. I acknowledge that every choice I make has consequences, and I take responsibility for the outcomes of my decisions. I release any attachment to the outcomes of my choices and trust that everything will work out for my highest good. I trust my choices. Choices create opportunities for personal development. I embrace the journey of decision-making with curiosity. Choices bring growth and learning. I align choices with my values and goals. I am grateful for the abundance of opportunities and choices available to me. I choose to focus on the positive aspects of my choices and release any negative thoughts or doubts. I will continue to constantly learn and grow through my choices, and I will embrace the journey with enthusiasm and curiosity.

# Create a New Life Filled with Positivity

**I am capable of creating a happy and enriched life by changing my thoughts and beliefs.**

I choose to focus on positive, empowering thoughts that align with my goals and dreams. I release any limiting beliefs that hold me back and replace them with new, empowering beliefs that support my growth and success. I am worthy of living a fulfilling and happy life. I trust that the Universe supports me in creating the life of my dreams. I take full responsibility for my actions and choices, and I make conscious decisions that align with my vision for a better, happier life. I choose to focus on abundance and prosperity, and I take inspired action toward creating the life I desire. I am grateful for all the blessings in my life, both big and small, knowing that they contribute to the life I want. I cultivate a spirit of gratitude and appreciation, knowing that gratitude leads to attracting more of what I want into my life. As the days go on, I will focus on the positive aspects of my life and let go of negativity and limiting beliefs.

# Reject the Victim Mindset

### I am not a victim, and I have the ability to shape a better, more satisfying life.

I decide to concentrate on the positive and seek solutions for obstacles instead of fixating on the negative. Bad things happen to good people, and I release any negativity or bad energy I carry with me. I am deserving of abundance, respect, and love, and I won't allow past experiences to restrict my potential. I forgive myself and others for any harm caused and choose to move forward with kindness and empathy. I have faith in the Universe's ability to lead me toward recovery and progress. I'm receptive to any new opportunities and experiences that will enable me to become stronger and less focused on self-pity. Every setback is a chance to learn and become a better version of myself. I am a survivor and a thriver, not a victim. My circumstances do not define me, and I refuse to let them hold me back from living my best life. Instead of giving in to negativity and self-pity, I choose to remain strong, resilient, and optimistic. I release the victim mindset and embrace my power to create positive change. I am worthy of living a life free from victimization and pain. I choose to let go of past hurts and traumas. I focus on my strengths and abilities rather than my limitations. I will continue to focus on releasing the victim mindset and creating a life filled with joy, love, and abundance.

---

— DAY 69 —

# Take Radical Responsibility

**I am radically responsible for my life, meaning that I am in control of my life and the decisions I make.**

---

I choose to take responsibility for all my actions and their outcomes. I refuse to blame others for my circumstances, and instead I focus on finding solutions and taking proactive steps toward achieving my personal and professional goals. I recognize that my thoughts and beliefs shape my reality, and I choose to focus on positivity, abundance, and gratitude in all areas of my life. I am committed to living a life of purpose, fulfillment, and joy, and I take full responsibility for creating the life I desire. I am open to feedback and constructive criticism, recognizing that this can help me improve and become the best version of myself. I am the author of my own life story and choose to write a narrative of strength and resilience. I release any attachment to negative labels and identities and choose to define myself on my own terms. I take responsibility for my own happiness and well-being. I'm the boss of me, and as time goes on, I will continue to make the decisions that will take me to the top!

# Realize Happiness Within

**I am full of an abundance of love, compassion, and joy within me that I can tap into at any moment.**

I'm like a treasure chest, and all the gems I need to live a rich and fulfilling life are already within me, just waiting to be discovered! I acknowledge that I have everything I need within myself to live a happy, fulfilled life. I am not defined by external possessions, accomplishments, or validation from others. I am complete and content within myself. I trust that the Universe has provided me with everything I need, and I am open to receiving more abundance in all areas of my life. I release any feelings of lack or scarcity and embrace the abundance that surrounds me. I am worthy of all good things, and I know that I deserve to live a life filled with happiness, love, and prosperity. I am grateful for the blessings in my life, both big and small, and know that they are a part of the reason I am happy within. I am content with what I have while also striving toward my goals and dreams. I will approach each day with positivity and patience, knowing it will fuel my inner happiness.

# Focus On Your Growth and Transformation

I am more than my past mistakes and trauma; though I may feel damaged, I choose to see my past struggles as opportunities for growth and transformation.

---

Life can be really tough, and it's okay for me to have moments of feeling broken after I experience challenging or traumatic events. I release the belief that I am damaged or unworthy of love, and I embrace my innate goodness. I trust that I am exactly where I am supposed to be in my journey toward healing and self-discovery, and I have the inner resources to overcome any obstacles along my way. I forgive myself and others for any past mistakes and pain, and I choose to focus on the present moment with compassion and understanding. I surrender my fear and self-doubt to a higher power, and I trust that I am guided and supported in every moment. I acknowledge my pain and trauma, but I am not defined by it. I am still whole and valuable. I am capable of healing and transforming my pain into wisdom and true self-love. I release any shame and self-blame and embrace self-love and acceptance. I am surrounded by love and support, and I choose to let this lift me up and help me heal. I am worthy of love, happiness, and abundance, and I am excited to see what the future holds for me. Every day, I will choose to focus on my resilience and strength rather than my wounds.

# Celebrate Your Uniqueness

### I am a unique person with a creative, authentic, and out-of-the box mind.

My uniqueness is my superpower. I embrace my individuality and use it to make a positive impact on myself and others. I am not meant to fit into anyone else's mold or expectations. I am meant to be myself and create my own future. My unique qualities and experiences make me irreplaceable. I will always use my traits to create a fulfilling life and inspire others. I will not compare myself to others or let their opinions of me dictate my worth. I am worthy simply because I exist and bring unique contributions to the world. By embracing my uniqueness, I attract people and opportunities that align with my authentic self. I celebrate my uniqueness and recognize it as a gift that makes me special and valuable. I embrace my individuality, and I am always expressing myself authentically and creatively. I am proud of my differences and recognize them as strengths that set me apart from others. I embrace the power of honoring and respecting the uniqueness of others. My uniqueness is needed in this world. As days go on, I will continue to be grateful for my unique perspective, experiences, and talents, which contribute to making the world a more diverse and interesting place.

# Become the Highest Version of Yourself

*I am constantly expanding and growing, and I trust that the Universe is conspiring in my favor to help me become the best version of myself.*

I am on a journey toward becoming my best self. My best self isn't a one-time destination, but a lifelong commitment to the process of my life. I am aligned with the energy of abundance, joy, and success, and I am attracting positive experiences and opportunities into my life that support my growth and evolution. I am the creator of my reality, and I have the power to manifest my highest potential by focusing intentions on my desired outcomes. I am constantly evolving into my highest, most authentic self. I trust in my ability to tap into my inner wisdom and guidance to reach my highest potential. I am open and receptive to opportunities that align with my highest good and purpose. I release any limiting beliefs and fears that hold me back from becoming my best self. I am committed to living a life that reflects my highest values and aspirations, and I work toward that every day. I am grateful for the journey of growth and self-discovery, and I will continue evolving into the highest version of myself, using my unique gifts and talents to make a positive contribution.

# Understand That You Are Protected

**I am protected, and I trust in the Universe to guide me toward the best outcomes for my highest good.**

I have faith in the divine protection that surrounds me, keeping me safe and secure at all times. I release all fear and negativity, knowing that I am spiritually protected and guided on my path. I am surrounded by positive energy and loving people who watch over me and keep me safe. I trust in my own inner resilience to conquer any hurdles that come my way. While I do stay vigilant and alert to my surroundings, I also won't let fear paralyze me or stop me from pursuing my goals and dreams. I trust in the Universe to keep me safe and lead me down the path I am meant to take. I am confident in my ability to set healthy boundaries and protect my energy from negativity and harm. I am surrounded by a powerful shield of protection that keeps me physically and spiritually secure. I am grateful for the loving protection of my loved ones and guides, who support me on my journey. I am protected from any harm while reaching my goals. As the days go by, I will embrace the protective power of love, which guides me toward positivity and empowers me to face any challenges with courage.

## — DAY 75 —

# Live in the Present Moment

**I am fully present now, and I find joy in this moment.**

I know that life can be full of distractions and chaos, but I am choosing to be entirely engaged with the here and now. I embrace and enjoy the present moment completely, knowing that it is a precious gift that will never come again. In this moment, I release any worries and regrets about the past and any fears and doubts about the future. The present moment is all there is, and I embrace it fully. I find gratitude for the simple pleasures of life, and I am fully here to appreciate all of them. The power to create a better future for myself is found in the now: I create a good future by creating a good present. I am focused on the task at hand, and I trust that by being attentive, I will achieve my goals with grace. I am at peace with the present moment, and I believe that by living fully right now, I am creating a positive and abundant future. I fully appreciate the beauty and uniqueness of the present moment. I live in the now, loving all its opportunities and possibilities. I am a cocreator of my present moment, and I embrace the power of my choices. As life goes on, I will be immersed in the present day's happenings, letting go of distractions and embracing the moment.

# Recognize Your Value to the World

### I am valuable to the world, and
### I am worthy of love simply because I exist.

My worth is not determined by external factors but by the inherent value I hold as a human being. Valuing myself means I believe in myself and my abilities, and I achieve my goals, which in turn helps the world a little bit at a time. I am grateful for my unique talents and perspective, as they add value to the world and make positive impacts upon it. I will always treat myself with kindness, respect, and compassion, knowing that in order to take care of the world, I need to take care of myself. I honor the value of my skills, talents, and experiences and use them to create positivity on this planet. I trust in my own worth and the value I bring to others. I embrace the value of mistakes and challenges, as they offer opportunities for me to learn how to become a more responsible global citizen. I recognize and appreciate the unique qualities and strengths that make me who I am, and I honor them fully. I am a valuable member of my community and the world, and I strive to make positive contributions to those around me. As I move forward in life, I will continue to find value in my contributions, treating the world with patience and respect.

# Love Who You Are

**I am a wonderful person, and I love every aspect of what makes me who I am.**

I love and accept myself fully and unconditionally, just as I am in this present moment. I embrace all my strengths and weaknesses, knowing they make me who I am today. I am worthy of love and respect just as I am. I cherish the person I am right now and the journey that has led me here. I choose to love and celebrate myself exactly as I am. I am grateful for my unique qualities and the experiences that have shaped me into the person I am now. I focus on the positive aspects of myself and my life, and I love and appreciate myself as I am in this exact moment. I am deserving of my own love and compassion, and I give them to myself freely. I respect the qualities and strengths that make me who I am, and I love myself for them. I embrace self-love as a powerful force for positive change. With each passing day, I will be committed to loving and caring for my present self, knowing that it is the foundation for living the life of my dreams.

# Work Hard to Prepare for a Successful Future

*I am so proud of all my hard work and dedication; it's prepared me for today and beyond.*

---

Every experience, every failure, and every success have helped shape me into the person I am today. I know that everything I have worked for has prepared me for this moment and the moments that are to come. I approach hard work with resolve and enthusiasm because each minute of labor brings me closer to my goals. I trust in my own abilities and commit to putting in the effort required to achieve success. I find satisfaction in the process of hard work, knowing that it helps me develop as a stronger person. I view hard work as a challenge to be embraced, and I am constantly inspired to push myself to new heights. I believe in the power of hard work to transform my life, and I am committed to making a positive impact through my efforts. I am grateful for the opportunities ahead, and I am committed to pursuing my dreams with gratitude. My hard work and effort are not in vain: I recognize that even the smallest actions make a difference in my life. I am resilient, and I persevere through anything. Through the toughest of times, I will be committed to staying focused on the task at hand, working diligently, and trusting the process.

# — DAY 79 —

# **Meditate to Unlock Your Potential**

I am aware that meditation is the gateway to my
inner world and a key to unlocking my full potential.

---

I recognize that the power of my mind is limitless, and through
meditation, I can tap into that power to create the life I desire.
I approach my meditation practice with an open mind and heart,
allowing myself to experience the present moment fully. I am
grateful for the peace, clarity, and healing that meditation brings
to my life, allowing me to let go of limiting beliefs and embrace a
new, empowered mindset. I am committed to making meditation a
regular part of my daily routine. My practice helps me center my
mind and approach life with intention. When I meditate, I feel a
sense of calm and inner peace, and my mind becomes clearer and
more focused. I am open and receptive to the transformative power
of meditation. Through meditation, I can heal and strengthen my
body, mind, and soul. Meditation helps me tap into the higher levels
of myself and my manifestation abilities. I am grateful for opportunities that allow me to connect with the Universe. I embrace
the journey of meditation with patience and compassion, knowing
that it is a process of self-discovery that unfolds over time. I will
prioritize my meditation practice every day, knowing that even a
few minutes of quiet reflection can have a profound impact on my
well-being and the direction of my life.

# Honor Your Emotions

**I am a sensitive human being, aware and enthused about the range of emotions I am able to experience.**

I honor my emotions as a valuable and essential part of who I am. My emotions allow me to work toward a life of authenticity and fulfillment. I recognize that suppressing or ignoring my emotions only leads to more suffering, so I choose to acknowledge and express them with compassion and understanding. I will not judge myself for any emotions that arise, but instead will observe them with understanding. My emotions provide me with valuable feedback and insight into my inner world and the world around me. I will not allow others to invalidate or dismiss my emotions, as they are a valid and important part of my experience. I prioritize my emotional well-being, taking the time to check in with myself regularly and practicing self-care and self-compassion to support my emotional health. I freely express my emotions because they exude courage, vulnerability, beauty, and commitment. I experience my emotions because they allow me to better understand myself and have compassion for others. By honoring my emotions, I can cultivate deeper self-awareness and a greater sense of purpose. With each passing day, I will be grateful for the power of my emotions, and I will always use them to create positive changes in my life.

# Pursue Your Desires

**I am worthy and deserving of all the abundance and blessings that I desire, and I joyfully receive them now.**

My desires are mine for a reason, and I know that by pursuing them, I will create a life that is aligned with my truest self. I believe the Universe reveals my desires to me for a reason, and that reason is to fulfill them in divine timing. I control my own destiny, and I can manifest whatever I desire. The power to create my reality lies within me, and I use it to manifest my dreams. I trust that the Universe is always working in my favor to bring my desires to fruition. I release all doubt and fear and embrace the feeling of already having my desires. With courage, determination, and a commitment to my dreams, I can achieve anything that I want. I will not let fear, doubt, and the opinions of others hold me back from pursuing my desires. I am grateful for the desires that I feel because they are the sparks that ignite my creativity, passion, and drive. My heart's desires are valid and worthy of being pursued. My deepest longings reflect my unique path and purpose in life. I am excited about the endless possibilities that lie ahead, and I am moving forward with a spirit of adventure and joy.

# Set Meaningful Boundaries

I am empowered by the boundaries I set
for myself and recognize that they define
who I am and what I stand for.

---

I develop a strong sense of self by setting and maintaining healthy boundaries in my life. I prioritize my self-care by providing and honoring boundaries that support who I am. My boundaries are important and deserve respect. I trust myself to set and maintain healthy boundaries. I communicate my boundaries clearly and assertively. Boundaries are a form of self-love that enhances my quality of life. I hold fast to my boundaries, even when faced with resistance or negativity. I recognize the importance of healthy boundaries in my relationships and make it a priority to establish them. I trust in my inner voice to help me set appropriate boundaries in all areas of my life. I honor my limits with confidence. I respect the boundaries of others and expect the same in return. I enjoy that boundaries create healthy relationships built on mutual respect. I am committed to honoring the boundaries of others and to cultivating relationships that are founded on trust. I am grateful for the sense of safety and security boundaries bring to my life. Throughout my life, I will communicate my boundaries with confidence and honor the limits of those around me.

# Release Inner Resentment

I am capable of releasing any lingering resentment, and I acknowledge that holding on to grudges and anger can negatively impact all aspects of my life.

---

With empathy, understanding, and forgiveness, I choose to address any resentment I am harboring. I refuse to let past pain dictate my present and future. By letting go of my resentment, I open myself up to inner peace, emotional freedom, and a greater sense of empathy for others. I recognize that holding on to resentment only imprisons me and prevents me from living a fulfilling life. I choose to practice forgiveness toward those who have caused me pain, knowing that it is the antidote to resentment and will bring peace and healing to my heart. I acknowledge the harmful effects of resentment on my relationships, career, and health. I choose to make choices with intention and purpose and to let go of any resentment that may arise as a result of my choices. I acknowledge my feelings of resentment without judgment, and I now let them go. I release all feelings of resentment, and instead I call in positivity and forgiveness. I approach situations with compassion and understanding rather than allowing resentment to take over. I am in control of my emotions and choose to respond with love and forgiveness, even in difficult situations. I am grateful for the lessons that come from experiencing resentment, and I will continue to use those lessons to become a better person.

# Look at Healing As a Journey

I am in the process of healing and am confident that whatever ails me will help me grow stronger.

---

I begin my healing journey with self-compassion and self-love, knowing that kindness and gentleness create the perfect space for healing to happen. Asking for help is a courageous act of self-care and personal growth, and I choose to reach out to others when I need support on my healing journey. I accept that healing begins with letting go of what cannot be changed and embracing the present moment with compassion and gratitude. I am worthy of healing, and I trust in my ability to heal. I release all that no longer serves me and welcome healing into my life. Every day, I am getting stronger and healthier. My body, mind, and spirit are capable of healing and renewal. I am grateful for the opportunity to heal, and I embrace the journey with open arms. Healing requires patience, self-compassion, and vulnerability, and I choose to face my inner demons with courage and a willingness to grow. I am deserving of wholeness, and I will love and accept myself unconditionally on this journey. Each day, I will approach my healing with an open heart and mind, knowing that the journey toward self-discovery, self-love, and inner peace is a transformative one.

# Practice Showing Dignity

**I am worthy of dignity and recognize the value and unique contributions of others as well.**

As I choose to focus on my own well-being, I affirm my commitment to honor my dignity and others' in all my interactions. I understand that every person, including me, is inherently deserving of respect and recognition. I approach every situation with empathy, kindness, and a deep sense of appreciation for the inherent value of all individuals. No external circumstances or actions by others can ever compromise my dignity, for I know that my self-worth comes from within. I hold myself to a high standard of conduct and integrity, and I maintain my sense of dignity even in the face of adversity. As I honor my own dignity, I am grateful for the opportunity to also honor the dignity of others. This practice cultivates healthy relationships and positive self-esteem, plus it also deepens my sense of empathy and compassion for those around me. I prioritize self-respect and self-love as essential components of honoring my own dignity, and I extend kindness, empathy, and respect to others, knowing that we are all equal and deserving of these qualities. With my unwavering commitment to my values and a willingness to act with courage and resilience, I will continue to create a positive impact in the world and inspire others to do the same.

— DAY 86 —

# Recognize the Power of Words

**I am mindful of my words and their influence, and I am in control of the power my words hold.**

My words have a powerful impact on my reality, and I will use them to expand my potential and create positive results. The words I use shape my beliefs and perceptions, and I will choose words that inspire me to pursue my goals. I am planting positive seeds in my mind through the words I use, knowing that they always grow into fruitful outcomes. I choose to use my words to heal, uplift, and inspire those around me. The words I use reflect my positive, loving, and peace-filled thoughts and feelings. I recognize the effect of my words, so I carefully choose to live a life full of abundant, joyful, and productive words. I only choose words to lift myself and others up, inspire, encourage, and empower. Words are powerful tools that can create positive change in the world. I recognize that my words have the power to shape my thoughts and actions, and I use them to cultivate positive beliefs, attitudes, and behaviors in myself. I let go of words that do not serve my highest good. My words can either heal or harm those around me. I believe that the words I speak have the power to do amazing things. Each day, I will be committed to creating a world of love, kindness, and compassion, where everyone is valued and respected, through the words I speak.

# DAY 87

## Allow and Enjoy Luxury in Your Life

### I am worthy of the best things and experiences life has to offer.

I am grateful for the abundance that I possess and enjoy sharing it with others. I trust in the Universe's ability to provide me with everything I am manifesting. I deserve luxury that feels comfortable and enjoyable, and I only surround myself with things that make me feel good. My desired luxurious life is not based on my bank account; it is determined by the abundance of joy that I feel in each moment. The ultimate luxury is the freedom to live life on my own terms. I am grateful for my freedom, and I use it to create the life I desire. I find luxury in simplicity and ease. I appreciate the comfort and beauty of everyday things. I prioritize beautiful and good things in my life, recognizing that luxury is not a necessity but a choice that enhances who I truly am. I am filled with a thankful heart when I think of how the Universe wants the best for me. I prioritize my time as my greatest luxury, savoring each moment and making the most of every precious hour. With every passing day, I will continue to be grateful for the luxury of the simple pleasures that bring me authentic happiness.

# Live Sustainably

### I am dedicated to living a sustainable and eco-friendly life.

I make choices that minimize harm and maximize sustainability. I am grateful for earth, the planet that we all share, and I am committed to doing my part to take care of it. I am thankful for the earth's natural resources. I understand that I am borrowing the earth from future generations, and I choose to leave it in a better state than how I found it. I choose to reduce waste, reuse items, and recycle whenever possible. I take responsibility for the future of the planet and acknowledge that it is my duty to take action to protect it. I make a conscious effort to support environmentally friendly products and companies. I believe that we all have a role to play in creating a sustainable future, and I choose to be an active participant in this movement. I appreciate the value of water, and I try to conserve and protect this precious resource. When I am living sustainably, I am creating a better future for myself, my community, and our planet. I strive to support environmentally conscious organizations, and I am always looking for new ways to reduce my carbon footprint. I will commit to incorporating sustainable practices into my daily routine, and I will take pride in my part in this movement that works toward a greener future.

## DAY 89

# Rest to Revitalize Yourself

**I am deserving of rest, and I honor this need in my life.**

---

I give myself permission to rest when I feel weary and rejuvenate my mind, body, and spirit before getting back to what I need to do. Rest is not laziness. Sometimes, lying on the grass under the trees, listening to water or watching clouds, is a much-needed break that helps me recharge. Relaxing helps me let go of stress. When life gets busy, it's easy to forget the joy of just being. This is why I take a moment to breathe, relax, and enjoy the present. I listen to my body and rest when I feel drained, refreshing myself physically, mentally, and spiritually so that I can feel renewed, energetic, and focused. Resting is a valuable use of my time and helps me revitalize my mind. When I remind myself to take a break and rest, it prevents burnout and renews my energy to keep going and not give up. Self-care is essential for me to be able to give my best to others. I love to take care of myself because it allows me to fill my cup and serve others from a place of abundance. I recognize that taking a break from my devices, work, and other obligations is important. By unplugging for a few minutes during the day, I will recharge, then return to my tasks with renewed productivity.

# Feel Secure in Yourself

I am a strong, secure person, and I am blessed
that security appears in my relationships
and all facets of my life.

As I love myself and strive to become better, the world around me becomes a more secure and loving place. I understand that security is not an excuse to give up, and I am committed to working hard toward my goals. I let go of the need to control every aspect of my life because I trust that true security comes from embracing change and uncertainty. I feel secure in the knowledge that I am always protected by my higher power, no matter what challenges or dangers I may face. I understand that true security cannot be bought or given to me by anyone else, but it is something that I can cultivate within myself. I build security through my own resilience and inner strength. I find comfort in knowing that the people I love are always with me, even when we are physically apart. I embrace the unknown with courage. I recognize that feeling secure within myself is a significant achievement that brings me greater peace than any external validation. From this point on, I will honor and cherish the unique qualities that make me feel secure with who I am and who I am becoming.

# Nurture Intuition for Personal Growth and Fulfillment

I am attuned to my intuition, trusting that the more confident I become in my inner voice, the better I become.

Trusting my intuition empowers me, strengthens me, and brings me happiness. In all facets of my life, including work, relationships, and creativity, my intuition plays a vital role in achieving success. As I continuously refine my intuition, my inner knowing expands, illuminating a clearer path before me. My intuition is my soul's voice, and I listen to and respect it. As I tune into my intuition, I gain insights and clarity beyond my rational mind. My intuition is the most valuable asset I possess, as it can lead me to my hopes and dreams. When I cultivate and trust my intuition, I access infinite possibilities and find my true purpose in life. My intuition is not meant to explain what is going on in my life, but it is there to lead me toward my highest good. I value my intuition above all else for helping me make decisions and navigate my path. I see the world through my soul and allow my intuition to guide me to achieve my deepest desires and aspirations. I listen to my inner voice and trust my instincts. The guidance I receive from my inner voice is rooted in a wealth of knowledge and experience that resides within me. Each day, I will embrace a deep sense of gratitude for the wisdom and guidance that my intuition graciously provides me.

# Put Faith in Yourself and the Universe

**I am faithful to myself and my journey, even if I cannot see the path ahead clearly.**

I trust that every step I take is leading me toward my ultimate destination. I believe in myself and all that I am. I know that I have the resilience to overcome any obstacle that comes my way. I have faith that the Universe is guiding me toward what is right for me. I approach life with optimism and hope, knowing that my faith in myself and my abilities will lead me toward success and achievement. I hold on to my faith in the face of changing circumstances. I trust that everything is happening for a reason and that I am exactly where I am meant to be at this moment. I feel the light even in the darkest of times, trusting in the unseen and the unknown. My faith is the strength that helps me emerge from any self-doubt or hate, even when my world seems shattered and broken. My faith is the key to my perseverance. With the power of my faith, I will continue to believe anything is possible in my life from now on.

# Believe In the Promise of the Universe

### I am trusting in the power of the promise of the Universe.

The heavier the darkness, the brighter the Universe's promises shine in my life. Even when I don't understand what's happening in my life, I trust that everything is happening for a reason. The Universe's promises shine on me equally, regardless of my past or present circumstances. The Universe's promises anchor my soul, provide hope and strength, and form my foundation. I don't have to earn the Universe's promises; they're a gift from the Universe and dependent on its ability to fulfill them. I believe, receive, and live out the Universe's promises in my daily life. The promises of the Universe shine brightly in my darkest moments, and they provide me with hope and comfort. I trust that when the Universe instructs me to do something, it will always provide me with the resources and means to accomplish it. The Universe's promises are the foundation of my belief, and I believe that the Universe will always be faithful to me. I take comfort in knowing that the Universe always keeps its promises and will never fail me. Like the rainbow after the rain, the Universe's promises remind me that there is always hope, even in the midst of life's storms. I will remind myself daily that I am blessed to have the Universe's promised love and support, and I will honor it in all that I do.

# Believe Your Achievements Are Limitless

I am a force of limitless potential, and
as a result, I believe in myself, take on challenges,
and conquer any deep-seated fears.

---

I refuse to let anyone bring me down because I know I've got this. The only limit I have is the amount of energy I am willing to invest in myself. My boundless goals help me become a better version of myself. Because of my ever-flowing optimism and determination, I am committed to nurturing my own growth and success. The only limits I have are the ones I create for myself. What I gain by achieving my goals is secondary to what I gain through the journey. I am capable of dealing with any challenge life presents to me because I do not impose limits and restrictions to my goals. I let go of the fears that hold me back and focus on achieving my goals with a positive mindset. I am deeply grateful for my potential and all the opportunities that await me. I welcome a limitless amount of abundance and success with open arms. Each day I am on this planet, I will continue to be grateful for my boundless potential and great destiny.

# Form and Sustain Habits

I am motivated to start new things,
and I sustain them with my habits.

My actions make me excellent, and my habits sustain my excellence. I form good habits and continue to cultivate them throughout my life. These habits make all the difference in my growth and success. I am successful and resilient, and I sustain this success with my habits. I acknowledge that my habits build the foundation of my life. Habits keep me going, and I am committed to building good habits that lead me to success. I create excellence in my life by developing positive habits and repeating them consistently. I choose to build a life of good habits that help me reach the outcomes that I desire. I have the power to create habits that serve me and help me achieve my goals. I trust that by creating positive habits that serve me, I can overcome feelings of laziness or lack of motivation. I am in control of the story I tell myself about my habits, and I choose to see them as opportunities for improvement. As I progress, I will use my motivation to develop positive habits, and I will depend on my habits to maintain my momentum and reach my goals.

# Do Some Inner Work

I am open to working on understanding my inner self,
and I will use this knowledge to grow and evolve.

I look within my heart to gain clarity and vision, knowing that looking outside only leads to dreaming. I know that I have the power to alter my life by changing my inner thoughts, and I am committed to doing so. I embrace the journey within myself, knowing that it is the only true journey that leads to self-discovery and fulfillment. I am dedicated to discovering the depths of who I am, and I welcome the lessons and insights that come with this exploration. I begin my journey toward self-acceptance by examining myself. Through self-reflection, I grow and learn in life. As I look into my own heart, my vision becomes clearer: I am now unlocking my true potential. I accept myself completely, even if there are parts of me that are hard to confront. My acceptance of myself frees me from oppression. I trust in the power of inner work to transform my life. I am excited to continue to explore my inner self, embrace my shadow, and unlock my full potential.

---
## DAY 97
---

# **Embrace a Role in Leadership**

I am inspiring and empowering others to do great things, and I embrace my role as a leader with humility and honor.

---

As a true leader, I have the confidence to make tough decisions, the courage to stand alone, and the compassion to listen to the needs of others. I strive to lead by example, empowering those around me to take charge of their own lives and reach their full potential. By taking care of those in my charge and nurturing their growth, I create a positive and supportive environment for all. I understand that true leadership is about producing more leaders, and I am committed to empowering others to step up and take charge of their own lives. I am open and receptive to feedback and constructive criticism because I know it is a necessary part of my development as a leader. I motivate and guide others to work toward a shared vision, and I cheer them on as they grow. Effective communication is crucial to my leadership success. So, I freely communicate my vision, goals, and expectations with clarity and openness. I am a thoughtful leader who takes responsibility for the outcomes of my leadership. I personally lead myself to greatness by delegating responsibilities, providing resources and support, and encouraging myself to take ownership of my work. As I keep growing as a leader, I will continue to set achievable goals, defining a path toward success for my team.

# Reject Perfectionism

**I am not perfect and choose to embrace my imperfections, seeing them as opportunities for growth and learning.**

I am open to the lessons that come from making mistakes and recognize that these mistakes are an essential part of my journey toward personal and professional development. I am not defined by my achievements or failures, and I release any attachment to external validation. I choose to focus on the present moment and give myself permission to make progress, not perfection. I recognize that perfectionism can be a source of anxiety and self-doubt, so I aim for accepting and growing from my mistakes. I am open and receptive to feedback and constructive criticism, knowing that it can help me improve and grow. Instead of a relentless pursuit of the unachievable, I honor my journey toward self-acceptance and strive to cultivate self-compassion in all areas of my life. I am perfectly imperfect, and I embrace my uniqueness and quirks with confidence and humility. I release the belief that perfectionism is the only path to success, and I embrace the power of progress. I am worthy of love and acceptance, regardless of whether or not I achieve perfection in everything I do. I am giving myself permission to make mistakes and learn from them, recognizing that growth comes from both successes and failures. As each day passes, I will recognize that my worth is defined not by achieving perfection but rather by my unique qualities and contributions to the world.

# Believe In the Law of Assumption

**I am a believer in the law of assumption, knowing that what I desire is already mine for the taking.**

I assume the fulfillment of my wishes and act toward them. The law of assumption is a key to realizing my desires, and I embrace it fully. I regularly cleanse my assumptions to let in the light and positivity of the world. I know that what I assume to be true will manifest in my life, and so I strive to assume the best in every situation. Assuming is my way of bringing my dreams into reality, and I do it with confidence. I put my faith in the law of assumption, and it brings me the fulfillment of my dreams. I assume the feeling of my wishes being fulfilled and observe the route that my attention follows. I change my assumptions to change my circumstances and create the life I desire. I assume I am who I want to be, and that assumption attracts all my worldly and spiritual desires. I am a cocreator of my reality, and I use the law of assumption to manifest my dreams into fruition. I will continue to be confident in my ability to assume the best, and I trust that it will lead me to a life of love, happiness, and success.

# Allow Detachment from Expectations

I am actively releasing my beliefs on how things "should" be, which allows me to fully experience the present moment and tap into the creative power of the Universe.

Detachment is key to unlocking a life of true freedom and abundance. When I detach from my thoughts, emotions, and the external world, I can access the realm of true manifestation. By holding a vision of what I want but also releasing my attachment to it, I allow the Universe to deliver my manifestations in perfect timing. Detachment is not about giving up or being passive but rather about trusting that everything is working out for my highest good. I commit to taking inspired action toward my goals without being attached to the outcome. When I detach from the need for things to be a certain way, I open myself up to new possibilities that I may not have even considered before. I trust that everything is happening for a reason and that it's happening the way it's supposed to. I am open to new experiences, and I trust that the Universe will bring me everything I need in its own time and in its own way. Each day, I will choose to let go of my attachment to outcomes and surrender to the flow of the Universe.

# DAY 101
## Dance to Heal

I am constantly amazed by the limitless possibilities of movement that exist within me, and I embrace dancing as a way to express myself and feel my emotions.

My body speaks a language that words cannot express, and dancing allows me to translate that language into movements that nurture my soul. When I dance, I feel alive, free, and connected to the rhythm of life. I use dance to embrace my quirks and imperfections. The art of dance helps me uncover the hidden language of my soul and express it with fluidity and grace. Whether I'm in a group class or dancing alone in my room, I allow myself to let go of any self-consciousness and surrender to the joy of movement. Moving my body helps me release any stress, anxiety, and negativity and fill myself with love, joy, and positivity. My body is an instrument of my soul, and dancing allows me to play sweet melodies that bring joy and harmony to my being. Through movement, I can heal and transform my physical, emotional, and mental states, creating positive change in all areas of my life. Dancing takes me out of my shell, making me feel more powerful, beautiful, and alive than ever before. This is my time to shine, and I embrace it with all my heart. I will continuously use dance to connect spiritually to the higher levels of the Universe.

# Explore to Find a Fulfilling Life

**I am ready to explore and take risks in order to experience all that the Universe has to offer.**

I approach life as an adventure, not a predictable journey. Even when faced with challenges or uncertainty, I am confident in my ability to navigate the storms of life with courage and resilience. I choose to live life to the fullest, embracing every moment with a sense of daring and adventure. I let go of any apprehension about trying new things and getting out of my comfort zone. I am excited to explore who I am and find my true purpose in life. I am adventurous and committed to living the life of my dreams. I let go of my fears and doubts and take the leap into new experiences because my biggest breakthroughs lie on the other side of the unknown. I recognize that simply existing is not enough, and I am committed to actively searching for a fulfilling and purposeful life. I am excited to embark on the greatest adventure of all: to live the life of my dreams and create a future full of possibility and abundance. I love to explore life because it leads me to better understand myself and my desires. I'm grateful for this journey and all the wonders that it holds. Every day, I will rise up with a childlike sense of awe and anticipation, eagerly seeking the treasures that await me.

# Notice and Celebrate Success

I am living a life worth celebrating, and I am eager to celebrate others' achievements as well as my own.

I release any negativity or pessimism that tries to dim my light. I celebrate my accomplishments, but I also raise the bar for myself, confident that I am capable of even more. I acknowledge the wins of others, accepting the positivity the Universe has to offer. I am important, and it is my duty to celebrate my existence, spread love, and focus on the good. Having a positive outlook is essential for creating a life of joy and abundance, and I focus on the things that make me happy. I celebrate my victories and cheer on those around me, believing that positive energy is contagious. When I celebrate, I invite joy and hope into my life, ever mindful that there is always something to be grateful for. I enjoy celebrating others' wins because I believe when I celebrate others, I am showing the Universe that I am also ready for blessings. I embrace the spirit of celebration, acknowledging the positive impact we can have on one another. Success is not just about me; it's also about sharing joy in achievements with others and instilling a confident attitude in others. Life is a journey, and I choose to celebrate every step of the way. As the years go on, I will celebrate my life, considering every moment a blessing and one to be grateful for.

# Recognize the Power of Restoration

I am resilient and strong, and my personal restoration process is a testament to my ability to overcome obstacles and rise above adversity.

---

I embrace the delicate process of restoration, anticipating unexpected discoveries and challenges that will help me grow and become stronger. I trust in the process of restoration. My scars are healing, my damage is repairing, and my beauty is now being reborn. I embrace a restorative mindset. I feel peace in the present moment and use it as a powerful tool for contentment and healing. Through restoration, I am able to reclaim my wholeness and rediscover my true self. I am receptive to the restorative powers of nature, music, art, and all forms of creativity. I approach every situation with a restorative mindset, transforming challenges into opportunities for personal development. I accept that my shortcomings are a natural part of my life, and I use a rehabilitative approach to learn, grow, and improve. I restore my personal happiness by honoring my vulnerabilities and taking care of myself, allowing me to be the best version of myself. Restoration allows me to create something new and beautiful out of what remains. As I live an authentic and healthy life, I will continue to lean on restoration to provide me with open doors to endless possibilities for transformation.

# DAY 105

## Nurture Your Daily Spiritual Journey

I am a spiritual being, and I prioritize my daily spiritual journey to cultivate inner peace and balance, even in the midst of challenges.

I make my spiritual journey a way of life beyond the daily act of meditation. I am committed to setting aside time each day to nourish my mind, body, and soul with practices that align with my inner self and the divine energy surrounding me. I am willing to explore new modalities and techniques that resonate with my soul, believing there are endless possibilities for spiritual expansion. My spiritual journey is continually helping me find peace and clarity in all my days. I release any hesitation around making time for my spiritual journey. I cultivate inner tranquility, love, and compassion toward myself and others through my spiritual practice. I recognize that a daily spiritual practice is a necessity, not a luxury, and I commit to making it a nonnegotiable part of my routine. I understand that spirituality is not limited to religion but is about connecting fully with my higher self. I learn so much when I am embracing my spiritual journey. It provides me with meaning and purpose in life. I undertake a journey of self-discovery through my spiritual practice, connecting with something greater than myself and understanding my true nature. I will continue to value my spiritual journey as a sacred part of my daily routine, and I will commit to nurturing it with love and dedication.

# Filter Out Harsh Criticism and Accept Constructive Feedback

I am gentle with myself, understanding
that the feedback of others may make way
for necessary and welcome change, and
I find peace within the chaos of life.

---

I am inherently deserving of love and acceptance, just as I am. I filter out harsh and unconstructive criticism from myself and others. I love and approve of myself, and I am deserving of all the love and affection from the Universe. The way I treat myself reflects my inner thoughts and feelings, and I choose to make them positive and constructive. I see clearly what amazing things happen when I approve of myself. I welcome criticism because it is a sign of progress and innovation. Criticism may be uncomfortable, but it helps me identify areas where I can improve. I am grateful for all that I am and all that I have, even though I know I must be receptive to change in order to grow. I continue to focus on the positive aspects of myself and others. I am brave and valiant, striving for my goals despite harsh criticism and failures. As the days go on, I will continue to focus on the positive, acknowledging feedback when it is constructive to my end goals.

# Listen to Internal
# and External Messages

I am open to receiving both internal and external messages that are meant to help me on my journey.

I trust in the power of the Universe to guide me, but I also look into my own heart to find clarity and awaken to my true vision. I love that the Universe speaks to me in so many different ways, whether it's through my intuition, signs and symbols, or the people and situations I encounter in my life. Everything and everyone in my life reflects my inner self, and there are lessons to be learned from every experience. I quiet my mind and become more receptive to the messages of the Universe. I am aware of the synchronicities and coincidences that occur, and they are not random coincidences but rather meaningful messages from the Universe. I trust in my own inner wisdom, and I am willing to listen to the guidance it provides. I believe that my intuition is always leading me in the right direction. I am open to the magic of the Universe, and I allow my mind to expand. I trust that all the dots in my life will connect in the future. I have faith in my potential. Every day, I will listen to my inner voice, which doesn't use words but rather feelings, and trust in both the internal and external messages I am receiving.

# Be Grateful for the Present and the Future

I am grateful for all that I have in my life, both the things that I can see and the things that I cannot.

I am grateful to the Universe for the now and for what is to come. I am thankful for the love and support of my family and friends, for the opportunities that have come my way, and for the challenges that have helped me grow. There is power in my thankful heart. I believe that my thoughts and emotions create my reality, so I choose to focus on appreciation and optimism. I know that when I am in a state of gratitude, I attract more abundance in my life. I am appreciative of and excited for what the future holds, and I trust that everything is happening for my highest good and personal growth. I am ready to receive even more things to be grateful for. I am already thankful for what is to come in my life, even though I don't see it and have yet to experience it. I feel so much peace and gratitude knowing that I am on the right path. I am filled with appreciation for all that I have and all that is coming. Thank you, Universe, for what you are doing and what you are about to do in my life. I know that I am blessed beyond measure. With each waking moment, I will continue to be thankful for every blessing, challenge, and encounter I have.

# Prioritize Mental Health

I am able to manifest my desires with freedom and hope when I attend to and prioritize my mental health.

---

My mental health means a lot to me, and I put in the work to make my mental health consistent and strong. I know that my mental health is just as important as my physical health. I engage in self-care practices that honor my mental health, like meditation, exercise, enjoying nature, and journaling. I'm also not ashamed to say that I occasionally need professional help. There's no shame in admitting that I need extra support on my personal journey. I'm all about focusing on my strengths and celebrating myself and the great life I live. I've surrounded myself with people who uplift me, and I guard my mind from any negative influences. I prioritize my mental health because it leads me to live a life that's full of purpose, joy, and resilience. When I am feeling my best, I show up for myself and for loved ones. I'm so grateful for all the tools and resources that are out there to help me take care of my mental health. Prioritizing my mental health means that I am proactive and take responsibility for my actions. I will continue to remind myself that my health is worth the effort and keep my best interests at heart when making decisions.

# Perform a Positive Nightly Check-In

*I am satisfied and comfortable with my
accomplishments each day,
and I'm happy I have a restorative
night's sleep ahead of me.*

As I prepare to rest for the night, I release all worries and stresses of the day. I know that tomorrow is a new day, full of opportunities and possibilities that align with my highest good. As I speak my affirmations before sleep, my subconscious mind is most comfortable and receptive to them, and this will work to make them come true. I am grateful for all that I have accomplished today, knowing I am on the path to achieving all my wildest goals. I choose to use this time to influence my subconscious mind positively so I can wake up with positive energy and the ability to quickly manifest my dreams. I banish negativity and now reflect on the world around me with a cheerful attitude. As I sleep, my subconscious mind is open to receiving words of affirmation that help reprogram my mind. I am grateful for my loved ones, and I send them love and positive energy as they rest as well. As I drift off to sleep, I visualize my dreams and goals, seeing myself accomplishing them with ease and grace. I will continue to check in with myself each night to express gratitude and maximize my manifestation journey.

# Trust Guidance from Angel Numbers

I am open and receptive to the messages
of angel numbers, and I trust that
they will lead me to my desired path.

---

The appearance of angel numbers in my life is a sign of divine guidance and support. Angel numbers are a reminder that the Universe is working in my favor. I get so excited when I see repeating numbers because they speak to me. The presence of angel numbers in my life fills me with peace, love, and positivity. I am open to receiving the divine messages and guidance that the angel numbers bring into my life. When I encounter angel numbers in my daily life, I am reminded that I am on the right path and that the Universe is supporting me every step of the way. I trust that the angel numbers are signs of my spiritual growth and evolution and that they will lead me to my higher purpose. As I see angel numbers and work with their messages, I am aligning myself with the highest and best version of myself and manifesting my dreams and desires with ease. As I continue to align my thoughts and actions with the messages of the angel numbers, I will manifest my desires effortlessly and gracefully.

# Embrace the Journey of Self-Discovery

**I am on a journey of self-discovery, and I am excited to explore every part of who I truly am.**

---

I am open to discovering my likes and dislikes, my passions, and my purpose. In spite of external pressure and expectations, I take the time to truly get to know myself and stay loyal to my values and goals. With an openness to discover and learn, I have the power to transform my life in ways I never thought possible. I am wise because I have taken the time to really know and understand myself. I know that there is no one else like me, and I am proud of the person I have become through introspection. Every day is a thrilling adventure as I explore the depths of my being and discover new aspects of myself. I am committed to staying true to the values I have forged and following my heart. I trust that by being true to myself, I am aligning myself with my highest purpose and living a fulfilling life. The path to fulfillment lies within me, and I am committed to embarking on this journey of self-discovery. I am courageous and willing to let go of what's comfortable in order to explore new aspects of the person I am. I will continue my journey of self-discovery with gratitude and excitement as I learn more about myself.

# DAY 113

## Utilize Your Imagination to Impact Life

**I am powerfully imaginative and have the mental fortitude to make my vision a reality.**

I use my creative thoughts to make a direct impact on my experiences and circumstances. I allow myself to dream big and imagine a life filled with abundance, joy, and love. My imagination knows no bounds, and it has the power to take me beyond my wildest dreams. I am grateful for the power of my imagination and believe that it is guiding me toward my best life. By embracing my imagination, I open myself up to a world of untapped potential. I know that my dreams and desires are not just fantasies but are seeds that I am planting to manifest my reality. I am free to soar the limitless skies of my imagination, reaching new heights with every passing moment. When faced with the realities of life, I use my imagination to visualize solutions for any obstacle. I imagine my ideal life with clarity and detail, using all my senses to create a vivid picture in my mind. My imagination unlocks a universe of endless opportunities and boundless creativity within me, allowing the right things to happen at the right times. Every day, I will embrace the strength of my imagination and put it to work so that I may achieve my ideal life.

# Visualize Your Goals

I am committed to acting toward my goals,
knowing that visualization is a key part
of the manifestation process.

My visualization practice is a powerful tool for achieving my dreams, and I bring my visions to life through my actions and intentions. I love to visualize because it brings me clarity and helps me detail what I desire. I set myself up for success when I put in the effort and dedication to visualize my goals. I believe that visualization allows me to connect with my desires on a deeper level, and it helps me align my thoughts and beliefs with my goals. I use all my senses to create vivid and compelling pictures in my mind, allowing me to take steps toward what I truly want. By visualizing my goals, I align myself with the Universe's infinite wisdom and guidance. I am in control of my own destiny, and by believing in myself and my capabilities, I can accomplish anything. I am creating powerful momentum toward my achievements when I use the power of visualization. As I vividly picture myself achieving my goals, I become increasingly motivated and inspired to take the necessary steps to make them a reality. I am grateful for the power of visualization, and I am excited to see my dreams manifest in the way they were always meant to. I will continue to visualize my goals each day, taking the needed steps to reach my desires.

# DAY 115

## Grow and Connect Through Vulnerability

**I am ready to present myself honestly and vulnerably to the world, even if it means risking rejection or judgment.**

My vulnerability allows me to build meaningful and authentic relationships. I have the courage to show up and be seen, even when the outcome is uncertain. I know that vulnerability is not a sign of weakness but a testament to my power and desire to grow. I trust that vulnerability is a necessary part of my human experience, and it is through my shared experiences of vulnerability that I can connect with and support others. I am committed to embracing vulnerability in all areas of my life, knowing that it is key to personal growth and development. I am willing to take risks and try new things, even if it means stepping outside my comfort zone. I am confident in my abilities, and I trust that my vulnerability will only make me stronger and more resilient. I know that by embracing vulnerability, I am opening myself up to new experiences and opportunities, and I will receive them with an open heart and mind. I am grateful for the power of vulnerability, and I am excited to see where it will take me in my journey of self-discovery and personal growth. I know that vulnerability is a key ingredient in living a life of purpose, joy, and fulfillment. Each day, I will commit to being vulnerable, allowing myself to flourish and connect with others.

# Commit to Learning

I am a lifelong learner and a student of life who knows that through new experiences, I can expand my understanding of the world.

I know that there is always something new to discover, and I will seek out wisdom wherever I can find it. I am open to new ideas, perspectives, and ways of thinking, and I am always willing to challenge my own beliefs and assumptions. I believe that learning is a never-ending journey and that the drive to learn will help me immensely in my personal and professional life. By investing in my education today, I am creating a brighter future for myself tomorrow. I know that by continuing to learn and grow, I create a life of purpose, passion, and fulfillment. I am grateful for the abundance of knowledge and resources available to me, and I am excited to explore new fields and areas of interest. I embrace new challenges as opportunities to learn and grow, even if it means stepping outside my comfort zone. Learning is a gift I give myself that no one can ever take away. As a lifelong learner, I am confident that there is no limit to what I can achieve. I approach every day with a sense of curiosity, living my life to the fullest while also making time to learn and grow. I will continue on this journey of personal development, knowing that every day is an opportunity to learn something new and change the world.

# Challenge Old Beliefs

I am open and willing to let go of old beliefs
that no longer serve me, and I welcome new beliefs
that will help me manifest my dreams.

---

I trust in my ability to grow and evolve, and I know that by letting go of old patterns and beliefs, I am able to create space for new possibilities. I am committed to exploring new perspectives and ways of thinking, knowing it will enrich my life and lead me to my goals. I am open to learning from others who will challenge my ideas, and I am excited to see how they impact my journey. My beliefs shape my reality, and I relinquish any limiting beliefs that do not align with my goals. I take risks and listen to different ideologies, even if it means stepping outside my comfort zone. By welcoming new beliefs, I am able to align myself with my deepest desires, expressions, and intentions. I am grateful for the power of the thoughts and beliefs that serve me, and I am committed to using them to manifest my dreams. I want to see the positive changes that will happen as a result of welcoming new beliefs. I know that by allowing outdated opinions to leave, I am creating a life of joy, abundance, and fulfillment. Each day, I will continue on a journey to find experiences and beliefs that I love, and I won't settle for anything less than what truly resonates with me.

# Tap Into Your Conscious Mind for Manifestation Mastery

**I am using my conscious mind to manifest my desires, and the Universe is responding to my thoughts and feelings.**

My conscious mind is essential to unlocking my true potential and manifesting all my dreams. When I tap into my conscious mind, I open up a world of possibilities for all my manifestations. The power of my manifestation lies within the conscious mind. My conscious mind is where thoughts and beliefs create reality. I am the creator of my own reality, and my conscious thoughts and intentions are shaping my future. My conscious thoughts and beliefs are powerful tools for manifesting my dreams, and the Universe is conspiring to make them a reality. By harnessing the power of my conscious mind, I am able to attract abundance, success, and joy into my life. I am in control of my thoughts and intentions, and I am using them to manifest the life I truly desire. The Universe is supporting me every step of the way. My conscious mind is a powerful tool for manifesting my deepest desires and dreams into reality. I trust that my focused thoughts and intentions have the ability to attract positive experiences and opportunities into my life. I am in control of my thoughts, and I choose to focus on positive and empowering beliefs that allow me to manifest my desires. Every day, I will continue to use my conscious mind with intention and clarity to manifest all that I desire.

# Embrace Your Potential

**I am limitless in my potential and capable of achieving anything I set my mind to.**

I know that I am a unique and valuable individual with my own strengths, talents, and gifts to offer to the world. Within me lie the strength, wisdom, and resilience to face any challenge that comes my way. I trust in my own abilities and believe in my potential to create the life I desire. I am courageous and committed to pursuing my dreams, knowing I have the ability to do hard work. I focus on the positive possibilities that are available to me rather than getting bogged down by negative self-talk. I release any limiting beliefs that hold me back from realizing my full potential and creating a bright future for myself. I pursue my passions and dreams, knowing that I have the power within me to make them a reality. I put in the time and effort necessary to achieve my goals, and I am confident in my ability to overcome any obstacles that may arise along the way. I focus my thoughts and energy on pursuing goals that bring me true happiness and fulfillment, trusting that my efforts and unbridled potential will lead me to a life of meaning. As each day passes, I will continue to believe in my own potential and take inspired action toward my goals, creating the life I truly desire.

# Foster Unconditional Love for Yourself and Others

**I am committed to nurturing an unconditional sense of self-love and self-acceptance, and this is the foundation for my meaningful life.**

I know that I am valuable, deserving, and worthy of love and respect—no strings attached. I extend this same level of unconditional love and acceptance to others, recognizing that everyone has a unique journey and unique experiences. My love is unwavering and unconditional, able to weather any storm and remain steadfast even in the face of change. I choose to approach others with compassion and understanding rather than judgment and criticism. I acknowledge and learn from my mistakes with no self-doubt, knowing that they do not define me. I know that by practicing unconditional love and acceptance, I am able to create a life filled with satisfaction, abundance, and peace. I am grateful for the unconditional love that is shown to me each and every day. To receive love, I must first give it freely and generously to others, fostering a spirit of kindness, compassion, and acceptance in all my interactions. I choose to live a life fueled by selfless love, letting go of anger, resentment, and bitterness in favor of a heart filled with kindness, empathy, and understanding. I am powerful and present, deserving of unwavering love and respect. By accepting and giving unconditional love every day, I will continue to create a better world for myself and those around me.

---

## DAY 121

# Act As If You Have
# Achieved Your Goals

**I am committed to taking inspired action toward my
goals, believing I have already achieved them.**

---

I choose to live my life as if my dreams have already come true. I
know that by acting as if I have already achieved my goals, I am able to
cultivate the feelings of joy, abundance, and fulfillment that are necessary for manifestation. I fully immerse myself in feeling like I have
accomplished my dreams, knowing that I am sending a powerful message to the Universe about my desires. I am open to receiving all the
abundance and blessings that are available to me, and I believe these
blessings are already on their way. I am more than able to cocreate
my reality with the Universe, and it has already given me what I truly
need. The journey toward my goals helps me grow into a better version of myself—a version of myself who has all the confidence that
comes with success. I know that my thoughts and emotions have the
power to create my reality, and I am committed to using them in a
way that supports my highest good. I am grateful for the abundance
and blessings that are already present in my life. I focus my attention
on the feeling of already having achieved my desires, and I trust in the
Universe. I will continue to be excited for the amazing opportunities
and experiences that are in store for my future.

# Persist to Manifest Your Goals

**I am committed to persisting in the manifestation of my desires, regardless of the challenges.**

I know that achieving my goals requires dedication, perseverance, and unwavering faith in the power of the Universe to bring my dreams into reality. I am willing to take consistent and focused action toward my goals, mindful that each step I take brings me closer to achieving my dreams. I know that setbacks are opportunities for growth and learning, and I am willing to embrace them with an open heart and mind. I am grateful for the consistent progress I have made toward my goals, and I choose to celebrate each step along the way. I know that by focusing on the positive aspects of my journey, I am able to cultivate the feelings of joy, abundance, and fulfillment that are necessary for moving forward. By persisting in the manifestation of my desires, I am sending a powerful message to the Universe about my intentions and my commitment to achieving my goals. I am confident in my ability to achieve my dreams, believing I am deserving and powerful. With each day, I will persist in my journey toward my desires, and I remain excited for all the amazing experiences and opportunities that are waiting for me.

# Respect Your Body

I am mindful of what I put into my body and how I treat it, knowing that my choices have a direct impact on my overall vitality.

---

I honor and cherish my body as my own sacred vessel that carries me through life. My body is a gift, and I am committed to loving and respecting it. I nourish my body with healthy and nutritious foods that support my physical, mental, and emotional health. I prioritize rest and relaxation, as my body requires adequate sleep and downtime to function at its best and heal. I honor my body as the temple of my spirit and treat it with gentleness and compassion. I am grateful for the strength and resilience of my body, and I choose to honor it by engaging in regular physical activity that brings me joy and support. I am open to exploring different types of movement and exercise, knowing that my body thrives on variety and change. By taking care of myself first, I can take care of everything else in my life. I am committed to listening to the signals and cues of my body, and I trust in its innate wisdom to guide me toward what it needs. I choose to see my body as a source of power and beauty, and I am committed to treating it well. As the years go on, I know that by honoring my body, I will be able to live a life of prosperity, contentment, and strength.

# Celebrate Yourself and Others

I am choosing to celebrate myself and others,
knowing that each of us has our own gifts, talents,
and contributions to offer the world.

---

I am able to cultivate feelings of joy, appreciation, and gratitude when I focus on positivity. I celebrate my achievements and strive to set the bar even higher with each success. My community gets stronger as we celebrate one another's successes and support one another through our struggles. Together we are able to create a strong and supportive environment that uplifts and inspires. I celebrate myself by embracing every part of who I am, including my beauty, flaws, strengths, and weaknesses. I am committed to sharing my gifts and resources with others with joy and enthusiasm. I am grateful for the diversity and richness of the people in my life, and I choose to celebrate each person with an open heart. I know that by celebrating the differences and unique qualities of myself and others, I am able to create a world that is more compassionate, loving, and accepting. I celebrate my uniqueness and stand out confidently in a world that often rewards conformity. Success comes from being true to who I am. I will create a life of joy, abundance, and fulfillment by celebrating myself and others every day.

# DAY 125

# Cultivate an Abundance Mindset

**I am grateful for the abundance that already exists in my life, and I am open to receiving even more.**

Having an abundance mindset is a powerful way of thinking that allows me to do exactly what I desire. I cultivate an abundance mentality by finding internal security, valuing my own worth, and not seeking external validation. I choose to focus on the limitless possibilities that exist all around me. I believe that there is always enough for everyone and that my own success does not come at the expense of others. I understand that abundance is not just about money but about feeling rich in all areas of my life. Because I cultivate an abundance mindset, fear, doubt, scarcity, and lack are no longer limiting me. I know that abundance can take many different forms, whether it be financial wealth, loving relationships, good health, or personal growth. I am open to receiving abundance in all its forms, and I trust that the Universe is always providing for me in ways that align with my highest self-interest. I focus on abundance rather than scarcity. I believe that my abundance mindset will bring me even more prosperity and success. I am grateful for all that I have and all that is yet to come, and I will continue to embrace an abundance mindset that will attract positive opportunities.

# Take Nothing Personally

**I am not responsible for the actions of others, and I recognize that the actions and words of others are not a reflection of my own worth or value.**

Taking nothing personally allows me to navigate life with a sense of inner peace and clarity. I understand that everyone is on an internal journey, dealing with their own struggles. I extend compassion and empathy toward others rather than taking their words or actions personally. When I release my attachment to their opinions and actions, I free myself from needless suffering. I am not a victim of my circumstances, as my inner peace and happiness are not dependent on the actions or opinions of others. I know that by taking nothing personally, I am able to let go of negative energy and create space for more positive experiences in my life. My own perception of myself is the most important thing, and I choose to honor and respect myself in all situations. Despite the challenges, hurt, and betrayal I may have experienced, I still choose to live my life to the fullest. By taking nothing personally, I can detach myself from external events and situations. I choose to live with a sense of balance, lightness, and freedom, unburdened by the weight of other people's opinions or actions. I will continue to be grateful for the peace and joy that come with taking nothing personally, and I will remember that this mindset will serve me well in all my endeavors.

# Mold Authentic Connections

I am connected to everything and everyone around me, and I seek out true connections with others, creating an enriching community.

I acknowledge the interdependence of all living things and nurture my connections with them. I show up authentically in my relationships, allowing myself to be vulnerable and open to the experiences and perspectives of others. I also recognize the importance of connecting with myself, taking time to listen to my own inner voice, needs, and desires. I create positive energy in my connections with others by listening with an open mind and heart, validating their experiences, and expressing gratitude for their presence in my life. I choose to connect with the world around me, finding beauty and wonder in the natural environment and in the everyday moments of life. I am grateful for the opportunity to experience the world through my senses and to connect with the life force flowing through all things. I know that by prioritizing true connections in my life, I am able to experience a deeper sense of meaning and purpose and to live in alignment with my values and beliefs. I am grateful for the connections that I have and for the opportunities to create new connections in the future. True connection is a reciprocal process, and I strive to support and encourage those around me to be their best selves. Each day, I will choose to live with an open heart and an open mind, allowing connection to be a guiding force throughout my life.

# Recognize Your Importance in the World

### I am important and needed in this world.

I positively impact the world, am useful and compassionate, and live honorably. I show up each day and work toward my goals with intention and determination. I am grateful for the opportunities that come my way in which I can use my skills and abilities to make a difference. I know that my presence in this world matters and that I am capable of creating positive change in my community and beyond. I am a source of light and positivity, lifting up those around me and spreading joy wherever I go. I understand that there will be challenges and obstacles along the way, but I will not relent—my goals are too important. I trust in my own resilience and perseverance, and I know that I am capable of achieving great things. I am needed by those people who love and support me. I am on this earth to help others and make a positive difference. By serving others, I find myself, my purpose, and my place in the world. I choose to show up fully in my relationships, offering my love and support to those around me. I embrace this truth with gratitude. Each day, I will acknowledge that my contributions matter and that I am making a positive impact in the world.

# Accept Your Inherent Value

### I am valuable just as I am,
### with all my successes and failures.

I recognize that my worth is not determined by external factors, such as my accomplishments, appearance, or status. I am valuable because of who I am, not just because of what I have achieved. I am grateful for my strengths and my weaknesses, for my successes and my failures, for the experiences that have shaped me into the person I am today. I choose to celebrate my individuality, recognizing that my quirks and imperfections make me who I am. I know that by embracing the value of my true self, I am able to live a fulfilling life and attract people and experiences that are aligned with my highest good. I release the need to compare myself to others, recognizing that each person's journey is unique. I am valuable simply because I exist. I am valuable just as I am, and I embrace this truth with love and gratitude. Mistakes are valuable opportunities for growth and learning, and they are an important part of my journey. Each day I will remind myself that I am worthy of love, respect, and happiness and that my life has meaning.

# DAY 130
## Embrace Your Freedom

*I am free, and I strive to live a
life of liberation and autonomy.*

Freedom comes from living authentically and according to my values and beliefs. Freedom is a state of mind, and I choose to release the limiting beliefs and fears that prevent me from fully living. I release the need to conform to society's expectations and the expectations of others, recognizing that true freedom comes from being true to myself and my values. I allow myself the freedom to make mistakes, for they are opportunities to improve. I choose to live my life with passion and purpose, pursuing the things that bring me joy and fulfillment and making a positive impact in the world. I am free to express myself authentically, follow my passions, and align my life with my deepest desires. I demand my freedom from those who threaten it, and I refuse to be oppressed by any force, external or internal. I free myself from attachment to material things and find the highest form of freedom is inside me. I am grateful for the freedom that I have, and I am committed to using it in a way that empowers others. I choose to be a beacon of light and hope in the world, living with intention and purpose and inspiring others to do the same. Each day, I will remind myself that I am free, and I will embrace this truth with delight.

# Believe Things Are Happening

I am a believer that things are happening,
even when I can't physically see changes.

I don't need to manage every aspect of my life, and I recognize that there are forces at work beyond my understanding. The Universe has a plan for me that is greater than I can imagine. I trust in the timing of the Universe, knowing that everything happens at the right pace and that the changes I seek are coming. Though I cannot see them, I choose to believe in the power of my thoughts, care, and intentions, knowing that my energy and focus have the power to attract positive opportunities. I believe I can manifest my dreams and goals, and I focus on the desired outcomes rather than the obstacles before me. I release the need to see immediate results, recognizing that change takes time, and that progress is not always visible. I trust in the process of growth and transformation, confident that every small step I take will lead to the bigger picture I envision. I believe in myself and in the Universe, even when things seem difficult or unpredictable. I trust that everything is working out for my highest good and that even in the moments of darkness or uncertainty there is a lesson to be learned and a path to be revealed. Just as I know that the sun will rise each morning, I will be certain that good things will continue to come my way, even when I can't yet see them.

# Revitalize Your Mind by Evaluating Your Mental Health

**I am committed to regularly evaluating my mental health in order to maintain my overall well-being.**

Mental health cannot be achieved overnight—it is a journey that requires consistent effort, self-care, and self-awareness. I will always prioritize my mental health by engaging in activities that promote mental fitness. I make time for self-reflection, meditation, and mindfulness practices that help me stay centered and focused. Through reading, taking courses, or engaging in stimulating conversations, I strive to challenge myself intellectually and revitalize my mental health. I pay attention to my emotions and practice emotional intelligence. I allow myself to feel my emotions fully, without judgment or criticism. I seek support from loved ones when needed and also seek professional help if necessary. I am proud of my strength and perseverance, even when others may not see the battles I am fighting. I prioritize exercise, proper nutrition, and adequate sleep, recognizing the connection between my body and mind. Setbacks and challenges are part of life, and I am not letting them define me or my mental health. I treat myself with kindness and understanding and celebrate my progress along the way. Each day, I will continue to put in the time and effort necessary to ensure that my mind is healthy and strong.

# Devote Time to Relaxation

**I am devoting time to relaxation because
I deserve to unwind and rejuvenate.**

I allow myself time to unplug, unwind, and recharge to help me function at my best. Life can be stressful, so relaxation is a priority in my daily routine. I am prioritizing self-care and making time for activities that help me destress. Whether I relax through meditation, yoga, a warm bath, or reading a book, I engage in activities that help me let go of any tension in my body. I give myself permission to rest and take breaks when needed. I understand that pushing myself too hard can lead to burnout, and I do my best to not let myself experience that. I make time for relaxation and self-care even when it seems like there's no time for them. I let go of the feeling of guilt for taking breaks, trusting that it is necessary. I don't let my mind wander to the stresses of the day or the to-do list that awaits me. Instead, I am focused on the present moment, and I allow myself to fully experience relaxation. I listen to my body and choose different relaxation practices as needed. I pay attention to how my body responds to different forms of relaxation and adjust accordingly to ensure that I am truly getting the benefits of rest. I will continue to be thankful for opportunities to relax so I can live a happier, healthier, and more rewarding life.

# Be Confident in Your Abilities

I am confident in my abilities and strengths, knowing
that they will lead me toward achieving my goals.

I believe in myself and all the many talents I have accumulated
throughout my life. Negative self-talk is not reflective of my true
abilities, and it hinders my progress. Instead, I am focused on positivity and affirmations that remind me of my strengths and abilities. I understand that growth and success often require taking
scary or uncomfortable risks. However, I am confident that I can
rely on my strengths to handle whatever challenges come my way,
and I am willing to do whatever it takes to achieve my goals. I do
not compare myself to others or let the opinions of others affect
my confidence. I focus on my own progress and successes and trust
that I am on the right path. I am capable of achieving anything I set
my mind to, and I trust in my own abilities and power. I am strong,
skilled, and resilient, and I have faith in my many strengths. I celebrate my accomplishments, no matter how small they may be.
I understand that building confidence takes time and that every
small step forward is a reason to celebrate. When I celebrate my
successes, I continue to build my confidence and stay motivated to
achieve my goals. I will continue to be thankful for the confidence I
exude daily, and I look forward to feeling my confidence grow with
time and experience.

# Manifest Your Desired Reality Through Mindful Intention and Action

I am the creator of my reality, and I trust in my power to manifest my deepest desires through conscious thought and action.

---

I am responsible for my life, but I am open to receiving the guidance and abundance that come from friends, family, and the Universe. I am grateful for every experience, knowing that they are all opportunities for growth and conscious creation. My thoughts and emotions are aligned with my vision for the future, and I trust that the Universe is conspiring in my favor to make it a reality. I take responsibility for my thoughts, emotions, and actions, knowing that they have the power to shape my reality and the world around me. I am open to the magical possibilities of the Universe, and I sharpen my mind to create a reality that aligns with my deepest desires. I am in control of my thoughts, and I know that changing them will change my reality. I take responsibility for my beliefs and use them to shape the outer conditions of my life. I believe in my ability to manifest the life I want and take action to make it a reality. Each day, I will continue to act with pure and loving intentions, bringing me exactly what I need in every moment.

# DAY 136

## Start a Revolution

I am a source of revolutionary change to my own life, and I make positive changes for the better.

My revolution is a continuous process of growth and transformation. I understand that revolutionizing my life requires a willingness to let go of old habits and beliefs and embrace new ways of thinking. I am willing to make sacrifices for my greater good, just as I would for any desire that I believe in. I understand that revolutionary change can be uncomfortable and scary, but I will step out of my comfort zone to grow and evolve. Revolution is necessary to reestablish justice and equality. I believe in creating positive change through peaceful means, but I am not afraid to speak out against oppression and injustice. Revolution is not an easy path, but it is essential for progress. I will fight for a better future, even if it means facing setbacks. I am not settling for a life that is less than what I deserve. I choose to live a life of integrity, knowing that it is good not only for me, but for the greater good. Throughout my time on earth, I will continue to revolutionize my life and make positive changes that will bring me closer to my goals and dreams.

# Believe In Redemption

**I am worthy of redemption, regardless of the mistakes and circumstances of my past.**

Redemption is possible for me, no matter what challenges I may have faced previously. I take the utmost responsibility for my actions and their consequences. I forgive myself completely for my past. I am accountable for my actions and am committed to making amends and taking steps to prevent similar mistakes from happening. I do not let my past mistakes define me or impede my success, and I live my current life in service to others. I show compassion and kindness to everyone I meet and do my best to help those in need. I seek forgiveness from those I may have wronged in the past. By making positive changes in my life and doing what is right, I can find redemption. Seeking forgiveness is not always easy, but it is necessary for healing and moving forward. I will learn from my imperfections and mistakes and use them to become a better person. Every blunder is an opportunity for growth and self-improvement. I am now becoming a better version of myself. With every day, I will remind myself that I am capable of redemption and that I am committed to taking the necessary steps toward making things better.

# Strive Toward Unity

I am actively working toward a united and harmonious future for my community.

Unity is possible among all people, regardless of our differences. Our differences are what make us special, and we can learn from one another's perspectives and experiences. Everyone has something valuable to contribute, and we can accomplish more when we work together. I find avenues to unite with others in positive ways. I listen with an open heart to those with diverse and differing viewpoints. By listening to others, I can gain a greater understanding of their experiences and perspectives, and this can help me better connect with others. When I treat others with kindness and respect, I create a positive environment in which unity can thrive. I acknowledge and work toward the progress and prosperity of my community, not just my own achievements. I speak up against hate and discrimination, working to unite others in love and peace. Hate and discrimination are barriers to unity, and I am committed to speaking out against them whenever I see them. Unity requires a powerful ongoing effort and commitment. As such, I cultivate positive relationships with people from all walks of life to create a peaceful world. Together, we can create a world where everyone is valued and included. I affirm that I will work toward building bridges of understanding and promoting peace and harmony among all people.

# Revive Your Sense of Self

### I am constantly reviving my sense of self and pursuing my passions.

Revival is possible for any aspect of my life that may have been stagnant or unfulfilling. I understand that revival requires a willingness to act toward positive change and to embrace new opportunities. By reviving my sense of self, I have the power to create my future and shape my destiny. I embrace the journey to awaken my soul. I trust in my ability to keep moving forward. With the dawn of a new day in my life, I create a vision that inspires me, and I have a purpose that is greater than myself. I am willing to let go of my old plans and embrace the new and exciting opportunities that are waiting for me. I let regrets die and am revived by making positive changes in the present to create a better future. I leap out of my comfort zone to try new things that can bring about a sense of renewal and revitalization. I am ready to experience personal revival to transform my physical, emotional, and mental health. I will continue to believe that it is never too late to become who I want to be.

# Pursue Financial Freedom

**I am ready to be disciplined, work hard, and plan smartly to be financially free.**

---

Financial freedom and independence are within my reach. I commit to creating a budget, saving money, and making wise financial decisions to achieve my financial goals. I am capable of achieving financial freedom by educating myself and putting in the effort to make it a reality. Financial freedom doesn't happen overnight but requires consistent effort and dedication. My debt does not define me; it shows the abundance that is possible in my life. I find peace and security not by acquiring more things but by living within my means and investing in my future. I am worthy of financial freedom, and I trust that abundance is on its way to me. I believe that I have the power to manifest financial freedom. I am constantly shedding old habits that hold me back so I can embrace a new mindset and reach financial freedom. I value financial freedom because it gives me the power to make choices that align with my goals and values. I am grateful for the abundance that surrounds me, and I welcome more financial abundance into my life. I am confident in my ability to create a life of financial freedom, and I trust that the Universe is conspiring in my favor to make it a reality. Each day, I will continue to believe in my ability to create a better financial future for myself.

# Be Grateful for Inspiring Relationships

I am grateful for the inspiring relationships
that already exist in my life, and I express my
appreciation for them every chance I get.

---

I prioritize building strong and meaningful relationships, knowing
that they directly impact my overall happiness and quality of life.
I am committed to doing all that is necessary to foster connections. I surround myself with people who make profound impacts
on my life. I prioritize building relationships with people who share
my values and aspirations, and I am open and honest in my communication with them. Quality time spent together is essential for
building strong, inspiring relationships, and I spend time with those
who matter most to me. I support and encourage those in my life to
pursue their dreams and goals. I build my relationships on a foundation of positivity and encouragement. I seek love that not only
accepts me for who I am but also challenges me to become the
best version of myself. I know that relationships are a precious gift,
and I am committed to doing my part in nurturing and cultivating these connections. I believe in fostering relationships that are
built on trust, mutual respect, and support, where both parties are
committed to growth and personal development. I firmly believe
in the power of positive relationships to bring joy, fulfillment, and
growth into my life for years to come. Each day, I will continue to
be grateful for the inspiring and meaningful relationships in my life.

# Work Toward Business Growth

### I am excited to see the future of my thriving and growing business.

I am committed to investing time in my personal and professional development to improve my skills. I seek out opportunities to expand my network and build relationships with others in my industry. I use networking as a tool for business and professional growth. Building strong relationships with others in my field can provide me with new opportunities and insights, and I am ready to do what it takes. I prioritize making a meaningful impact through my business endeavors, trusting that success will naturally follow. I set clear goals and objectives for my professional growth, knowing that sometimes change is an unexpected (and vital) key to success. I take ownership of my business's wins and recognize the value of growing as my own boss. I am strong, talented, and determined to make my business dreams a reality. I channel my energy into building a better future and career. I take calculated risks to achieve growth in my business and profession. I am resilient in the face of challenges and setbacks. I approach my business with a growth mindset, and I celebrate my successes along the way. Each day, I will affirm my ability to succeed, and I am committed to seeing my actions and plans for success through.

# Pursue Honest Reflection

### I am honest and nonjudgmental
### when I reflect on my choices.

---

As I reflect on my life, I have so many moments to be grateful for, whether they were full of happiness or challenges. I make time to reflect on my thoughts, actions, and experiences to help provide me with clarity about my life's journey. Reflection does not need to be a time-consuming task—even a few minutes of quiet contemplation can be beneficial. Through reflection, we gain meaning in our lives, making every moment worth living. I approach reflection with an open mind and heart. Reflection is the compass that guides me toward intentional actions and prevents me from creating unintended consequences. Reflection helps me identify areas of my life that require attention and can provide me with solutions for moving forward. As I deepen my reflection, I enhance my effectiveness in all areas of my life. Change can be overwhelming, but reflection helps me process it. I understand that reflection is a privilege and that being able to take time to reflect is a gift. I believe reflection without action is meaningless, and I am committed to taking the necessary steps to bring positive changes. I am committed to making reflection a part of my daily routine. I will continue to believe in the power of reflection to bring meaning, awareness, and lasting change into my personal journey and to express gratitude for this gift.

# Become Unstoppable

**I am unstoppable and am committed to achieving my aspirations no matter what.**

I have an unshakable belief in myself and my abilities. No obstacle is too big for me to overcome. I trust in my passion, and I won't settle for anything less than what I deserve. Mistakes are simply opportunities to learn and grow, and I keep going until I find solutions. My courage keeps me moving forward, and I will never give up on my dreams. I understand that the road to success may be long, but I am committed to staying the course. I am not afraid to fall because I know that every time I get back up, I become stronger and more resilient. I am persistent, and I believe in myself completely. I am grateful for the gifts of perseverance, determination, and support that I exude. My unstoppable mindset helps me persevere through anything. I believe that I can overcome any adversity because I am a powerhouse of strength and tenacity. I am fueled by my passion and purpose. I am always moving forward, growing, and evolving. I never settle for mediocrity, and each day I will strive to be better than I was the day before.

# Heal the Planet

**I am unwavering in my commitment
to healing and protecting our planet.**

---

I honor the earth by preserving it for future generations, as it is not ours to destroy. I recognize that our well-being is intimately connected to the health of the earth and that our actions have a significant impact. I deeply respect and cherish the magnificent and reliable earth. With mindful intent, I make conscious choices in my everyday life. I actively contribute to sustainable development that nurtures and protects our environment, ensuring it remains unharmed. I cherish the planet we share, knowing it is the only home we have in common. Education is a powerful tool for change, and I will continue to educate myself and others about the importance of healing our earth. When our earth is healing, I am healing. I choose to make sacrifices today for a better tomorrow, not just for myself but for future generations. I appreciate the natural beauty of the planet and celebrate it through my actions. I am dedicated to creating a future where humanity lives in harmony with nature. I embrace the opportunity to create a positive change by acknowledging the influence of my actions on the environment. As a guardian of our planet, I hold the unique ability to restore the damage caused, and I wholeheartedly accept this responsibility. Although the journey toward a healthier planet may be long and challenging, I affirm that I will remain steadfast in my efforts and never give up on our collective mission to create a more sustainable world.

# Bless and Honor Your Home

I am committed to blessing my home and creating a peaceful and loving environment that nurtures and supports me and others.

My home is a sacred space, and I am grateful for its warmth. I bless my home with kind energy and promise to maintain its harmonious environment. The energy I bring into my home affects the energy of the space, and I am steadfast in my efforts to create a positive, uplifting atmosphere. My home reflects my abundance mindset, and I cultivate a sense of gratitude and abundance in my home. I bless my home with love, connection, inspiration, and restoration. I honor my home as my healing space, and I am committed to creating a space that supports my physical, emotional, and spiritual well-being. I understand that my home can serve as a space for creative expression and inspiration, and I am determined to cultivate an environment that supports my creative endeavors. My place of residence is a space to celebrate life's blessings and moments of joy. I affirm that my home is a place of comfort, where I can find solace and recharge my spirit. I use tools such as candles, sage, and crystals to add warmth, cleanse, and balance as a way to bless my home. My home reflects my inner world, and I will continue to commit to creating a nourishing and uplifting space.

# Dress As an Expression of Yourself and Your Mental State

### I am proud of the clothing I wear, as it is an expression of me.

I honor my attire and belongings, realizing their impact on my spiritual growth. My clothing can affect my mood and energy, so I choose pieces that reflect my style and make me feel good. My fashion choices reflect my authentic self and unique personal style. My attire reflects who I am, and I am grateful for the joy and elation it brings me. I believe what I wear represents who I am, and I enjoy showing my personality through the clothing I wear. I feel good, and I look incredible showcasing my style through clothing and accessories. I am not afraid of wearing something unique and true to me. My attire conveys my inner world and kind heart. I express myself through my accessories and clothing, and those items uplift my mood and energy. I take pride in my appearance and understand my style is an offshoot of who I am. I invest in quality clothing pieces that make me feel confident and empowered. I wear my personality with pride, for it is the most important thing I can wear. I embrace my unique beauty and style, choosing colors that complement and enhance my natural features. Throughout my life, I will use fashion as a way to express myself and communicate my personality and values to the world.

# Get Inspired by Water

**I am like a drop of water in an ocean of possibilities, able to create waves of change and transformation.**

I am grateful for the abundance of water in my life, recognizing it as a precious resource and using it as a source of inspiration. Water inspires me to be fluid and adaptable, able to navigate life's twists and turns with grace and ease. Like a calm lake reflecting the beauty around it, I am peaceful and centered, radiating tranquility to those around me. Just as water can carve through solid rock over time, I am patient and persistent, able to achieve my goals through consistent effort and dedication. Water is a symbol of connection, and I embrace the interconnectedness of all things. We are all part of the same channel of energy and life. I go with the flow of life, like a leaf floating in a river. As I immerse myself in the healing power of water, I allow myself to let go of what no longer serves me and make space for positive growth. Water teaches me the importance of balance, reminding me to find harmony between my inner and outer worlds. I am like a raindrop falling to earth, nourishing the world around me with my unique gifts and talents. I am always evolving and growing. Water is a reminder of the cycles of life, and each day I will embrace change and transformation as necessary parts of my journey.

# Practice Meditation for Inner Peace

### I am able to find a state of deep relaxation and peace through meditation.

Meditation allows me to connect with my inner self and access my intuition. I am patient with myself as I learn to meditate, knowing that with practice, it will become easier and more natural. I am not trying to silence my mind through meditation, but rather I am uncovering the peaceful stillness that already resides within me. I am open to receiving insights and clarity during my meditation practice. I am learning to observe my thoughts without judgment and to release any control they have over me, knowing this will lead to inner peace. Meditation helps me reduce stress and anxiety, allowing me to approach life with greater calmness and resilience. I am able to let go of negative thoughts and emotions through meditation, creating space for balance and positivity to flow in. My meditation practice is a sacred and important part of my self-care routine. I trust that my meditation practice is helping me become more relaxed, grounded, and centered. By focusing on the present moment and my breath during meditation, I am able to conquer anxiety and find feelings of calm and peace. Meditation is a tool that empowers me to live my life with greater intention, mindfulness, and purpose. I will continue to make time for meditation each day, prioritizing my mental health and stability.

# Inspire Yourself Through Music

### I am able to feel fully connected to my emotions, inspired, and energized through the creativity of music.

Music has the power to uplift and inspire me at any time. I am grateful for the many different genres of music that exist, each with its own unique flavor and style. Music has the ability to transport me to another time and place, inspiring my understanding of people as a whole and creating fond memories. Music fills my life with meaning and purpose, making each day brighter. It is a universal language that brings many people from different backgrounds and cultures together. I am open to exploring new genres and artists, broadening my horizons, and expanding my musical tastes. The lyrics and the vibrations of songs inspire me to connect to the power of the Universe. When I play music, I am able to express myself in an authentic way. I am constantly inspired by the creativity and artistry of musicians and performers. The melodies and rhythms of music awaken my soul and inspire me to cherish the beauty in all things. Music helps me concentrate, allowing me to be more productive and efficient in my work. Music is a source of entertainment and enjoyment in my life, adding color and vibrancy to my daily routine. I am grateful for the transformative power of music. Each day, I will appreciate the music that lifts my spirits and creates magic in my life.

# DAY 151

## Recognize Your Past and Future Achievements

*I am deserving of recognition for my past and future achievements, and I trust that my abilities bring joy and fulfillment into my life.*

I embrace my talents, as they have helped me achieve everything I have worked for up until this point. I appreciate my experiences and the value they bring to my life as a whole. I have the courage to follow my inner voice to the places where it leads me, as it has led me to succeed throughout my life. I honor and nurture my talents to help them flourish. My achievements are unique to me and cannot be replicated by anyone else. I am willing to put in the hard work to continue succeeding. I am open to exploring new skills to diversify what I can offer and better achieve my goals moving forward. I am grateful for the opportunities that my intelligence, hard work, and persistence have brought into my life. My talents make me stand out from others and help me achieve my goals. I am thankful for my past, present, and future experiences, and I will use them to make my world a better place. I release the need to criticize myself. I let go of any doubt about my abilities, and I allow the energy of confidence to overtake me. I am ready to continue my success in this world. My pursuit of my talents is a journey of self-discovery. I will continue to improve myself through reflecting on my past successes and keeping my eyes on future success.

# Fulfill Your Mission

I am dedicated to my mission to create positive change in the world, and I will take the necessary steps to make it a reality.

---

The Universe has chosen me for my mission, and I am ready to use my strength, heart, instincts, and wits to accomplish it. I am inspired and motivated by my purpose and work continuously to achieve it. I believe in myself and my mission, and I know that I have what it takes to succeed. My mission gives me direction and purpose, like a rudder guides a ship. I am focused on my mission, and I do not allow distractions or obstacles to deter me from my goal. I am grateful for the opportunity to be on a mission that is meaningful and purposeful to me. My purpose is greater than myself, and I am honored to contribute my skills and talents to its success. I am making progress toward my mission every day, and I celebrate even the smallest wins along the way. I trust that the Universe is supporting me on my mission, and I am open to receiving help and resources as needed. My mission is unique to me, and I embrace that individuality as I pursue it. I am enthusiastic and dedicated to my purpose. By focusing on my purpose, I create a better future for myself. Every day, I will wake up with purpose and passion, knowing that I am on a mission to make a difference.

# Build Momentum

**I am worthy of building the momentum necessary to make my dreams a reality.**

Each small step I take contributes more momentum. I trust that as I act, my momentum will grow stronger. I am energized by the progress I make each day. My momentum is fueled by my commitment to my goals and values. I do not let indecision paralyze me; I swiftly decide and move forward. I embrace challenges as opportunities to build momentum and overcome obstacles. I am grateful for the support and encouragement of those around me in building momentum toward my desires. Momentum comes to me when I take leaps of faith, and I have the power to create positive momentum in any situation. The Universe is conspiring in my favor as I build momentum toward my goals. Passion is the fuel that propels me forward toward greatness. I keep searching until I find the things that ignite my soul. I am patient with myself as I build momentum, knowing that progress takes time. Success and failure will come, but what matters is my willingness to persist in the face of obstacles. I trust in my abilities and keep pushing forward, knowing success is within my reach. I am confident in my ability to build momentum and achieve my desired outcomes. With each passing day, I will celebrate every small victory as momentum is building with me.

# Face Rejection with Grace

I am resilient and can handle rejection
with grace and positivity, as rejection is
not a reflection of my worth.

Rejection is not the end but rather a redirection toward something better. I trust that the Universe has a plan for me, even in the face of rejection. Rejection provides me with the motivation to rise up and try again. Each rejection that I accept with dignity and grace brings me closer to the right opportunity or person for me. I am proud of myself for having the courage to put myself out there and risk rejection. Rejection does not define me; it helps me refine my goals and approach. I am open to feedback and constructive criticism from rejection, which can help me improve. Rejection is a natural part of life, and I am not alone in experiencing it. I believe in my destiny, embrace rejection, and enjoy the journey toward my manifestations. I accept that receiving rejection is an art that all humans must learn to master in order to thrive. I focus on the opportunities and lessons that come from rejection rather than dwelling on the disappointment. I am grateful for the rejections that have led me to better paths and experiences. I will look at every rejection I face as a step on the right path for me.

# Chase Your Dreams

**I am capable of achieving my dreams
with determination, and my dreams
are valid and worthy of pursuit.**

My abilities can turn my dreams into my reality. Every small step I manage to make brings me toward my dreams. I am grateful for the inspiration and motivation that my dreams provide. I believe in myself and my dreams, even in the face of doubt or adversity. My dreams have the power to positively impact not only my life but the lives of others as well. I trust that the Universe is working in my favor to bring my dreams to fruition. I choose to let go of limiting beliefs and negative self-talk that may hold me back from achieving my dreams. I am excited about the possibilities that my dreams hold and am committed to seeing them through. I trust in the journey toward my dreams and am grateful for the lessons and experiences that come along the way. I have the courage to pursue my dreams, and each and every one of them is coming true. I choose to pursue my passions and create a life that feels like an adventure, full of possibilities and excitement. It's never too late for me to set new goals or chase new dreams. My dreams are keys to unlock the best version of myself. I will remain committed to taking action toward my dreams every day, even when it looks like I will fail.

# Create a Heaven on Earth

I am committed to doing my part in creating a more peaceful and harmonious world—a heaven on earth.

I focus on the good in the world and actively seek out progressive change, adding peace and prosperity to my community. I am open to new perspectives and ideas that can contribute to creating a true utopia. I believe in the power of love, kindness, and compassion to transform our world. I am grateful for the opportunity to contribute to creating a better world for myself and others. I am committed to living my life in alignment with my values and principles for my vision of an earthly utopia. I am open to learning and growing from others who share the vision of creating heaven on earth. I trust that every small positive action I take has the potential to create a ripple effect of positive change. I believe in the power of collective action and collaboration toward making earth a paradise. I am now making my earthly experience heavenly. I choose to lead by example and inspire others to join in the movement toward a paradise. I am worthy of contributing to creating a more peaceful and loving world for all. I am grateful for the beauty and wonder that exists in the world and am committed to preserving it for future generations. A better world for tomorrow is possible with our hard work today, and I will continue to be excited for my part of the movement.

# Believe In Limitless Possibilities

**I am open to limitless new experiences and opportunities that expand my horizons.**

---

I believe in the endless possibilities that life has to offer me. In trusting the Universe, I am guided toward the opportunities that reflect my purpose and values. I am excited about the limitless potential for exploration in my life. I am worthy of experiencing abundance and prosperity in all areas of my life. I choose to embrace uncertainty and see it as an opportunity for boundless discovery. I believe that I have the power to create my own reality and shape my own destiny. I am grateful for the endless possibilities that exist within me and around me. The Universe is always reminding me of my limitless abilities. My imagination has the power to remove any barriers and open up unlimited possibilities. By taking proactive action, I uncover numerous possibilities that await me. I push beyond the limits of the impossible and into the possible to discover my true potential. I choose to let go of limiting beliefs and self-sabotaging thoughts that may hold me back from achieving what I am capable of. I trust that the Universe is conspiring in my favor and that endless possibilities for joy, growth, and fulfillment are available to me at all times. Day after day, I will embrace my enthusiasm and believe in the infinite opportunities for learning.

# Let Go of Doubts

*I am letting go of the power my doubts
have over me, acknowledging their existence
but not letting them control me.*

I trust in my abilities, the decisions I make for myself, and the validity of my goals. I choose to focus on my strengths and past successes to boost my confidence. I refuse to let my doubts of today limit my potential for tomorrow. I am open to seeking guidance and support from others who can help me overcome doubt. I will not let my doubts extinguish my dreams. I do not let my fears and doubts overshadow my potential to achieve great things and my ability to always pursue my goals. I choose to reframe doubt as an opportunity for self-improvement, knowing that it has something to teach me about my inner self and ultimate goals. I trust that my intuition will guide me toward the right decisions. I am strong and resilient, and I can overcome any doubts or obstacles that come my way. I am deserving of self-compassion and self-care, especially when I experience doubt. I trust in the journey toward my goals and dreams, even when doubt tries to shake my confidence. Goodbye, doubt, you are not welcome here as I grow and manifest the life of my dreams. Each day, I will affirm that self-doubt will no longer hold me back from reaching my full potential.

# Excel at Emotional Availability

I am capable of excelling at emotional availability
and expressing my emotions in a healthy way.

When I am emotionally available, I am able to authentically receive love and support. I am committed to being present and actively listening when others share their emotions with me, respecting their vulnerability as I expect them to do for me in turn. I am open to seeking professional guidance when I need support with my emotions, accepting that it may be challenging. I believe in the power of empathy and compassion in building deeper connections with others. I trust in my own emotional intelligence and intuition to guide me in my interactions with others. As I continue to learn about myself, I gain more clarity and knowledge about the range of my emotions and how to handle them. I am grateful for the opportunity to connect with others on an emotional level and share in their experiences. I am capable of holding space for others' emotions without taking them on as my own. I am deserving of healthy relationships that allow for emotional openness. I choose to communicate honestly and respectfully with others about my emotions and needs. I understand that emotional availability is critical to building healthy relationships, and I prioritize being emotionally available to those I care about. I am committed to growing in my emotional intelligence to better connect with myself. I will work toward creating a safe and supportive space for all emotions to thrive.

# Be a Magnet for Positivity

### I am a magnet for good things and positive experiences in my life.

I attract abundance, prosperity, and joy effortlessly into my life. I focus on positivity and gratitude, which attracts more of the same into my life. I attract blessings and gifts from unexpected sources. I believe that the power of attraction is within me, and I use it to manifest my dreams and desires. I understand that my energy is magnetic, and I am mindful of the people and things I allow into my space. I am committed to acting toward my goals and aspirations every day, which helps me attract positive outcomes. I choose to let go of what does not serve me and may block me from attracting good things into my life. I now embrace the things I love about myself, knowing that they are what make me magnetic to those who love me. I am open to learning from every experience and using these lessons to attract more positive outcomes in the future. To recharge my battery, I surround myself with uplifting, inspiring, and positive people and experiences. Each day, I will strive to create a life that attracts good things aligning with the Universe's plan for me.

# Choose Secure Attachments in Life

### I am deserving of secure attachments in my relationships.

I choose to cultivate healthy communication and emotional intimacy in my relationships. I trust that the Universe has my best interests in mind and will guide me toward the right people. I am worthy of love and respect in all of my relationships, and I choose to set healthy boundaries to ensure this. I believe in the power of vulnerability and expressing my needs and desires in my stable relationships. I am a securely attached individual with high self-esteem, resilience to stress, and the ability to form strong and supportive relationships. I am committed to building and maintaining trust in my relationships through being open and honest. My secure attachment style is the foundation for my emotional resilience and personal growth. I navigate interpersonal relationships with ease and few conflicts, thanks to my secure attachment style. As someone with a secure attachment style, I communicate openly and honestly, manage conflict effectively, and prioritize emotional intimacy. I choose to let go of past hurts and limiting beliefs that may hinder my ability to have secure attachment. I am grateful for the people and experiences in my life that have helped me cultivate secure attachment. I will trust that my desires are manifesting in the perfect way, and I will embrace the journey toward them with anticipation.

# Believe In Energetic Exchange

**I am worthy of receiving as much energy as I put out, and I choose to set healthy boundaries to ensure this.**

---

I believe in the power of equal energetic exchange in all my relationships and interactions. I trust in my own intuition and instincts to guide me toward relationships and experiences that are based on equal exchanges. I am mindful of the energy I allow into my space, knowing that positive and negative energy alike are contagious. I am committed to treating others with respect and kindness while also expecting the same in return. I choose to bring positive energy into every situation, knowing that it shapes my perceptions, receptions, and radiations to the world. Equal energetic exchange fosters mutual respect and growth in all relationships. I am grateful for the people and experiences in my life that embody inviting energy. I align my energy with the reality I want to create, knowing that everything is energy and I have the power to manifest my desires. I am committed to building and maintaining healthy and fulfilling relationships based on mutual giving and receiving. When I give and receive in balance, I create abundance and flow in all areas of my life. I live my life with integrity and respect for myself and others through equal energetic exchange. I will continue to be intentional about the energy I give and receive in every interaction, knowing that I have the power to either give or drain energy.

# Overcome Struggles

I am stronger than any struggle—
whether within myself or from an opposing force—
that tries to hold me back.

I can overcome anything and can easily bounce back from setbacks. I am committed to acting toward my goals and pushing through any resistance or discomfort. I welcome the challenges that life presents to me, knowing that they test my courage and willingness to change. I am ready to overcome every challenge. I am grateful for the adversities that come my way, as they allow me to use my mind and experience to create outcomes that once seemed impossible. I believe that every challenge is an opportunity to become a better version of myself. I am open to new ideas that can help me overcome any obstacle. I believe in myself and my abilities, knowing that my positive mindset helps prepare me for wins in the days ahead. I choose to stay focused on my goals, even in the face of adversity. I am committed to self-compassion, knowing that taking care of myself is essential to tackling challenges. I choose to surround myself with supportive people who believe in me and my ability to surmount any obstacle. I believe that I am capable of achieving anything I set my mind to, and I am ready to overcome any struggle that comes my way. Each day, I will choose to be motivated by difficulties, knowing that they serve as catalysts for my growth and strengthen my spirit.

# Experience Exponential Growth

I am worthy of experiencing exponential
growth in all areas of my life.

I trust in my own potential and believe that I am capable of achieving many great things over time. I am committed to acting toward my goals and making consistent progress. I believe that every experience, positive or negative, is an opportunity for learning. I trust in the powers of perseverance and consistency to help me achieve exponential growth. I am grateful for the resources and support that I have to help me reach my goals. I choose to embrace challenges and use them to my advantage. I am forever growing and changing, and that excites me. I embrace my failures as opportunities for growth and choose to rise every time, knowing that my strength lies in my resilience. Every step I take toward my goals brings me closer to exponential growth and success. I understand the power of exponential growth and choose to harness it to my advantage by continuously learning and working on self-improvement. I recognize the limitless potential of my exponential growth, and I am committed to using this force to drive progress and innovation in my life. I am open to constructive criticism to help me achieve my goals. I trust in the process of growth and know that it takes time, effort, and patience. I will continue to believe that exponential growth is mine for the taking, and I am ready to embrace it fully.

# Transcend the Boundaries of Your Extraordinary Reality

### I am capable of shifting my reality to create a better life for myself.

I trust in the power of my positive thoughts and beliefs to shape the life I am living. I am open to new possibilities and experiences that can help me shift my reality. I have unwavering faith in the transformative power of change, recognizing that it requires a delicate blend of time, dedicated effort, and unwavering patience. I can adapt and change in response to new situations, demonstrating my intelligence and flexibility. I am in charge of my own reality and can create the life I desire. I act toward my goals and make the necessary changes to shift my reality. I am grateful for the resources and support that I have in my life to help me shift my reality for the better. I choose to focus on what I want to create in my life rather than what I don't want. I believe that I am deserving of a positive and fulfilling life, and I am making that happen. My reality is shifting and moving in the right direction. I eagerly embrace the future and am ready to embrace whatever changes it brings to my reality. I trust in the power of the Universe to support me in my journey toward shifting my reality. What I am experiencing now is not necessarily a reflection of what I will experience in my future. I believe that as I manifest and shift my reality, I will create a life of joy, abundance, and fulfillment.

# Find Fulfillment Within Yourself

**I am whole and complete just as I am,
and I can find fulfillment and joy within myself.**

I choose to let go of the need to fill a void with external things or experiences. I believe that I have everything I need within me to feel content and happy. I am open to new experiences and relationships that can add value to my life, but I don't rely on them to fill any voids I have. I choose to cultivate a positive and optimistic mindset to create a fulfilling life. I trust in the journey of self-discovery and know that it takes time and effort to find true fulfillment. I am committed to self-improvement and personal growth to help me find inner peace and happiness. I focus on positive, uplifting thoughts to attract joy and abundance into my life, knowing that these thoughts help me achieve my truest desires. I take responsibility for my own happiness and choose to engage in activities that fulfill my needs. I acknowledge the presence of a spiritual void in my heart but am seeking to connect with the Universe to bring meaning into my life. I trust in the process of healing and know that it is possible to move beyond pain and loss, and I know I will feel even more whole as I move past my suffering. Each day, I will work on filling the void within myself, knowing I can create a life full of purpose, joy, and meaning.

# DAY 167

# Be Sympathetic to Others

I am a kind and sympathetic person who
seeks to understand others. I choose
to listen without judgment or bias.

I believe that everyone deserves to be treated with respect and empathy. I am committed to being there for others in times of need. I choose to see the good in people and look beyond their flaws. I cultivate compassion in my heart to bring happiness to others and myself. I serve others with my sympathetic heart and help those in need. I trust in my ability to connect with others on a deeper level and offer support and comfort. I am open to learning about different perspectives and experiences to broaden my understanding of the world. I practice sympathy by actively listening to others and learning about the world from their perspectives. I believe that small acts of kindness can make a big difference in someone's life. I choose to extend grace and forgiveness to others when they make mistakes. I trust in my intuition and instincts to guide me in showing compassion toward others. I offer support to people in need without expecting anything in return. I am grateful for the abundance in my life and share it generously with others. I believe that by showing sympathy toward others, I can create a more loving and harmonious world. With every passing day, I will choose to live with a kind and sympathetic heart, spreading love and positivity wherever I go.

# Give Off and Receive High Vibrations

**I am a magnet for high vibrations and positive energy.**

I radiate positivity and attract abundance in all aspects of my life. My thoughts, energy, and actions are filled with love, kindness, and gratitude. My energy is vibrant, magnetic, and contagious, giving off pure and high vibrations. Due to my positive energy, I am always surrounded by uplifting people who support my growth and success. I am connected to divine energy and receive guidance and blessings every day. I choose to see the good in every situation and maintain a positive attitude, knowing that even the smallest number of good vibes can make a big difference. I am open to receiving abundance and blessings from the Universe. I connect to high levels of vibrations that match my desires. I am a vibration match to my manifestations. I am mindful of the energy I bring to each moment, knowing that my thoughts and emotions have the power to shape my life experience. I release all negative energy and thoughts and embrace positivity and high vibrations. I am grateful for all the blessings in my life and appreciate them fully. I am a beacon of light and inspire others with my positive energy and high vibrations. Each day, I will find that my life is full of positive vibrations that bring me abundance.

# Make Wise and Intentional Choices

### I am selective and make choices that align with who I am.

I trust my instincts and know when to say no to opportunities that don't serve me. I am intentional about my time and energy and focus on what truly matters. I choose to carefully consider my options and make wise decisions that lead me to success. I am selective about the company I keep and surround myself with positive, supportive people. I am confident in my decisions and trust that they will lead me to my desired outcome. I am in control of my life and make choices that benefit my growth. I choose to engage in activities that bring me joy. I prioritize my time and energy by saying no to things that do not align with my goals, and this helps me achieve true success. I am patient and take the necessary time to achieve my dreams, knowing that doing it right is more important than doing it fast. I stay true to my values and priorities by saying yes to anything that supports my journey toward a meaningful life. I stay focused on my goals and make choices that bring me closer to achieving them. I am mindful of my thoughts and emotions in every circumstance. I am selective in what I consume, whether it be food, media, or information, and I choose what nourishes me. I will continue to be empowered and make choices that reflect my highest self.

# Open Your Heart

I am actively opening my heart,
allowing love to flow freely into my life.

My heart is soft, kind, and compassionate toward myself and others. I release all judgments and embrace acceptance and understanding. I choose to see the good in others and appreciate their unique qualities. My heart is strong and receptive to the beauty and goodness in the world around me. My loving heart is open to new experiences, connections, and opportunities. I am patient and compassionate with myself as I navigate life's challenges. I embrace simplicity and choose to show love, respect, and gratitude to others. I am willing to take risks and step out of my comfort zone with an open heart. I discover my true self by serving others with kindness and compassion. I contribute to a more peaceful world by choosing to love and understand others. I am connected to my intuition, opening and trusting its guidance in matters of the heart. I am grateful for the love and kindness that surround me, and I attract more of these blessings every day. I prioritize kindness over being right, and I listen with empathy and compassion to the needs and perspectives of others. I am gentle with myself and treat myself with love and kindness. Each day, I will continue to radiate love and kindness to all those around me and, in turn, receive them back in abundance.

# Experience Breakthroughs

**I am open to experiencing, and ready
to embrace, breakthroughs in my life.**

I welcome the challenges and breakdowns that I have encountered, knowing they are opportunities for breakthroughs and growth. I am focused and determined to break through any limiting beliefs that hold me back. I step outside my comfort zone and embrace new experiences, knowing that with every internal wall I knock down, I am working toward a better future. I am committed to doing the work necessary to experience breakthroughs in my life. I view defeats as learning experiences that help me understand myself better and discover my resiliency. I am worthy and deserving of experiencing breakthroughs in all areas of my life. I let go of all fear and doubt and trust that my improvements are coming. I celebrate every small victory on my path to breakthroughs. I am grateful for every aha or eureka moment I have experienced in my life. I choose to focus on positivity and possibility as I work toward my dreams. I know that my current circumstances do not determine my potential, and I am capable of achieving great things, no matter where I start. Each morning, I will affirm my enthusiasm about the breakthroughs that are coming my way.

# Embrace Your Unforgettable Qualities

**I am unforgettable, and I embrace my individuality.**

I leave a lasting, positive impression on everyone I encounter. I am confident in my identity and the value I bring to the world. I am memorable because I allow myself to stand out, and people remember me long after we meet. I am unforgettable because I radiate positivity and make others feel good about themselves. I am authentic and true to myself, and I bring my unique perspective to every situation. My creativity and originality set me apart. I am passionate and enthusiastic about life. My kindness and compassion toward others make me unforgettable. I am proud of the qualities that make me who I am, and I recognize that no one else in the world is quite like me. I am confident in my own skin and am unapologetically myself. I have a way of leaving a lasting impression on everyone I encounter. Whether it's through my words, my actions, or my energy, I have a way of making people feel seen, heard, and valued. I am committed to having a positive impact on those around me, and I know that my presence has the power to uplift and inspire. I make a conscious effort to radiate good vibes and kindness, and I know that the energy I put out into the world comes back to me in abundance. Each day, I will remain unforgettable because I will leave others feeling better than they did before they met me.

--- DAY 173 ---

# Start Each Morning with Positivity and Gratitude

### I am grateful for this great new day and the opportunities it brings.

I am filled with positive energy and am ready to tackle anything that comes my way. I trust in my ability to handle any challenges that arise today. I am open to receiving abundance and high vibrations in all areas of my life. I wake up each morning with an enthusiastic spirit and focus on making today count toward my goals and aspirations. Each morning, I wake up healthy, strong, and capable. As soon as I open my eyes, I choose to focus on the positivity and let go of any negative thoughts from yesterday. I start today with a positive mindset and energy. I am grateful that today is an opportunity to take one step toward living the life I truly desire, and I embrace each moment with excitement. I am deserving of happiness, peace, and success. I am confident in myself and my abilities. I begin today with clarity and intention, knowing that my positivity-fueled actions today will shape my future. I am grateful for the lessons I have learned and the experiences that have brought me to this moment. I am in control of my uplifting thoughts and emotions, and I choose to focus on what serves me best. I am excited about the opportunities that this day holds for me. Each morning, I will wake up grateful for the new day and the potential it holds for me to grow, learn, and thrive.

# Live in the Now

I am fully present in this moment,
and I embrace it with an open heart and mind.

I focus on the now. I gratefully acknowledge the lessons from my past, yet I liberate myself from their constraints, refusing to be defined, shamed, or hindered by them. I am excited about the possibilities of my future, but I don't let them distract me from the beauty of today. I appreciate the simple pleasures of life happening right now. The present moment is my gateway to all opportunities and possibilities in life. I trust my present inner voice to advise me wisely and earnestly, letting go of the past and not worrying about the future. I discover profound gratitude within this present moment. I am open to the wonders and mysteries of life that exist in the present moment. I appreciate the relationships I have today. I am fully engaged in my work, my hobbies, and my passions. I recognize the preciousness of the now and strive to make the most of it. I see the beauty and wonder of nature that surrounds me in the present moment. I am grateful for this moment, and I cherish it as a precious gift of life. As tomorrow comes, I will continue to be fully aware of the present moment, and I know I will continue to find true happiness and fulfillment.

# Believe In Self-Transformation

## I am capable of transforming my life in positive ways.

I embrace change and see it as an opportunity for growth and transformation. I am empowered to create the life I desire through the power of transformation. I trust the journey of transformation, and I allow it to unfold in its own perfect way. I am open to learning new skills and acquiring new knowledge that will support and fully change me. I am deserving of a life of abundance, joy, and fulfillment, and I am committed to changing myself, or my goals, to make that a reality. I am grateful for the challenges that have led me to this point of transformation. I have the power to transform my life by shifting my attitudes and beliefs. I am committed to the process of transformation, recognizing that there will be highs and lows and that each experience is an opportunity for growth. I am capable of transforming my pain into something positive and meaningful. I am excited about the endless possibilities of transformation and the new experiences it will bring. I am actively engaged in my own growth, and each day I become a better version of myself. I am confident in my ability to transform my life in meaningful ways. I release any fears and doubts about transformation and welcome it with open arms. I will continue to be grateful for the transformational journey that I am on, and I will trust that it is leading me toward something great.

# Move Past Insecurities

I am worthy and deserving of love and
acceptance regardless of any insecurities I have.

---

I choose to focus on my positive qualities and strengths rather than my insecurities. I am confident in my abilities and trust that I can handle a variety of challenges. I release all unhelpful thoughts and beliefs about myself and replace them with positive affirmations. I am learning to love and accept myself, flaws and all. My unique qualities make me who I am! I am proud of the progress I have made in overcoming my insecurities. I am learning to cultivate a sense of belonging within myself, knowing that I am enough just as I am. I surround myself with individuals who lift me up. I release the need to compare myself to others and focus on my own journey and growth. I am committed to building my self-confidence and rejecting the negative effects of my poor self-esteem. I recognize that my insecurities are rooted in fear, but I choose to confront those fears and believe in my own worth. I am confident in my unique path and trust that it will lead me to where I need to be. I am powerful and capable of achieving my goals, and I refuse to give up that power by succumbing to thoughts of powerlessness. Each day, I will continue to embrace my imperfections and use them as learning experiences.

# Take Accountability for Your Actions

I am aware of my own issues and take responsibility for working through them.

I choose to communicate my feelings and concerns in a healthy and productive manner rather than projecting them onto others. I trust that others are capable of working through their own issues and do not need me to fix them. I am committed to creating healthy boundaries and not taking on other people's issues as my own. I release the need to control others and their behaviors, and I focus on my own growth and development. I am committed to being the best version of myself in my relationships. I am taking responsibility for my personal growth and addressing my own inner demons to avoid future pain. I am committed to creating a safe and supportive environment where others feel comfortable sharing their feelings and concerns. I am capable of recognizing when I am projecting my own issues onto others, and I take responsibility for addressing them. I am free to forgive myself for projecting my issues, and I focus on moving forward with grace and patience. I choose to take ownership of my own attitude. I am grateful for the opportunities that projections provide for self-awareness. I will continually cultivate healthy and authentic relationships that align with who I truly am, and I will continue to take accountability for my actions.

# Cherish Your Inner Child

*I am choosing to cherish my inner child, knowing that nurturing this part of myself is an act of self-love.*

I honor and respect my inner child's needs and desires. Learning from my inner child comes from tapping into my past and accepting my intuition. My inner child is full of creativity and imagination. I allow my inner child to play and have fun without judgment. My inner child is safe and protected within me. I love and accept the playful and curious spirit of my inner child unconditionally. I appreciate the innocence and purity of my inner child. I nurture my inner child's joy and happiness. My inner child is capable of healing and transforming old wounds. I learn through the lessons of my inner child, and I embrace their vulnerability and authenticity. My inner child deserves love, compassion, and understanding. My inner child is a source of strength and resilience. I acknowledge and nurture my inner child, and these actions help me live a more fulfilling and joyful life. I embrace that my inner child is full of wonder and curiosity. I release any shame or guilt I may feel toward my inner child and forgive myself for past mistakes. I give my inner child permission to express themselves freely. As I learn more about myself, I will gain clarity and become more in touch with my inner child.

# Embrace the Flow While Manifesting for a Better Life

I am focusing my conscious mind on what I desire, allowing my positive intentions to manifest in my life.

I embrace the law of allowing, trusting that everything happens perfectly in its own time and way. Instead of resisting change, I embrace it as an opportunity for growth and transformation. I join the dance of life, allowing my path to unfold before me. I trust that everything happens for a reason, and I allow the natural flow of life to guide me toward my highest good. I let go of attachment to specific outcomes, and I allow the Universe to surprise me with unexpected blessings and opportunities. I understand that change is inevitable, and I allow myself to grow and evolve with each new experience. I release any need to control or micromanage situations, allowing them to unfold in their own perfect way. I trust in the inherent wisdom and goodness of the Universe, and I allow myself to receive all the abundance and joy that it has to offer. I allow myself to feel every feeling I experience because it gives me strength to face whatever is next for me. I release my hurt and resentment and open my heart to love and acceptance. With every moment, I will not need to control my manifestations because I willfully trust that the Universe is handling everything and creating the best path for me.

# Appreciate the Beauty of Romance in Life

**I am choosing to see the beauty in every moment of my life.**

I am surrounded by love, romance, and positive energy. I am worthy of experiencing a passionate and fulfilling life. I allow myself to indulge in the simple pleasures of life. I appreciate the beauty of nature and its ability to inspire me. I am grateful for the relationships in my life that bring love and connection. I allow myself to slow down and savor the little moments that make life special. I am worthy of experiencing deep, meaningful, and beautiful connections with others. I believe in the power of love to heal and transform my life. I trust my intuition and follow my heart. I deserve a life that is full of love, romance, and adventure. I am a magnet for fun and exciting experiences that bring me joy and laughter. I choose to embrace the beauty of reality and find joy in the imperfections. I allow myself to get lost in the magic of the moment and live life to the fullest. My life is full of romance and loving experiences. With each passing moment, I will choose to appreciate the beauty and romance in my life.

# Choose to Respond Rather Than React

**I am in control of my emotions and respond with calmness and clarity.**

---

I choose to respond with compassion and understanding instead of reacting impulsively. I honor my feelings and respond in a thoughtful way that aligns with my values and beliefs. My reactions to unpleasant events have a greater impact on my overall experience than the events themselves. It's important for me to cultivate a positive mindset and learn to respond to challenges in constructive ways. I release the need to react impulsively and choose to respond in a way that brings peace and harmony. While it may be difficult to control my thoughts, I have the power to choose how I respond to them. Instead of letting negative thoughts and emotions consume me, I can learn to acknowledge them and let them pass without allowing them to dictate my actions. I am patient and give myself time to consider my responses rather than reacting impulsively. I choose to respond in ways that empower me. I respond with love and understanding, even in moments of conflict. When faced with hard, uncontrollable circumstances, I must look inward for the appropriate responses and find ways to adapt and grow to meet future challenges. Thoughtful responses are powerful, and I choose to respond in ways that bring positive change. Each day, I will affirm that responding is a more mindful and intentional way of communicating that creates deeper connections and understanding.

# Accept That You Are Deserving of Good Things

### I am worthy and deserving of love, happiness, and fulfillment.

I believe in my worthiness and trust that I am deserving of the best. I honor my worth and recognize that I deserve to be treated with kindness and respect. I am enough just as I am, and I deserve to live a life that reflects my worth. I am worthy of success, abundance, and prosperity in all areas of my life. I release any limiting beliefs that hold me back from recognizing and embracing my worth. Manifestation involves identifying what I want and then aligning my thoughts, feelings, and actions toward that goal until it materializes. I am worthy of receiving compliments, praise, and recognition for my accomplishments. I embrace my unique qualities and trust that I am deserving of acceptance and love. My beliefs determine my limitations, so it's essential for me to challenge them and recognize that I am capable of more than I think. I release the need to prove my worth to others and trust that I am inherently deserving. I am deserving of forgiveness and compassion, both from myself and others. I recognize that my worth is based on what lies within. From now into the future, I will proclaim that I am deserving of my dream life and that it's within my power to make it a reality.

# Navigate Survival Mode

### I am currently in survival mode and give myself permission to take care of myself.

I acknowledge that I am strong and capable of navigating through any difficult time in my life. I trust that I have the resources and inner strength to overcome challenges. I recognize that being in survival mode is a natural response to stress and trauma. Survival is not just about physical strength but also about having the right mindset to overcome challenges. I choose to prioritize self-care and give myself grace during this time. When experiencing hardship, I have the will to survive, and this helps drive me toward success. I release my inner criticism for being in survival mode and choose to be kind toward myself. I allow myself to feel all emotions, knowing that this experience is part of the healing process. I trust that I will come out of survival mode stronger and more resilient. When faced with adversity, I am amazed at how much I can bear as I stay strong and flexible, but I will seek help when I need to. During tough times, it's okay for me to prioritize survival over personal growth. My resilience will help me thrive later. I choose to celebrate my progress, no matter how small it may seem. I will find a way to thrive, even in the midst of difficult circumstances.

# DAY 184

# Build Confidence to Face Your Fears

*I am a brave warrior, fearlessly
charging ahead toward my goals.*

With each step I take, I am fueled by courage and determination. I am doing what I need to do even if I am scared. My courage isn't the absence of fear; rather, it manifests in the moments when I triumph over fear. I prioritize my dreams over my doubts and act boldly with courage. I am capable of facing any difficulty, for I have the strength to overcome. I have the courage to keep going, learn from my experiences, and move forward with determination. I breathe in courage and exhale doubt. I choose a brave heart over comfort. I refuse to let fear define me, for I am defined by my resilience, my determination, and my unwavering commitment to my goals. When I face my fears directly, I gain a sense of empowerment, knowing that I am in control of my own destiny. I trust myself to make bold and daring choices, even when the outcome is uncertain. I now let go of the fear of the unknown because I know how to put my full trust in the Universe. I am grateful for my bravery, for it allows me to live a life of passion, purpose, and fulfillment. My bravery is leading me to wonderful experiences in this lifetime. I will continue to build my confidence so that when new and daunting challenges come, I can face them fearlessly.

# Expand Your Perspective and Embrace New Ideas

I am open-minded, always ready to seize
opportunities and face challenges with grace.

---

I welcome this new beginning, this new day, these new feelings with an open mind. My mindset shapes my experiences and creates endless possibilities. Change is not a threat to me but rather a chance for ultimate growth and transformation. I welcome transformation with open arms, and I embrace its lessons and adapt to new circumstances. Like a skilled sailor navigating a storm, I learn and adapt to whatever comes my way. In the face of adversity, I am courageous and determined, using it as an opportunity to grow and become stronger. When something doesn't align with my vision, I am not afraid to make changes or adjust my perspective. I embrace the chance for a new and better reality lying within me, and I am always working to manifest my dreams into reality. I have an open mind because it is key to building deep connections with others. By putting myself in someone else's shoes, I gain a new perspective and can relate to them on a profound level. I keep my mind open to new ideas and experiences, continuously evolving and growing. Intelligence is not just about being smart but also about being adaptable and flexible. I am resilient and ready to take on whatever the Universe throws my way. With every new challenge, I will expand my perspective so I am prepared to navigate the ups and downs of life.

# Overcome Social Pressure and Cultivate Self-Acceptance

I am letting go of the habit of comparing myself to those around me, on social media or otherwise.

I choose to find joy in my own unique journey. I release the need to compare myself to others and instead focus on cultivating self-love. I honor my authentic path and reject the oppression of comparison against myself. I choose to love and accept myself as I am. I recognize that comparison only leads to feelings of inferiority and loss of confidence. I choose to focus on my own strengths and accomplishments and celebrate the successes of others without comparison. I focus on my unique vision and avoid the trap of comparison. I am capable of creating my own path and achieving my own success. I embrace my differences and value the diversity of others. I reject the idea that comparison is necessary for creativity. I trust in my own creative abilities and honor my ideas and perspectives. I see that my beginning is not the same as someone else's middle or end. I accept my own route and trust that I am making progress in my own way and at my own pace. Each day, I will concentrate on my own progress and will value the efforts of others.

# Focus On Strengthening Your Hobbies

**I am capable of achieving the next steps in my hobbies because my determination is unshakable.**

---

I believe in myself and my ability to focus on the activities that bring me joy. I have the power to shape my future through the choices I make and actions I take today. To start working toward my goals, I only need to take that first step. Even my hobbies and interests hold power to create the life that I desire. By engaging in activities I love, I harness their transformative power to manifest my deepest desires and aspirations. I understand that having the desire to achieve is only the first step—it's putting time aside for my hobbies that truly counts. I am ready and willing to learn more about my passions, no matter how big or small. I am moving closer to my desired outcome. Success requires passion, drive, and dedication, and I am doing my best to embody all three and more. I am willing to light the fire within me and take bold action to make time for the activities I love. I am turning my dreams into tangible realities. I am committed to exploring my passions and finding work that fulfills me. I won't settle for anything less than a fulfilling and meaningful life that makes me truly happy. I will wake up every day with the intention of making my passions a larger part of my life.

# DAY 188

# Stay True to Your Strong Moral Compass

### I am committed to doing what is right and truthful, even when it is difficult and even when no one is watching.

---

I have real integrity, and I always fight for my morals. I am a respected leader with unshakable integrity, and I always keep my word. My character is defined by my actions, and I consistently demonstrate my integrity through my behavior. I understand that integrity is essential for true success, and I prioritize it in all aspects of my life. My integrity is central to me, and it sets the tone for all my other values. I choose to live with integrity by making decisions based on my values, not just personal gain. I embrace integrity by being honest with myself and others in all aspects of my life. My integrity is unwavering, and I always strive to be a person who upholds the truth and ethics in every situation. My inner image of myself is one of honesty and trustworthiness, and I will always strive to maintain that image, regardless of the circumstances. As I build my character, I recognize that integrity is the foundation upon which it is built, and I will always strive to maintain my strong moral compass. Today and tomorrow, I will choose to be honest with myself and with others, staying true to my strong belief system.

# Build a Strong Foundation to Thrive

I am building a strong foundation
because it is crucial for me to thrive in life.

Just like a house, my life needs a solid foundation to support my growth, development, and progress. I believe that a strong foundation is built on principles such as self-awareness, self-care, and self-development, and it provides the basis for my personal and professional success. Self-awareness is an essential element of building a strong foundation for me. This aspect of my foundation involves understanding my thoughts, emotions, and actions as well as recognizing my strengths, weaknesses, and values. By developing self-awareness, I can make better decisions, set meaningful goals, and create a clear vision for my future. Self-care involves taking care of my physical, mental, and emotional health, which helps me stay focused, energized, and motivated. Self-care practices range from regular exercise and healthy eating to meditation and spending time with loved ones. Self-development means I can increase my confidence, expand my opportunities, and achieve my goals. Creating an unshakable foundation is essential for me to thrive in life. Each day, I will focus on creating my foundation so I can work toward my personal and professional growth, resilience, and success.

# Establish a Professional Mindset to Manifest a Successful Career

## I am a professional powerhouse, and I am here to excel in my career.

I wake up every day ready to conquer the challenges that come my way. With my positive attitude, I am always ready to face the world and take on new professional opportunities. My mindset is laser focused, and I know that every step I take is leading me closer to my ultimate career goals. I have a clear vision of what I want to achieve at work, and I won't let anything get in my way. I have the drive and determination to succeed, and I never give up on my dreams. I embrace change and welcome new ideas from subordinates, leadership, and peers. I understand that the world is constantly evolving, and I am always adapting to stay ahead in my field. I jump at opportunities to learn new skills, expand my knowledge, and improve my craft. I am a true professional, and I take pride in my work. I am always willing to go the extra mile to ensure that my clients are happy and satisfied. I treat everyone with respect and kindness, knowing that building positive relationships is key to success. I am a force to be reckoned with, and I am unstoppable in my pursuit of greatness. I know that with my professional mindset, I can achieve anything I set my sights on. I will continue to remind myself that I will succeed, and I am excited to see where my career takes me.

# DAY 191
## Create Your Own Luck

I am a magnet for positive energy and opportunities, and I fully embody the lucky energy that flows through my life experiences.

---

I am surrounded by luck because I work hard and always strive for my goals. I am fortunate because I take on every opportunity and seize responsibility for my future. I am lucky because I practice and improve every day, and my efforts lead to success. Luck does not appear for me by chance; it's a result of my dedication to myself. I am prepared for every opportunity. I am balanced, and I can navigate the thin line between survival and disaster with ease. With my imagination, I can recognize the culmination of my desires. Everything exists within me. Anything I imagine, I have now. I create my own luck by putting in the work and being prepared for any opportunity that comes my way. The more effort and dedication I put into my work, the luckier I become. I have the talent and ability to make the most of every opportunity that comes my way. It is natural for me to feel the energy of luck in many situations in my life. I am blessed beyond measure. I will continue to believe that my lucky energy will attract abundance and success in all areas of my life.

# Manifest Love and Build Lasting Relationships with Yourself and Others

**I am capable of experiencing a love that ignites my soul and brings peace to my mind.**

I am now manifesting a love that is beyond my imagination. I show my love through my actions and make a positive impact on my loved ones. I find happiness in knowing that I can create my own joy and that I don't need external validation to feel fulfilled. I am calling in the love I desire by sharing love with those around me. Love inspires me to express myself creatively and eloquently, and I am fueled by matters of the heart. Love and compassion are essential qualities that I embody, and they are critical for my personal growth and for forming relationships with others. Through the power of love, I can make connections with people who were once my enemies. Possibilities are limitless when I use the power of love. Everything is happening effortlessly. I am blissfully happy with an unending amount of love for myself and others. Love is within me, and it will find me at the perfect time and place. Love requires sacrifice, and I am willing to make sacrifices for the people and causes I care about. I am capable of loving myself, and self-love is the foundation for building healthy relationships with others. Love is an unstoppable force, and I will continue to trust the journey of love and let it guide me to my destiny.

# Give and Receive Support from a Network of Allies

## I am grateful for the unwavering support of my friends, family, and network of supporters.

Their encouragement helps me persevere through tough times and chase my dreams. My support system is a blessing, and I cherish each and every person in this network. Even when I receive constructive feedback, I embrace it as an opportunity for personal growth because I know any feedback is meant with love. The guidance from my supporters helps me become the best version of myself. I spread kindness and positivity, and in turn, I am uplifted by the kindness and support of those around me. I may not be able to help everyone, but I can make a difference in the life of at least one person, and that is worth striving for. By serving others and helping them find their own paths, I find purpose and fulfillment. Together, we can shape the future generation with love, kindness, and empathy. Collaborating and lifting one another up is key to achieving greatness. I believe in leaving a positive mark on the world, and each day I will continue to uplift others (or allow others to uplift me) as a vital part of that journey.

# Rediscover Your Purpose and Passion

I am on a journey of self-discovery and growth, and every step I take is a step closer to my true purpose and path.

---

The feeling of being lost is a natural part of this journey, and I trust that I will find my way back to what excites me. I refuse to settle for anything less than what sets my heart on fire, and I am determined to seek it out until I find it. Feeling lost and uncertain is a sign that my life has meaning and purpose. I choose to surround myself with people who inspire me, uplift me, and bring positivity and joy to my life, as they are essential in fueling my motivation. While I can't control external circumstances, I have the power to adjust my mindset and approach and always move toward realizing my goals and dreams. Being lost presents an opportunity for me to explore new paths and possibilities, and I embrace it as part of my personal growth. It's a reminder that there is always something to be found, and I trust that my journey will lead me to where I am meant to be. In moments of uncertainty, I return to my true self and find strength and clarity within. Even when I feel lost, I will remain committed to learning, growing, and becoming the best version of myself.

# Embrace Your Calling

**I am always able to set new goals
or dream new dreams.**

---

I embrace the possibilities that each new day brings. I was born for a reason, and my calling is waiting for me to discover it. I trust in the journey of life and am open to the signs that guide me toward my destiny. I have the courage to follow my heart and pursue my calling with determination and persistence. I am open to listening and learning from others, knowing they may help me make it to the next step of my journey. I recognize that the integrity of my home and family is the foundation of my strength and the solution to many problems. I commit to the principles of love, respect, and compassion in all my relationships. I follow the principles that guide me toward my goals and dreams while also being flexible and adaptable. Through discipline and commitment, I am empowered to achieve my goals and live my best life. By following the calling within me and doing what I love, I open myself up to experiencing magic in my life. When I am obedient to my inner guidance, I am in alignment with my purpose and destined for greatness. By embracing my calling and being true to myself, I will continue to bring forth amazing possibilities and opportunities from the Universe.

# Cultivate Positive Energy for Yourself and Others

I am a magnet for all things positive.

Everywhere I go, I radiate positivity and attract uplifting experiences and people into my life. My infectious energy spreads joy and love to those around me, and I'm all about that good stuff. Every action I take propels me closer to achieving my dreams and desires. I trust that the Universe has my back and is constantly providing endless opportunities for abundance and happiness. I desire for everyone to experience the uplifting embrace of positive energy, empowering them to live their most vibrant lives. My positivity is like a beacon of light and love, shining brightly for all to see. My energy precedes me, and I'm constantly spreading optimism and light wherever I go. I believe that my positive energy can make a difference in the world, and I'm committed to spreading love and happiness wherever I set foot. Even when things get tough, I focus on the good and find the best in every situation. I refuse to let negativity bring me down or hold me back. My life overflows with an eternal river of unbridled joy, unwavering love, and relentless positivity. This is true testament to the profound influence of my thoughts and vibrations. I'm living my best life by matching my frequency with the reality I want to create. Every moment, I will align myself with the highest good, and my reality will reflect that alignment.

# Transform Yourself and Create Your Dream Life

**I am in the driver's seat of my life, and I am empowered to make changes whenever necessary.**

---

If I can't change a situation, I can always shift my perspective and attitude to create a new outlook on life. I am constantly embracing new levels of growth. I can reinvent myself whenever I desire. I have faith that my passion and hard work will lead me to my purpose, and I refuse to settle for anything less. Every day is a new adventure, and I am creating the future of my dreams. I know that I can learn from both my successes and failures, and I am determined to persist in pursuit of my goals while remaining open to new solutions. I have the power to create the life I want, and I am constantly reinventing myself to become the best version of myself. I am in love with what I do, and I trust that by following my passion, I will do great work and achieve my dreams. It's never too late to pursue my dreams and become the person I was meant to be. I am capable of transforming my life and creating a bright future. Universe, I am ready to take on anything that comes my way, and I am excited to see what the future holds. I will remind myself each day that I am a force to be reckoned with, and I won't stop until I am living my best life.

# Identify the Vibrational Energy That Shapes Your Life

**I am in tune with the vibration of the Universe, and I attract my desired reality by matching its frequency.**

My mind is a powerful producer of positive frequency, drawing abundance and joy into my life. My high frequency empowers me to attract positivity and achieve my goals, guided by my inner wisdom. I am matching the frequency of the reality I want, and I'm open to the blessings of the Universe. My energy frequency determines what I experience, and I choose to raise my frequency to attract positive experiences. The Universe responds to my positive and loving vibrational attitude. The Universe is a mirror of what I am, and I choose to be loving, friendly, and helpful to manifest the same in return. I love and accept myself, and my self-love attracts gestures of love from others. I am vibrating with positive energy and attracting abundance into my life. I match my frequency with the reality I desire, and I manifest it effortlessly. I create a powerful electromagnetic field with my thoughts and feelings, transforming my dreams into reality. My positive frequencies are on full blast, and I'm attracting nothing but amazing experiences and people into my life. With contagious energy, I'm spreading joy and love to all those around me. With my powerful energy, I will create a life overflowing with abundance, joy, and positivity!

# Cleanse Yourself Through Healthy Experiences

I am now cleansing my body through healthy habits, allowing for a deeper purification of my mind and spirit.

As I purify my mind through spiritual practice and self-love, my mental strength increases each day. I commit to purifying not only my body but also my speech and mind, creating a more peaceful and positive environment for myself and those around me. With each health-conscious experience, I become more focused and better able to discern what is truly important in my life. I practice mindfulness for the purification of my mind, allowing me to find inner peace and balance in my daily life. With each breath, I release what weighs me down and invite pure energy to fill me, restoring balance and harmony. Through the process of purification, I burn away all that is untrue and unreal, revealing my essential and true self. As I purify my heart, I am opening myself up to the path of enlightenment and a more profound spiritual experience. I am committed to the process of inner transformation, allowing for true purification of my mind, body, and spirit. I embrace the continuous journey of purification, shedding old habits and beliefs and embracing new, positive ones. I am a vessel of purification, clearing away all that no longer serves me and allowing love and light to flow freely. With each step toward purification, I will connect more deeply with the divine and experience a higher level of consciousness.

# Surrender to the Universe's Will for Your Highest Good

*I am surrendering to what is and letting go of what was, trusting that the Universe's plan for my life is always for my highest good.*

Surrendering to the Universe's will transforms my life, bringing me into harmony with its plan and opening up endless possibilities and blessings. I trust in the Universe's plan for my life and surrender to its calling, knowing that it has a purpose and a plan for me. I let go of my attachment to outcomes and surrender to the divine, trusting that the Universe's plan is always for my highest good. Trusting the divine is a strength, not a weakness. I surrender to the Universe and open myself up to receive its abundance and blessings. As I release myself to the Universe, I let go of my resistance to what is and allow myself to flow with the natural rhythm of life. I align myself with the highest good, allowing my dreams and desires to manifest effortlessly. I trust in the divine plan and have faith that everything is unfolding perfectly. I open myself up to infinite possibilities and trust that everything is happening wonderfully for me. Every day, I will release the burden of control and surrender to the Universe, experiencing the joy and beauty of life with ease and grace.

# Release Negative Emotions to Experience Genuine Joy

**I am a vibrant being, and I choose to release negative emotions to experience genuine joy.**

I know that holding on to negative emotions only weighs me down and prevents me from living my life to the fullest. I choose to let go of anger, resentment, and frustration. I understand that these emotions only cause harm to me and those around me. Instead, I embrace positivity, love, and gratitude. I am kind to myself and others, and I radiate positive energy wherever I go. I acknowledge that negative emotions are a natural part of life, but I don't let them consume me. I am in control of my emotions, and I choose to release negativity as soon as it arises. I live in the present moment, and I enjoy every second of it. I find joy in the simple things in life, like spending time with loved ones, reading a nice poem, or admiring the flowers. I know that my compassion, understanding, and optimism are key to experiencing genuine joy and happiness. I am a joyful being, and I am grateful for every moment of my life. I choose to release negative emotions and embrace positivity, love, and gratitude. I am free to be myself, and I am confident in my ability to create a life filled with joy and happiness. I will release any negativity within me so that I may embrace the joy in life.

# Embrace Your Beauty

**I am carrying a beautiful and vibrant light within me, shining brightly from the depths of my heart.**

I radiate love and joy to all those around me. My confidence is my most beautiful accessory—I wear it with pride, and it empowers me in all areas of my life. Even on the days when I don't feel my best, I gently remind myself of my innate worth. I am beautiful simply because I am me. I honor and accept all aspects of myself, both the light and the shadow. The true beauty that I possess comes from my soul. I nurture my inner beauty through acts of kindness, compassion, and love toward myself and others. I am comfortable in my own skin, allowing my true beauty to shine through to the world. I am beautiful because I choose to be myself, without apology or compromise. I honor my uniqueness and celebrate my individuality. I embrace my imperfections and recognize that they are what make me truly beautiful. My beauty radiates from within, fueled by my self-confidence and self-love. I nurture my inner flame and allow it to shine brightly for all to see. My inner beauty is what truly captivates others, drawing them in with my kindness, compassion, and love. I am truly beautiful inside and out, and I will cultivate my inner beauty each day through my thoughts, words, and actions.

# Manifest Money to Create a Dream Reality

**I am financially abundant today and every day.**

Money is a tool that I use to create the life I desire, and today I take time to visualize my dreams. I am in control of my finances and use them wisely to achieve my dreams. I believe that I am worthy of abundance and success. I use my financial security as a tool to support my goals and aspirations—while staying grounded in my values. I attract wealth and prosperity into my life through my positive thoughts and energy. I use the law of attraction to manifest the money and financial opportunities that I need to achieve my goals and live my best life. I trust that the Universe will provide me with the financial resources I need to live my best life. My doubts and fears about money do not define me. I am capable of manifesting wealth and abundance through positive thoughts and actions. I have the power to manifest my dreams, shaping them exactly to my desires and creating an environment that reflects my unique vision. Every aspect of its appearance, from the architecture to the smallest details, is under my control. I am not defined by my bank account nor by my material possessions. I am rich in the experiences and joy that life has to offer. I will continue to trust in my own abilities and use them to manifest financial abundance and prosperity in my life.

# Allow Forgiveness for Your Past Mistakes

### I am deserving of my own forgiveness for any faults I have.

I forgive myself for my past mistakes and release any guilt or shame. I am free to move forward with a renewed sense of purpose and hope. Self-forgiveness is a powerful tool for personal growth and healing. I am willing to forgive myself, knowing that it will bring me closer to my true self. I understand that self-forgiveness is an ongoing process, and I am patient and kind with myself as I work toward it. I release the heavy burden of guilt and embrace the lightness of self-love. Forgiving myself is an act of courage and self-compassion. I am willing to take this journey toward healing and know that it will lead me to greater peace and happiness. I acknowledge that making mistakes is a natural part of the human experience. Forgiving myself is an act of liberation. I release the chains of guilt and regret that have held me back, and I move forward with hope and freedom. I am willing to let go of the past to create a brighter future for myself. Self-forgiveness is a powerful expression of self-love. I am gentle and compassionate with myself, even in my darkest moments. When I forgive myself, I display self-empowerment and strength. I embrace the transformative power of self-forgiveness. I will move forward with grace and resilience and allow myself to forgive any past mistakes.

# Persevere to Overcome Adversity

I am determined to stay focused on my path,
taking one step at a time, knowing that
I will get there in the end.

---

Perseverance is the act of getting up after I fall. I choose to embrace my failures as lessons and continue moving forward toward my goals. I must take consistent small steps toward my aspirations. I acknowledge that perseverance can be challenging, but I choose to see it as an opportunity to grow and improve myself. I am willing to do the work even when it's hard, knowing that it will pay off in the end. I am becoming stronger and more resilient, trusting in my abilities and the power of my spirit to lead me toward success. I understand that perseverance is not about achieving success overnight but about committing to a process of growth and self-improvement. I am determined to keep working hard, trusting that my efforts will pay off. I choose to remain focused, motivated, and committed in the face of adversity, knowing that every step I take brings me closer to my ultimate goals. I am a warrior of perseverance, and I fearlessly charge forward toward my goals with unyielding courage and conviction. Each and every day, I will remain steadfast in my determination to surmount any obstacle.

# Ask For What You Want and Receive What You Deserve

### I am a confident creator, and I know that I can ask for what I want and receive what I desire.

I am not afraid to speak up and express my needs. I understand that by asking, I am opening myself up to new opportunities and possibilities. I trust that the Universe is always working to get me my desired outcomes. I know that I am worthy of receiving all the good things that life has to offer. I am not afraid to dream big and go after what I want with all my heart. I stay focused on my goals, and I keep a positive mindset no matter what. I know that by doing so, I am attracting more abundance into my life. I know that I don't have to do everything alone, and I am not afraid to ask for help when I need it. I surround myself with positive, like-minded people who support and uplift me. I trust my intuition, and I follow my heart. I don't settle for less than what I deserve, and I always strive for more. I am a powerful creator, and I am excited to see what the Universe has in store for me. By continuing to ask for what I want, I will receive what I desire, and I will create a life filled with joy, love, and abundance.

# Acknowledge Your Wants and Needs Without Guilt

I am worthy of all my desires, and I believe the Universe wants to make them my reality.

I proudly acknowledge my desires as my source of motivation. I choose to commit myself fully to pursuing my goals with determination and excellence. I recognize that change requires a strong desire for something new, and I release any guilt attached to my wants. I choose to prioritize my desire to grow rather than staying in my comfort zone, and I am open to the possibilities that come with it. I release the limiting belief that I cannot have what I desire. I embrace my deepest desires and believe that they are within my reach. My wants are the starting point for my achievements. I choose to act in pursuit of my goals and nurture my inner flame of passion and purpose. I believe that anything is possible if I have the courage to pursue it. I choose to acknowledge my desires as the stepping stones to my dreams, and I am willing to do what it takes to make them a reality. Everything in my life happens for a reason, and my desires are a road map to my destiny. I will continue to acknowledge what I want and need, and I will not feel guilty for expressing my desires.

# Recognize Your Worth to the Universe

### I am valuable, and the world needs my unique contributions and mindset.

I have the power to make positive changes in my life and contribute to the greater good. I am not just here to make a living; I am here to enrich the world and fulfill my purpose. I have the capacity to be great and make a difference through service and love. The Universe needs me, and I am here for a reason. I believe in my own importance and trust that my contributions to the world are significant. My calling is important, and honoring it is the greatest gift I can give to myself and the world. I believe in my own importance. I am a powerful force of positive energy. I believe in myself and my abilities, and I am capable of overcoming any challenge that comes my way. I am a unique and valuable individual with a purpose to fulfill in this world. When I stand up for my beliefs and refuse to settle for less, I open myself up to infinite possibilities for growth and success. I have the courage and determination to pursue my dreams and make a positive impact in my life and the world. I am important, and my presence in this world matters. I will continually remind myself that I am a unique and valuable individual, and I will embrace my worth with self-love.

# Break Old Patterns
# and Build New Habits

**I am excited about developing positive
patterns and habits to create my fulfilling life.**

---

I believe in my ability to break negative patterns and replace them with positive ones that align with my goals and values. I acknowledge that change takes time and effort, and I commit to making consistent progress toward developing positive habits that support my physical, emotional, and mental well-being. I am in control of my patterns and choose to create ones that serve me well and bring me joy. I break negative habits and replace them with positive ones. I trust myself to make conscious choices that align with my intentions and goals, and I am open to learning and growing from my experiences. I choose to celebrate small wins and progress toward creating positive patterns and habits, knowing that even small steps can lead to significant changes over time. Seeking support and guidance when needed is a sign of strength, and I am willing to do so to help me create lasting positive changes in my life. Ultimately, I am deserving of creating habits and patterns that bring me happiness, and my efforts will have a ripple effect in all areas of my life.

# Commit to Becoming Your Best Self Through Self-Care

### I am dedicated to becoming the best version of myself by loving and caring for myself.

Self-care is not selfish; it is an essential part of my well-being. I recognize that taking care of myself enables me to better care for others and live a fulfilling life. I prioritize self-care as an act of love and respect for myself. I am worthy of investing time and effort in my physical, emotional, and mental health. I choose to make self-care a daily habit, and I integrate small acts of self-love into my routine. This could include taking a relaxing bath, going for a walk in nature, practicing meditation, reading a book, or taking a few deep breaths to center myself. I am intentional in carving out time for self-care, knowing that it is crucial for my overall well-being. I also acknowledge that self-care can take many forms, and what works for one person may not work for another. Therefore, I am open to exploring different self-care practices and discovering what works best for me. I trust myself to know what I need to feel refreshed and rejuvenated. Taking care of myself is not a luxury but a necessity. Every day, I will release any guilt or shame around prioritizing self-care, knowing that it is an essential part of my overall health and journey to becoming my best self.

# Deepen Your Connection with the Divine Through Spiritual Rituals

### I am committed to the rituals I create to connect to myself and the Universe.

Rituals are powerful tools that connect me with my roots and provide a deeper sense of belonging. When I embrace the power of ritual, I create a structure that restores harmony in my life and in the world around me. Through these simple acts, I find meaning and purpose in my daily life, and I honor the sacred presence within myself. As I elevate the ordinary to the realm of the sacred, I cultivate a deeper connection to my spirituality and find beauty in the simple things. Each ritual I participate in strengthens the bonds of connection and community, bringing positive change into every area of my life. When I create a sacred space for transformation and growth, I invite abundance and positivity to manifest in my life. I am reminded that I am part of something greater than myself and that my existence has purpose and meaning. By tapping into the divine within me through ritual, I unlock my full potential and manifest my highest self. Each ritual I create becomes a powerful tool for transformation, helping me tap into the sacred presence within myself. I embrace my spiritual journey with the power of ritual and find deep meaning, purpose, and harmony in my life. By honoring my traditions and connecting with the Universe, I will live a life filled with abundance, positivity, and spiritual growth.

# Unlock Divine Abundance and Prosperity

I am open to receiving unexpected blessings
and miracles from the Universe.

I trust in the supernatural provision that is available to me in all areas of my life. Abundance flows to me effortlessly, as the Universe provides what I need. I am worthy of receiving abundance, prosperity, and blessings beyond my imagination. I acknowledge that supernatural provision comes in different forms, and I am open to receiving it in whatever way it manifests. I am grateful for the divine blessings that have already shown up in my life, and I trust that more are on their way. My awareness of the magic in the Universe sharpens my intuition and allows me to recognize opportunities for supernatural gifts. Love and blessings are my birthright, and I trust that the Universe is storing them up for me in abundance. I choose to let go of control and trust in the divine timing of supernatural provision in my life. I am deserving of living a life filled with joy, peace, and abundance. Opportunities for abundance and success will continue to surround me, and I will trust that the Universe will provide me with the resources I need to achieve my goals.

# Live a Purpose-Driven Life

**I am trusting that I have a unique purpose
in this world, and I am driven to fulfill it.**

---

I am open to discovering and embracing my purpose with clarity and confidence. I choose to align my thoughts and actions with my purpose to create a meaningful life. I am worthy of living a purpose-driven life that aligns with my passions, skills, and values. I acknowledge that my purpose may evolve and change, and I am open to exploring new possibilities. I am grateful for the experiences and lessons that have brought me closer to my purpose. I choose to trust the journey of discovering my purpose and enjoy the process. I am willing to take inspired action toward my purpose, even when it feels challenging or uncertain. I trust that my purpose serves a greater good and contributes to the well-being of others. I choose to let go of comparison and trust that my purpose is unique and valuable. I am capable of making a positive impact on the world through my purpose. I am deserving of a purpose-driven life that brings me joy, abundance, and fulfillment. I trust that the Universe supports me in fulfilling my purpose and that the resources and opportunities I need will be provided. I choose to stay aligned with my purpose, even when faced with distractions or obstacles. I will continue to be grateful for my purpose and its impact on my life.

# Release Shame
# and Embrace Healing

**I am now releasing any shame that has held me
back from living my life to the fullest.**

---

I am worthy of love and acceptance, despite any mistakes I've made or imperfections I have. I confront my shame with compassion and understanding rather than avoidance or denial. Shame is a natural emotion, but I am not defined by it. I am capable of healing from shame and transforming it into self-love and acceptance. I let go of any shame that no longer serves me and move forward with confidence. I am deserving of forgiveness and compassion, both from myself and from others. I am capable of owning my mistakes and using them as opportunities for growth and learning. I release any shame around my past experiences and trust that they have led me to where I am today. Shame is not a reflection of my worth or identity. I am grateful for the lessons that shame has taught me and the opportunities for healing and growth it has provided. I am willing to seek help and support when dealing with shame and its effects on my life. I trust in my ability to overcome shame and cultivate a sense of self-love and acceptance. I choose to let go of any shame that has been passed down to me from others and create a new narrative of self-worth. Each day, I will slowly break free from the grip of shame and embrace a life of joy and fulfillment.

# Live Spontaneously

**I am embracing my spontaneous side and trusting the excitement it brings to my life.**

---

I love the thrill of not knowing what's next and following my heart in the moment. Spontaneity brings me joy, laughter, and unforgettable memories. I allow myself to be open to unexpected opportunities and adventures. I am spontaneous and free-spirited, allowing myself to let loose and have fun. I trust my intuition and embrace the unpredictable nature of life with enthusiasm. Being spontaneous is a natural part of who I am, and I celebrate this part of myself. I release any fear of the unknown and trust that everything will work out in the end. Spontaneity allows me to break free from routine and experience new things with a fresh perspective. I welcome spontaneity into my life with open arms, knowing it will lead to exciting experiences and personal growth. I trust that my spontaneous decisions are aligned with my higher purpose and bring me closer to my goals. I choose to let go of any need for control and allow spontaneity to guide me toward what's meant for me. I am grateful for the moments of spontaneity that have brought magic and joy into my life. Being spontaneous allows me to connect with myself and others in a deeper and more authentic way. I am capable of balancing my spontaneous nature with my responsibilities, and I will cultivate a life of fun and fulfillment, embracing spontaneity.

# Understand the Power of Karma

### I am confident that my good deeds are bringing positive karma into my life.

My actions carry consequences, and I choose to make choices that align with my highest good and the good of others. I release any negative energy and welcome positive karma into my life. I attract good karma by being kind and compassionate toward others. I believe that what goes around comes around, and I am grateful for the positive karma in my life. I am aware of my actions and their consequences, and I choose to create good karma every day. I am a magnet for positive energy and good karma. The seeds I sow today will determine the fruits I harvest tomorrow; I choose to plant positivity. I focus on the present moment and make choices that align with positive karma. I am thankful for the lessons that negative karma has taught me, and I use them to grow and improve. I am grateful for the abundance of positive karma in my life. I trust that the Universe will balance out any negative karma with positive karma. I am a conscious creator of my karma and choose to manifest positive outcomes. I choose to see challenges as opportunities for positive karma and growth. I will continue to trust that my good intentions will bring positive karma into my life and the lives of those around me.

# Have the Courage to Change

*I am brave enough to admit when
I need to change, and I am committed
to my growth and self-improvement.*

I choose to let go of fear and embrace the courage it takes to make positive changes in my life. I trust that admitting I need to change is the first step toward positive growth and transformation. I am capable of making the changes necessary to live a fulfilling and joyful life. I am open to constructive feedback and willing to make changes that will benefit my relationships and my personal growth. I choose to be honest with myself and others about the areas of my life that need improvement. I release any shame and guilt about past mistakes and trust that I have the courage to make positive changes moving forward. I trust that the Universe supports me in my journey toward self-improvement and positive change. I choose to embrace the discomfort that comes with change and trust that it is worth it in the end. I am proud of myself for having the courage to admit I need to take a new path in life. I am open-minded and willing to try new things in order to create positive changes in my life. I trust that by admitting I need to change, I am opening myself up to new possibilities and opportunities for growth. I affirm that I will have the courage to overcome any obstacles and challenges, ultimately making positive changes in my life.

# Understand the Feeling of a Successful Manifestation

I am capable of imagining my dreams
into reality, feeling their manifestation,
and receiving their manifestation.

I choose to focus on the positive outcome I desire and imagine it in vivid detail. I feel the joy and excitement of my dreams already being manifested, and I trust that they are on their way to me. I release any doubts and fears about my ability to manifest my dreams. I trust in the power of my thoughts and emotions. I am worthy of receiving all the abundance and joy the Universe has to offer, and I trust that my dreams are already on their way to me. I choose to focus on the present moment and imagine the positive future I desire as if it is already happening. I trust that by feeling the emotions of having reached my desired outcome, I am attracting it to me with ease. I trust that the Universe is conspiring in my favor and aligning all the necessary resources for me to manifest my dreams. I will continue to live my life as though I am deserving of love, joy, and abundance from the Universe and show that I am ready to imagine it, feel it, and receive it.

# Use Powerful Words for Positive Change

*I am always using my words wisely and speak only words of positivity, abundance, and love.*

---

My words have the power to shape my reality, and I choose to use them to create the life I desire. I am mindful of the words I use, knowing that they have the power to uplift me and others or bring us down. I trust that my positive words have the power to attract more positivity into my life and the lives of those around me. I release any negative self-talk and replace it with words of love and affirmation. The power of my words lies in my ability to choose the intention behind them. My intentions are full of love, kindness, and positivity. I am worthy of speaking words that uplift and inspire me. I am mindful of the impact my words have on me and others, and I choose to use them for the highest good. I believe that my positive words have the power to create helpful changes in my life. I am open to receiving the fantastic outcomes that come from speaking words of love, gratitude, and abundance. I am grateful for the ability of my words to heal and transform. I choose to speak words of encouragement and support. Each day, I will live empowered by the knowledge that my words are powerful and use them to create positive changes in my life and the world.

# DAY 220
# Discover Your
# Inner Warrior's Strength

*I am a warrior, strong and capable of overcoming any challenge that comes my way.*

I embrace my warrior spirit and use it to fuel my determination to succeed. I am courageous and fearless, and I face challenges with a warrior's mindset. I am a fighter, and I never give up on my dreams and goals. I am resilient and bounce back from setbacks with the strength and determination of a warrior. I am disciplined and focused, and I stay committed to my path no matter what obstacles arise. I am a warrior of light, and I use my strength and power to bring positivity and healing to the world. I am a force to be reckoned with, and I use my power to create positive change in my life and the world around me. I am worthy of success and abundance, and I claim it with the strength of a warrior. I am empowered by my fighting spirit, and I use my will to fight to conquer my fears and doubts. I am grateful for the challenges that have made me a stronger warrior and brought me closer to my goals. I am unstoppable and fearless, and I use my warrior spirit to inspire and motivate others to overcome their own challenges. I will continue to be a warrior of love and use my strength and power to spread kindness, compassion, and positivity wherever I go.

# Thank the Universe
# for All Blessings

**I am now saying thank you for the
abundance of blessings in my life.**

I am grateful for all the opportunities that come my way, and I say thank you for each one. Thank you for the love and support of my friends and family. I am thankful for all the lessons I've learned, even the hard ones. Thank you for the beauty and wonder of the world around me. I am grateful for the good health and vitality of my body and mind. Thank you for the freedom to make my own choices and live my life on my own terms. I am thankful for the teachers and mentors who have guided me on my path. Thank you for the moments of joy and laughter that light up my days. I am grateful for the challenges that have helped me grow stronger and more resilient. Thank you for the abundance of opportunities to learn, grow, and evolve. I am thankful for the power of gratitude, which helps me attract even more blessings into my life. Thank you for the simple pleasures in life that bring me happiness and contentment. Thank you for the gift of life itself, with all its ups and downs, joys and sorrows. And thank you for the opportunity to make a difference in the world. When the gift of tomorrow comes, I will still be grateful for the abundance of love, compassion, and kindness in the world.

# Stay Focused and Motivated to Keep Moving Forward

*I am focused on my vision and moving toward it with intention and determination.*

---

I am confident that I am moving in the right direction toward my greatest desires. Every day, I take steps toward my goals with confidence and purpose. I am committed to my growth and evolution, and I trust that I am moving in the right direction. I release any fears and doubts that may be holding me back, and I move forward with confidence and conviction. I trust my intuition to guide me toward the path that is right for me. I am open to receiving guidance and support from others who can help me on my present journey. I am confident that I am on the right path, and I am excited to see where it takes me. I am grateful for the lessons I have learned along the way, and I apply them to my journey moving forward. I trust in my own abilities and strengths, and I can quickly and fiercely overcome any obstacles that may arise. I am aligned with my purpose and my values, and I move forward with clarity and focus. With every step I take, I will move closer to my dreams, and I will remain grateful for the progress I am making.

# Remember That Everything Is Working in Your Favor

I am a magnet for positivity and abundance,
and everything flows to me with grace.

---

The Universe is conspiring in my favor, and all things are working toward my highest good. I trust that everything that happens is leading me toward my best path and purpose. I am grateful for all the blessings and opportunities that come my way, knowing that they are meant for me. I have faith that even when things seem tough, everything is happening for a reason and will ultimately work out in my best interest. I choose to focus on the positive outcomes and possibilities, knowing that everything works out in the end. The Universe is always providing for me, and everything I need comes to me in perfect timing. I am blessed beyond measure, and each person and thing that comes into my life serves a purpose for my greater good. I am worthy of all the good that comes my way, and I accept it with an open heart. I choose to see every situation as an opportunity for growth and learning, knowing that everything is working for the best. I am grateful for the challenges that come my way, assured that they are providing me with strength. Every day, I will trust the process of life and surrender to the flow of the Universe, knowing that everything is unfolding in my favor.

# Honor Your Intentions to Create a Better Life

I am empowered to create the life I desire with unwavering faith and crystal-clear intentions.

I trust in the power of my thoughts and beliefs to manifest my deepest desires into reality. My intentions reflect my highest purpose, and I am fully aligned with them. As I focus on my intents, I know that they will come to fruition. Every thought and action I take is in alignment with my positive intentions, bringing love and abundance into my life. I am open to receiving the opportunities that will help me achieve my goals, and I am grateful for the support of the Universe in manifesting my intentions. With gratitude and positivity as my guides, I am always moving forward toward my intents. I trust the process of manifestation and know that my intentions will be realized when I align my thoughts and actions with them. I am deserving of my intentions, and I am grateful for the clarity that comes with setting them. I am excited for the opportunities that will come my way as I continue to focus on my positive intents. I trust in the Universe to bring me everything I need to manifest my desires, and I am ready to receive them with open arms. I know that my intentions are already being fulfilled. With each passing day, I will be one step closer to manifesting my deepest desires and living the life of my dreams.

# Give Time and Love Freely to Others

**I am committed to making a difference
every day by freely giving to others.**

---

My life is full of love and kindness, shining brightly for all to see. I understand that even the smallest actions can make a positive difference in someone's life. Time is precious, and I choose to use mine to show love and compassion toward others. The love I put out comes back to me every time. When I am with those I care about, I am fully present and engaged. I extend a hand of kindness and support to those who need it, and I believe that love and charity go hand in hand. I am committed to giving to those in need, whether it's my time, resources, or love. I understand that serving others is a path to finding fulfillment and purpose in life. True love is not just a feeling but a willingness to make sacrifices for others. I am committed to being there for those I care about. I believe that even the smallest acts of kindness can make a big difference in the world. I am grateful for the opportunity to love others well and to make a positive impact. My life is a testament to the power of love and kindness, and I will continually commit to spreading that love wherever I go.

# Trust In the Universe's Magic

## I am surrounded by the magic of the Universe.

I am open to receiving infinite blessings from a higher power. I trust that the Universe is always providing magic in my life, and I know that anything is possible. I trust in the Universe's ability to bring me what I need at the perfect time. Whether it's an opportunity, a person, or a situation, I know that the Universe will deliver it to me when I truly need it. I am in awe of the Universe's magic, and I am constantly amazed by its power. I see magic in the beauty of nature, the kindness of strangers, and the synchronicities in my life. I trust the Universe's magic to guide me on my path. I know that even when things seem uncertain or challenging, the Universe is always working behind the scenes to bring me closer to my goals and dreams. I am grateful for the magic in my life, and I am excited to see what my higher power has in store for me. I know that the Universe has my back, and I trust in its power to create miracles in my life. I am a cocreator with the Universe's magic, and I am ready to manifest my deepest desires. I know that by aligning my thoughts, feelings, and actions with the Universe's energy, I will continue to create a life filled with abundance, joy, and love.

# Inspire Others by Being the Light in the Darkness

**I am a firm believer that each one of us has a bright inner light, showing us our path in the darkness.**

---

We all possess unique talents, gifts, and abilities that we can use to make a positive difference in the lives of those around us. I choose to embrace this power and let my light shine brightly, inspiring others to do the same. I understand that life is not just about making a living but also about making a difference. When we use our inner light, we shine, enriching the world and leaving a lasting impact. I am committed to using my own unique talents and gifts to make the world a better place, whether it's through small acts of kindness or bigger initiatives. In a world that can sometimes feel dark and uncertain, I choose to be a beacon of hope and positivity. I believe that by radiating peace, love, and kindness, I can create a ripple effect that spreads far beyond my own little corner of the world. Whether through a kind word, a helping hand, or a listening ear, I am committed to making a difference in the lives of those around me, no matter how small the gesture may be. I believe that the light within me is stronger than any darkness outside of me. I will continue to nurture my inner light, letting it shine brightly and guide me through any challenge or obstacle that comes my way.

# Step Into the Role of the Hero

I am the author of my own life story,
and I choose to make it a masterpiece.

I now take the main character's role in my story, controlling my destiny and making my dreams a reality. I am the creator of my own opportunities and success, and I radiate a heroic power in everything I do. I believe that doing what I love is key to success. I pursue my passions with vigor and determination and never settle for anything less than my greatest desires. My truth is my power, and I embrace my story with the energy of a main character, unapologetically and authentically. I am the hero of my own story. I face my challenges head-on and emerge victorious because I am strong, capable, and resilient. I manifest my dreams and desires with my unique heroic energy, knowing that the Universe supports my every step. I understand that my life is my story, and I am committed to writing it well. I shape my narrative and lead my journey toward greatness. I release the negative and embrace the positive so that my legacy will inspire others for generations to come. I know that my story is my legacy, and I make it a good one. Each day, I will embrace my role as a hero so that I can leave a positive impact on the world around me.

# DAY 229

# Embrace That Change Is
# As Natural As the Seasons

I am embracing change, and I see the seasons
as a reminder that life is a journey full of new
beginnings and endless possibilities.

---

Just as nature revives with the changing seasons, so too can my soul. I am open to the newness and growth that each season brings. I am resilient and adaptable, able to thrive through the changes of the earth's phases. Like the leaves that change with the seasons, I am constantly evolving and becoming more beautiful with each passing day. Winter is a time of reflection and renewal, a celebration of the inner strength that sustains us through the changing seasons. Summer is the season for vibrant joy, endless possibilities, and cherished memories. I embrace the stillness and find joy in the simple pleasures of life. I welcome the changes of life and use them as a catalyst for growth. My experiences shape me, and every moment presents a chance to start anew. Life is a cycle, and each new phase brings new opportunities for growth and expansion. The changing seasons inspire me to embrace the present moment and live fully in the here and now. With every changing season, I trust that the Universe has something beautiful in store for me. I will continue to be grateful for the changing seasons of life, as they remind me that I am constantly evolving and becoming the best version of myself.

# Foster a Safe Environment for Your Relationships

I am safe and protected in all my relationships.
I am worthy of love and respect, and I feel safe
expressing my true self.

I trust my intuition and know that I am always guided toward safe and healthy relationships. I choose relationships that support my growth and make me feel safe and secure. I release any fear and anxiety about past relationships and trust that I can create safe and healthy relationships in the future. I am surrounded by people who love and care for me. I set clear boundaries and communicate my needs, which helps me feel safe and secure in my relationships. I trust that the Universe will bring me the right people, who will make me feel safe and loved. I am grateful for the safe and healthy relationships that I have in my life. I am deserving of love and respect, and I feel safe receiving them from others. I choose to let go of toxic relationships and surround myself with people who make me feel supported. I am confident in myself and my ability to create healthy relationships. I am surrounded by positive energy and love, which helps me feel secure. Every day, I will be at peace knowing that I foster a safe and protective space in all my relationships.

# Master Patience and Navigate the Journey of Manifestation

### I am grateful for the process that is required to achieve my goals and dreams.

Every step I take brings me closer to the manifestation of my vision, and I am patient and persistent in the pursuit of my aspirations. I understand that manifestation is not just about thinking positively but also about taking aligned action toward my goals. I am taking inspired action toward my goals and making progress every day. I am focused on the present moment and enjoying the journey, knowing that the manifestation of my desires will be even sweeter when I get there. I believe that my success is inevitable, and I am manifesting my desires with positive thoughts, feelings, and actions. I know that the power of manifestation lies within me, and I am using it to create the life I desire. I am confident in my abilities, and I trust that the Universe is conspiring to bring me everything I need to achieve my goals. The journey toward my manifestations may take time, but I am patient and persistent. As I continue to take aligned action toward my goals and remain patient and persistent, the manifestation of my desires will become my reality.

# Cultivate Inner Strength and Overcome Adversity

**I am cognizant that my strength is not just limited to my physical form; it emanates from the depths of my being.**

Even in moments when I feel physically weak, I know that my inner strength will sustain me. As I face the challenges of life, I am discovering the depth of my resilience and power. With each obstacle I overcome, I am learning that I am capable of more than I ever thought possible. I choose to stand firm in the face of discomfort and controversy. I recognize that it is through these difficult moments that I have the opportunity to grow and become even stronger. I am unafraid to speak my truth and stand up for what I believe in. I am stronger than I think, and I am stronger than I feel. I approach each challenge with curiosity and openness, knowing that I have the inner resources to overcome it. I am grateful for the strength that I have gained through adversity. I am brave enough to face difficult situations head-on. Rather than shrinking away from challenges, I embrace them as opportunities for growth and self-discovery. I trust in my own ability to overcome obstacles and emerge stronger on the other side. My strength is within, and my resilience helps me overcome any challenge. I bend, but I never break, with the Universe's strength within me. Each day, I will remind myself that adversity is an opportunity to show off my ultimate inner strength and growth.

# DAY 233

# Find Balance by Utilizing Purpose and Prioritization

### I am actively working to create balance in all aspects of my life.

I understand that balance is not something that I can find but rather something that I must intentionally create through my thoughts, actions, and decisions. I strive to maintain balance in my work and personal life, my physical and mental health, and my relationships with others. I believe that true happiness comes from living a balanced life where there is order, rhythm, and harmony in everything I do. I take time to reflect on my purpose and priorities and make intentional choices that align with my values and goals. I am mindful of my needs and the needs of those around me, and I strive to find balance in my relationships. I am attuned to my own sense of balance, and I know when I need to adjust in order to maintain it. I listen to my body, my mind, and my heart, and I trust my intuition when it tells me that something is out of alignment. When I feel off balance, I take time to reflect on my priorities and make changes as needed so that I can regain my equilibrium and live my life with purpose. I will continually recognize the great powers that exist within and around me, and I will honor them by maintaining balance in my life.

# Embrace Self-Confidence

### I am successful because
### I believe in myself and my abilities.

My self-confidence is strong and unwavering, guiding me toward my goals. My self-concept is shaped by my past and present experiences, beliefs, and values. I keep my focus on positive self-talk and affirmations that remind me of my strengths and abilities. My greatest accomplishment is being true to myself, even when the world tries to make me something else. I honor my unique qualities and embrace my individuality. I embrace my flaws and imperfections as parts of what makes me special. My self-confidence includes my awareness of my faults, and I do not let my flaws hold me back from achieving my goals. My self-concept is a compass that directs me toward a fulfilling life. I trust in myself and my abilities to navigate challenges and pursue my dreams. I truly believe that I am capable of accomplishing anything I set my mind to, and I approach each day with enthusiasm and determination. I am confident in my ability to overcome challenges and conquer my fears. I believe in myself and my resilience, and I refuse to let anyone bring me down. I have a positive self-concept, and I am committed to cultivating a healthy and positive self-image. I am strong, capable, and unstoppable. Each day, I will continue to honor myself and my strengths, letting my self-confidence shine and grow.

# Take a Leap of Faith to Create Peace

**I am willing to step outside my comfort zone and take risks, knowing that peace in life is a fabulous reward.**

---

I embrace fear and uncertainty as prerequisites for calmness ahead, and I trust that my courage and resilience will carry me through any challenges. I know that taking a chance on peace requires faith, and I am willing to take that leap knowing that peace will be the last word of history. I believe that every small step toward peace can make a difference, and I am willing to take those steps. I have faith in myself and in the Universe to guide me on my path. I know that taking the first step in faith is often the hardest, but I am willing to do so, trusting that the rest of the staircase will appear. I believe that every step I take toward peace will reward others with tranquility. I am open to taking risks and learning from both my successes and failures. I recognize that failure is an important part of growth and that every experience teaches me something valuable. I know that finding my true calling requires perseverance, patience, and faith. I am committed to exploring different opportunities and finding calm for my community and inner self. Each day, I will resolve to take a leap of faith in order the find the serenity inside myself.

# Pursue Radical Self-Acceptance

**I am ready to face my fears and embrace my true self.**

---

I embrace my unique beauty and authenticity, knowing that I don't need to be accepted by others to feel worthy. I choose to accept myself fully and unconditionally, without judgment or criticism. I am willing to confront the parts of myself that scare me the most, knowing that radical self-acceptance is key to living a fulfilling and joyful life. Accepting myself completely means acknowledging my strengths and weaknesses, my light and shadow, and integrating all aspects of myself into a cohesive whole. I am enough just as I am. I have nothing to prove to anybody, including myself. My worth is not determined by external validation or achievements but by my inherent value as a human being. I choose to love and accept myself exactly as I am, without conditions or expectations. I refuse to be in an adversarial relationship with myself. I know that self-acceptance is a powerful act of self-love, and I am committed to treating myself with kindness, respect, and compassion. I know that accepting myself fully means embracing all parts of myself, even the ones that I may have previously rejected or judged. I am ready to release the self-imposed limitations and embrace my true potential. I am willing to take bold steps toward radical self-acceptance, even if they initially scare me. As I journey to accept myself fully, I will inspire myself to discover so many amazing things about myself.

# Journey to Find Transformation

I am embracing the journey of transformation,
knowing that both mountaintops and
valleys are essential to my growth.

By understanding my thoughts and focusing on my goals, I can make a positive change in the world. I am committed to growing and transforming into the person I am meant to be. I create space in my life to allow for transformation and growth. I am engaged in the present activity of transformation, embracing the journey and welcoming positive change. My focus is on the size of my own personal growth rather than the size of my problems. I understand that transformation is a journey, and I am committed to taking the necessary steps to become the best version of myself. Change starts within me. By changing my own thoughts and actions, I can positively impact the world around me. I embrace change and move with it, confidently joining the dance of life. I am committed to letting go of who I was in order to become the person I am meant to be. I am willing to embrace the pain that comes with growth and change, knowing that staying stuck in a place where I don't belong is even more painful. I release the mindset that halted my growth and embrace a new way of thinking. With each passing moment, I will choose radical transformation, not trapped by the dogma of others, and I will make the most of my time in this world.

# Shift to Giving Thanks Instead of Complaining

I am capable of effecting change,
and I refuse to let a sense of powerlessness
turn my complaints into excuses.

---

Complaining doesn't change anything, and I remind myself of this whenever I feel the urge to be dissatisfied. I recognize that complaining is a waste of my energy, and I choose to instead focus on taking positive action. I understand that complaining is not a viable strategy for achieving my goals, and I am committed to working with the world as it is. I refuse to be a victim of my circumstances. Instead, I choose to leave, change, or accept the situation and move forward with clarity and purpose. I have the power to change my attitude by shifting my perspective and embracing a positive mindset. I am aware of the ego's desire to complain, and I am committed to maintaining an optimistic outlook and finding solutions rather than dwelling on problems. I have the power to control my attitude in every situation. I focus my efforts on achieving my goals. I will continually commit to breaking the habit of complaining and instead choose to focus on the positive, take action, and create the life I desire.

# Venture Toward Self-Discovery

I am reminded that this path to self-discovery
is not just about discovering my true self but
also about healing and growth.

---

By facing my fears, confronting my shadows, and learning from my challenges, I can develop a greater sense of self-awareness, resilience, and compassion. I understand that self-discovery is not a destination but a continuous process of self-improvement and self-evolution. It requires me to be open to learning, to remain curious about myself and the world, and to be willing to embrace change. On this journey, I am also reminded of the interconnectedness of all beings and the importance of cultivating empathy and compassion toward others. As I discover more about myself, I also develop a deeper understanding and appreciation of the diversity and beauty of humanity. I am committed to being kind to myself and to others along this journey, recognizing that we are all on our own paths of self-discovery. I trust that by living authentically, I can inspire others to do the same and contribute to a more compassionate and harmonious world. I am grateful for the opportunity to embark on this journey of self-discovery and am excited to see where it leads me. I will trust that the path of my self-discovery is full of love, joy, and abundance, and I will be excited to embrace it fully each day.

# Harness Vibrational Alignment for Manifestation

**I am a powerful magnet, attracting into my life what is in harmony with my dominant thoughts.**

My life is in perfect harmony with the vibrations of the Universe. I trust that the Universe is constantly sending me messages, and I listen and respond with alignment. My personal energy frequency reflects my life experiences, relationships, and thoughts, and I choose to align it with positivity and abundance. The law of attraction is always working in my favor, and I align my thoughts and emotions with what I want to manifest in my life. My vibrational alignment is constantly improving, as I am open to the flow of positive energy in the Universe. I trust in the process of life and know that my vibrational frequency is always in tune with my highest good. My inner being is in perfect vibrational alignment with my desires, and I allow this alignment to guide me toward my goals. I embrace the power of my thoughts and emotions, knowing that they shape my vibrational frequency and attract abundance into my life. I am a magnet for positivity and abundance, as I maintain a high vibrational frequency through daily practices of gratitude and self-care. My positive energy is powerful enough to quickly bring my manifestations into my reality. I am amazed at how powerful I truly am. There will continue to be so much vibrational energy out there just for me, and I will manifest every day with the gratitude of already experiencing it.

# Focus On Resilience and Growth in the Midst of Adversity

### I am committed to staying true to my values and purpose.

In the face of adversity, I choose to be better, not bitter. I recognize that challenges are a part of life, and how I respond to them determines the direction of my journey. I am resilient when encountering adversity. I know that I cannot control what happens to me, but I can choose how I respond to it. I refuse to be reduced by my circumstances; instead, I use them as opportunities to learn, grow, and become a stronger, more compassionate person. I am in control of my mood, regardless of what is happening around me. I choose to approach each day with a positive attitude, knowing that my thoughts and feelings have the power to shape my reality. I am grateful for all the blessings in my life, and I focus on my positive growth, even in the midst of challenges. I am brave and capable in the face of storms. I recognize that adversity is a natural part of life's journey, and I trust that I have the skills and resources to navigate any challenges. With passing time, I will cultivate more positivity in my life and use it as a protective castle, shielding me from negativity and doubt.

# Collaborate with Others to Manifest Positive Changes

I am open to new ideas and approaches from others, knowing that diversity of thought and experience encourages positive changes in the world.

---

I embrace the power of collaboration, knowing that together we can achieve more than we could alone. I cocreate with others in a spirit of harmony and mutual respect, recognizing the unique strengths and perspectives that each person brings to the table. I trust that the Universe brings me opportunities for collaboration that align with my values and purpose. I contribute my skills and expertise to collaborative projects with enthusiasm and dedication, knowing that our joint efforts will make a positive impact on the world. I value the diverse perspectives and ideas that come from cocreation. Trust is the foundation of collaboration, and I work to build strong relationships with those around me. Through teamwork, we can achieve great things at a faster pace. I understand that the success of any team depends on the ability to work together toward a common goal. I commit to maintaining this focus in all collaborative efforts. Together, we will continue to be an unstoppable force for positive change in the world.

# Send a Message to Your Younger Self

**I am sending love and compassion to my younger self, knowing that I did the best I could at the time.**

---

I trust that everything I experienced in the past has led me to where I am now. I release any regret and guilt I may have about my past actions and decisions. I embrace the lessons and growth that have come from my past experiences. I forgive myself for any mistakes I made in the past. I am proud of my younger self for persevering through challenging times. I honor the still-present resilience and courage of my younger self. I recognize the unique gifts and talents my younger self possessed. I acknowledge the progress and growth I have achieved since then. I trust myself today and know that I have all the knowledge and power I need within me! I am grateful for the positive memories and experiences from my past. Life is a journey, so I'm choosing to enjoy the ride and stay patient through all its ups and downs. I give my younger self permission to dream big and chase their passions. Even if they strike out, they'll learn and grow from the experience. Every day is a new opportunity to live life to the fullest and make the most of each moment. I will continue to honor my inner child with every positive and impactful action I take.

# Recognize Meaning in Life's Coincidences

I am open to experiencing the synchronicities in my life, and I trust that they are a sign of the Universe guiding me on my path.

I recognize that coincidence is the language of the Universe, and I trust that everything that happens is part of a greater plan. I believe that there are no real coincidences in life and that every person who enters my life is there for a purpose, even if it is not immediately clear to me. I trust that the coincidences in my life are not random but are rather a convergence of events that have a significant purpose. I believe that we are all connected in the Universe, and I am open to the coincidences that bring people and opportunities into my life. I am inspired to see the synchronicities in my life as a reflection of my path and purpose, and I am grateful for the guidance they provide. When I look back on my life, I see how the Universe was always aligning situations in my favor. I have a smile on my face when I remember times when I was hurt or rejected because they really were blessings in disguise. I find joy in reflecting on the favor over my life. I will continue to recognize the power of coincidences, and I will look forward to where the Universe is leading me in the future.

# Cultivate a Clear Mind and Concentrated Effort for Fulfillment

I am focused on my goals and dreams,
using them to guide me toward fulfillment.

---

I channel my energy and effort toward what truly matters. I work toward clarity on my desires and aspirations, allowing them to become powerful sources of motivation and inspiration. I concentrate my thoughts and actions on the task at hand, unleashing my full potential and creativity. I harness the power of concentration, accessing the infinite intelligence and abundance of the Universe. My mind is clear and focused, allowing me to see the path ahead. I cultivate a deep sense of concentration and discipline, using it to fuel my progress and growth. I declutter my mind so that I can concentrate on what is in front of me. My thoughts and actions are precise, cutting through distractions and obstacles to achieve my goals. I tap into my inner wisdom and intuition, using them to guide me toward a path of clarity, focus, and success. I am fixated on the good in my life to attract even more from the Universe. My mind is clear, and my heart is open. Each day, I will be ready clear my mind and concentrate in order to experience my desires.

# Work Toward Freedom and Authenticity by Surrendering Control

I am embracing the freedom that comes
with letting go of total control in life.

I understand that clinging to my past only brings me unnecessary pain and suffering. I acknowledge that the only person I have control over is myself and choose to let go of things that no longer serve me. I release beliefs that bring pain and suffering and invite in beliefs that bring peace and joy. I let go of things that weigh me down, trusting that it will bring a sense of lightness and freedom to my life. I embrace the opportunity to start over. I choose to release negative stories about who I am and what I am capable of, knowing that I can then access a greater sense of freedom and authenticity. I surrender the need to control every aspect of my life, and I trust in the flow of the Universe. I choose to let go of the need to please others and seek their approval because authenticity comes from aligning with my own values and beliefs. Every day, I will embrace the unknown and surrender control over the future, as this action will allow me to live in the present moment and experience life with greater clarity and authenticity.

# Achieve Your Desires Through Positive Thoughts and Beliefs

I am committed to thinking positively and envisioning my success, and I allow my mind to expand and grow beyond its current limitations.

---

I believe in my dreams, and with a positive mindset, the Universe helps me achieve them. I understand that my mind has incredible power, and I am conscious of the thoughts I think and the person I choose to become. Positive thoughts create desirable outcomes, and my mind is a source of endless optimism. I trust in my ability to conceive and believe in my dreams and make them my reality. I recognize that my mind is a powerful tool, and I am capable of shaping my thoughts to manifest my desires. With a kindled mind and a heart full of positivity, I attract abundance and success into my life. I am thinking and believing wonderful things about my future. With this commitment, I consistently see positive changes in my life. I am achieving all that I desire with the positive shifts I am making in my everyday life. Life feels so good when I am thinking and believing positively. I am aware of the power of my thoughts, and I will continue to cultivate positive, nourishing thoughts that will blossom into a beautiful garden of abundance and fulfillment.

# Understand Your Chakras for Enhanced Balance and Wellness

### I am excited to use all my chakras to align myself with my inner being.

My chakras are powerful energy centers that, when open and aligned, bring me greater physical, emotional, and spiritual well-being. By keeping my chakras balanced and aligned, I ensure that life force energy flows freely through my body, promoting my health and wellness. My root chakra is my foundation, providing me with a sense of safety, security, and stability in life. The sacral chakra is my creative center, giving me the power to express myself, enjoy pleasure, and experience intimacy. My solar plexus chakra is my power center, allowing me to cultivate self-confidence, personal power, and a strong sense of self-worth. The heart chakra is my center of love and connection, enabling me to give and receive love freely and to cultivate compassion and empathy for others. My throat chakra is my center of communication, allowing me to express myself authentically, speak my truth, and listen deeply to others. The third eye chakra is my center of intuition and insight, giving me the ability to access higher wisdom, connect with my inner guidance, and see beyond the physical world. My crown chakra is my connection to the divine, enabling me to experience oneness with the Universe, access higher consciousness, and deepen my spiritual practice. With each passing day, I will continue to be thankful for my chakras working together for my highest good.

# Optimize Your Time and Productivity to Achieve Your Goals

**I am productive because I manage my time efficiently to make the most out of each day.**

Every hour is a valuable opportunity to work toward my goals and dreams, and I make the most of my time. I choose to use my time wisely and prioritize what truly matters in my life. Time is a gift, and I make sure to use it in a way that aligns with my values and purpose. By scheduling my priorities, I ensure that I am making progress toward my goals and living a fulfilling life. I manage my time wisely to align my actions with my deepest desires and bring my dreams into reality. I prioritize my daily tasks and schedule my time in a way that allows me to work toward my goals with ease and joy. I choose to let go of distractions and focus on what is truly important to me, making time for what brings me joy and fulfillment. By using my time intentionally and purposefully, I am able to manifest abundance, success, and happiness into my life. I trust in the power of my time management skills to help me achieve my dreams and live a life of purpose and meaning. Time is on my side. Every day, I will use my time wisely to create the life of my dreams and achieve my ultimate goals.

# Develop Self-Awareness and Strengthen Relationships

I am in tune with my emotions and use this awareness to make thoughtful decisions that ultimately strengthen my connections with people.

I value empathy and use it to connect with others, building meaningful relationships and creating positive change in the world. I practice self-compassion and self-care, recognizing that my emotional well-being is important for my social health. I embrace the power of emotional intelligence to navigate challenging situations with other people, learning and growing from each experience. I choose to approach every interaction with emotional intelligence, understanding that it is a key factor in fostering positive communication, collaboration, and understanding with others. I am aware of my own emotions and the emotions of those around me, and I use this knowledge to guide my thoughts and actions. I get along with others and influence their actions positively and productively. I choose to recognize, understand, and control my emotions and use them to guide my interactions with others. I use my emotions as beneficial tools to help me expand my connections with people. I know how to express and manage my emotions effectively, which allows me to communicate my thoughts and feelings with clarity and confidence. I will continue to strengthen the relationships I have with others.

# Find Calm Amid Anxiety and Stress

*I am present in this moment, and*
*I find peace in my breath, knowing that*
*I can conquer any anxiety in my life.*

Today, I find strength within myself to face any hardships that may come my way. I release the stress caused by wanting to be somewhere else because I am exactly where I need to be at this moment. I have the power to focus on positivity and gratitude, which helps me overcome any stressors in my life. I may stumble at times, but I will never give up. Every time I fall, I will rise again, more resilient than before. I am capable of handling any challenges that come my way, and I trust in my ability to overcome them with grace and ease. I focus on the present moment, and I let go of any worries and fears about the future. Right now, I am safe and secure. I release any tension that I am holding on to, and I allow myself to relax and find peace within. I am worthy of self-care and self-compassion, and I prioritize my own well-being as I traverse life's ups and downs. I am learning how to feel calm whenever I notice anxious thoughts creeping in. I remind myself that I can navigate my anxiety because it does not control me nor influence who I am. I will continue to view stress as an opportunity for growth and learning, and I will approach each situation calmly and with an open mind.

# Connect with Your Passion to Create a Meaningful Life

I am on a journey to connect with things
that excite me, and I am eagerly anticipating the day
when my passions lead to a meaningful life.

I embrace the interesting and fun experiences that life presents to me, and I fearlessly seek out new adventures to enrich my journey. I trust that when I follow my passions, I will find true fulfillment and satisfaction in my work. I choose to pursue my passions, knowing that success will follow when I am aligned with my true desires and values. I am committed to living a life that blends work and play, so that I can enjoy every moment and thrive in all areas of my life. I am open to exploring my interests and talents, and I trust that my passions will guide me toward my purpose. I believe that I have a unique purpose in life, and I am committed to discovering it through self-exploration and growth. I embrace the journey of finding my passion and purpose, knowing that every step I take is leading me closer to my true calling. I trust that when I align my actions with my values and passions, I will experience a sense of joy and fulfillment that cannot be found elsewhere. I love to discover new things about myself to connect myself to my purpose. I am worthy of a life filled with purpose and meaning, and I will keep pursuing my passions with enthusiasm and dedication.

# Overcome Procrastination to Achieve Your Goals

**I am committed to starting small on a task and building momentum over time.**

I choose to act now and avoid the pain of procrastination later. I am capable of achieving my goals and making progress each day. Every small step I take will lead me closer to my desired outcome. I am pushing myself to get things done at the right time. When I show up for myself, I make small steps toward getting rid of the procrastination habit. I am focused on acting, no matter how small my action or how uncertain the task in front of me may seem. I value my time and understand that it's important to make the most of each moment. I choose to avoid procrastination and seize opportunities as they arise. I am in control of my time and my life. I make each day count and avoid the trap of putting things off until "someday." I trust in my ability to act and make progress toward my goals, one task at a time. Time is a precious gift, so I choose to use it wisely. Every journey begins with a single step, so I embrace the unknown and start with courage. I turn my dreams into reality by making some progress every day. The time to start is now, and I will commit to working toward my goals.

# Advance Your Career

I am worthy of a fulfilling and successful career,
and I pursue work that aligns with my passions,
values, and strengths.

I choose to act toward my career goals today, knowing that my future success depends on the effort I put in now. I am committed to finding work that I love so that I can experience a sense of fulfillment and joy in my career. I believe that I can achieve great things in my career by aligning my passions with my work. I choose to pursue work that I truly enjoy and find meaningful. I am worthy of a fulfilling and satisfying career, and I choose to focus on doing work that aligns with my values. I know that success is not determined by my past failures and achievements but by my courage and determination to continue moving forward toward my goals. I choose to embrace courage and move forward with confidence and resilience in my career. I am committed to investing in my personal and professional development, knowing that it will help me reach my career goals and unlock my full potential. I believe in my ability to overcome obstacles and setbacks in my career journey, and I choose to approach challenges with a growth mindset and a willingness to learn. I am grateful for the opportunities and experiences that have shaped my career thus far, and I will use these lessons to guide me toward even greater success in the future.

# Master Decision-Making and Problem-Solving

## I am in control of my future, and I choose to make decisions that align with my goals and values.

When faced with a decision, I trust my intuition, knowing that even a wrong decision can teach me valuable lessons. I see problems as opportunities for learning, and I approach them with a positive and solution-focused mindset. I embrace the complexity of decision-making and problem-solving, and I choose to weigh different perspectives and options before making informed choices. I believe that every problem is a chance to become a better version of myself, and I use my creativity, resilience, and resourcefulness to find effective solutions. I trust in my ability to make wise decisions and solve problems with clarity and ease because I align my thoughts, feelings, and actions with my desired outcomes. I release any doubts, fears, and limiting beliefs that may hinder my ability to manifest my goals, and I approach decision-making and problem-solving with a sense of curiosity, wonder, and gratitude. I remain open to unexpected solutions and synchronicities along the way. I will continue to be a powerful decision maker and problem solver, capable of manifesting my dreams and desires with clarity, purpose, and joy.

# Embrace Aging in a Healthy and Prosperous Way

I am grateful for the wisdom and experience that come with age, and I embrace each day as an opportunity to learn, grow, and contribute to the world around me.

---

I honor my body and mind by nourishing them with healthy foods, exercise, rest, and self-care, knowing that a vibrant and healthy life is desirable. I release any fears and limiting beliefs about aging and embrace the natural process of life. Every stage of life brings new adventures, challenges, and opportunities that I do not want to miss. I am a valuable and respected member of society, and I contribute to my community in meaningful ways. I choose to focus on the positive aspects of aging and longevity, and I approach each day with a sense of joy, vitality, and curiosity. I recognize that playfulness, creativity, and a childlike sense of wonder are essential for a fulfilling and meaningful life, and I cultivate these qualities in my daily activities. Every day is an opportunity to discover new possibilities, learn new skills, and deepen my understanding of myself and the world around me. I embrace the challenges and opportunities that arise as I grow older. I have the power to shape my own aging process, and I will continue to make choices that support my physical, emotional, and spiritual well-being, knowing that each day is a gift to be cherished.

# Build a Thriving and Innovative Business

*I am a visionary entrepreneur, and I have the courage and creativity to turn my innovative ideas into successful ventures.*

---

I am open to new ideas and perspectives, and I embrace the power of innovation to transform my business and my life. I am a trailblazer, and I am constantly seeking new, interesting ways to overcome challenges and achieve success. I am a resilient and adaptable entrepreneur, and I approach failure as an opportunity to learn, grow, and innovate. I am a confident and inspiring leader, and I use my skills and expertise to empower and motivate others to pursue their own entrepreneurial dreams. I am a leader in my field, and I embrace unique solutions to distinguish myself and bring value to the world. I am ready to act on my entrepreneurial dreams, and I commit to turning my ideas into reality. I am a creative problem solver, and I approach innovation by taking existing ideas and putting them together in new and exciting ways. I embrace risk and change as necessary elements of innovation, knowing that taking risks is the only way to achieve success in a rapidly changing world. Each day, I will remind myself that I am an entrepreneur at heart, and I will commit to turning my passions and interests into a profitable and fulfilling venture.

# Explore the World of Consumerism with Awareness and Intention

I am mindful of the things I consume and the impact they have on the planet, and I am committed to making conscious choices that reflect my beliefs.

---

Every purchase I make is an opportunity to support companies and products that align with my values and vision for the world. I believe that small, intentional choices can lead to big changes in the world, and I take responsibility for the impact of my actions as a consumer. I am not perfect, but I try every day to make more conscious and responsible choices about the things I buy and the companies I support. I understand that the true cost of a product goes beyond its price tag, and I consider the environmental and social impacts of my purchases. I am empowered to make mindful choices as a consumer and positively impact the world through my purchases. My buying decisions have the power to create a ripple effect that can inspire others to make more conscious choices as well. I support companies and products that prioritize sustainability, ethical practices, and social responsibility. By consuming mindfully, I am able to reduce my environmental impact and contribute to a more sustainable future for all. With each purchase, I will learn more about the impact of my consumption habits and make changes that align with my vision for a better world.

# Use Your Heart As a Guide

I am open and receptive to the messages
of my heart, and I listen to its guidance
with compassion and curiosity.

---

I follow my heart, while also consulting my mind, on my journey. I am connected to my heart's deepest desires. I listen to my heart to guide me through life. My heart holds reasons and passions that my mind may not understand, and that's okay. When I look into my heart, my vision becomes clearer, and my dreams turn into reality. I trust my heart to guide me toward the right path, even when my mind is uncertain. My intuition is powerful and helps me experience life fully. My heart is the compass that guides me toward my true purpose and passions. I trust the wisdom of my heart to lead me toward a life of love, joy, and fulfillment. When I honor and express my emotions, I unlock the power of my heart and unleash my true potential. My emotional intelligence is my greatest asset, allowing me to cultivate deeper connections and a richer life experience. The more I connect with my heart, the more I discover the beauty and magic of the world around me. I will keep honoring the unique voice of my heart and will allow it to guide me toward a life of authenticity and abundance.

# Write and Speak Goals for the Future

**I am a powerful manifester, and I know that writing down my goals is an important step toward bringing them to life.**

By putting my goals on paper, I am making a clear and precise declaration to the Universe about what I want to achieve. I speak my goals into existence, and I am filled with joy as I watch them unfold before me. Every time I write down my goals, I am giving them life and energy, and when I speak them aloud, I know the Universe can hear my desires. I am creating a tangible reminder of what I want to achieve, and I am aligning my thoughts and actions with my deepest desires. I take pleasure in the process of writing down my goals, knowing that each word is infused with my intentions and dreams. I am constantly revisiting my list, adding new goals, and crossing off accomplished ones. With every goal achieved, I am reminded of my power to create my own reality. As I speak my goals into existence, I am affirming to the Universe that I am ready and willing to receive them. My words carry weight, and I know that my positive energy will attract even more abundance and blessings into my life. I am confident in my ability to manifest my deepest desires, and I am excited to watch my dreams come true. I will continue to be grateful for the power of writing down my goals and speaking them into existence.

# Manifest a Loving, Compatible Relationship

I am committed to building a lasting, fulfilling relationship with a person who is compatible with me.

I believe that true love is not about finding someone who is perfect but about accepting their flaws and growing together as a couple. When I meet someone who truly understands me and brings out the best in me, I know that I have found a kindred spirit. I trust that the Universe is bringing me a partner who complements me and helps me grow. I know that love is about giving and accepting, and I choose to love my partner unconditionally for who they are, flaws and all. I understand that true love is about building a strong foundation of trust, respect, and understanding. I trust that the Universe is bringing me a partner who shares my values and goals. I believe that a healthy relationship is built on mutual respect, trust, and communication, and I am committed to fostering these qualities with my partner. I know that true compatibility is not about finding someone who is exactly like me but about celebrating our differences. I am worthy of a partner who appreciates and accepts me for who I am—and with whom I can be my authentic self. I will continuously remind myself that compatibility arises naturally when two people are aligned in mind, body, and spirit, and I will manifest that relationship for myself.

# Create a Sense of Inner Security

I am secure in thinking and feeling the way I do, and I choose to focus on the positive, safe aspects of my life.

---

I cultivate feelings of security by embracing the present moment and trusting in my ability to handle whatever challenges come my way. I find purpose and meaning in serving others, and this brings me a sense of fulfillment and security. I recognize that my sense of security is a precious gift that comes from within, and I nurture it by focusing on the positive aspects of my life. I believe that true security comes from knowing that I am loved and valued for who I am, and I surround myself with people who uplift me. I understand that inner security is not about having all the answers or being in control but about cultivating trust in myself and the Universe. Everything happens for a reason, and the Universe is always working in my favor, which brings me inner peace. I am secure in my ability to handle any challenges that come my way, and I trust that I have the inner resources to overcome any obstacles. I understand that true security comes from within, and each day, I will find security in cultivating self-awareness and self-love.

# Avoid Burnout by Prioritizing Self-Care and Recharging Mentally

I am committed to replenishing my mental, spiritual, and emotional reserves, and I recognize that this is necessary in order to make a positive impact on the world.

---

I realize the importance of taking breaks and unplugging from technology, and I make time to recharge my mind, body, and spirit. I am now feeling recharged and ready to tackle the day. I prioritize self-care and take care of my own needs before I tend to others, knowing that by doing so, I am better equipped to help others. I understand that rest and renewal are essential for my well-being, and I make time to refresh and recharge myself on a regular basis. I honor my body as the temple of my soul, and I take care of it by eating well, exercising, and engaging in activities that nourish my spirit and bring me joy. I give myself permission to take the time I need to rest and recharge, knowing that I will then be able to give things my all. I am worthy of care and attention, and I make self-care a priority in my life in order to nourish my mental and physical selves. Every day, I will commit to taking care of myself, and I trust that by investing in my own well-being, I am creating a foundation of strength and resilience that will support me throughout my life.

# Create Authentic Partnerships and Friendships

I am grateful for the connections I make with others, knowing that these relationships bring joy and meaning to my life.

I recognize that true partnerships are built on foundations of shared values, mutual respect, and willingness to support one another on the path of growth. I understand that friendships are essential to my well-being, and I am committed to authentically nurturing these connections. I believe that love and magic are present in all my relationships, and I am open to receiving the gifts that each connection brings. I trust in the power of connection to bring people together and create positive change in the world, and I am honored to be a part of a Universe that is filled with limitless potential for love and friendship. I am surrounded by amazing people who inspire and support me. I am grateful for their presence in my life, and I am committed to nurturing our relationships with kindness, compassion, and respect. I believe that my partnerships and friendships reflect my inner world. When I cultivate love, understanding, and positivity within myself, I attract similar energy from the people around me. I understand that every connection I make, no matter how brief or insignificant it may seem, has the potential to transform my life in meaningful ways. Within the long and promising path of life, I will continue creating many authentic relationships.

# Embrace the Wisdom of Spirit Guides

**I am tapping into a divine source of wisdom and guidance today.**

My inner guidance system connects me to the Universe and helps me navigate through life. I trust the whispers of the Universe, knowing that my spirit guides are always with me, leading me toward my highest good. My spirit guides support, teach, and direct me on my journey. The speech of my spirit guides may be subtle and hard to hear, but the message is very powerful. When I learn to tune into their words, I unlock a whole new level of insight and support on my journey. My spirit guides are like the GPS of my soul, keeping me on track with my purpose and guiding me through challenges. I am grateful for my spirit guides, the wise and loving beings who are with me always. When I open myself up to the guidance of my spirit guides, I tap into an infinite source of wisdom and love that supports me on my journey. My spirit guides are my wise and loving companions, helping me trust my intuition and follow my path with confidence. I believe that my spirit guides are always with me, providing me with guidance, protection, and support as I navigate life's challenges. By continuing to listen to the whispers of my spirit guides, I will open myself up to the infinite wisdom of the Universe and be guided toward my highest good.

# Transform Life with Divine Love

I am connected to the highest power
in the Universe, which is divine love.

---

Love is the great miracle cure. Love from the Universe heals all wounds and unites us all. Divine love is within me and around me always. It is unconditional and infinite and is the foundation of my spiritual path. I am bridging the gap between myself and everything else by using the power of love. The essence of my being is love, and I express that love through my thoughts, words, and actions. I embody the energy of divine love, which is the antidote to fear, hatred, and separation. Love is the highest vibration, and I tap into this energy on a daily basis, leading me to unity, harmony, and peace. By cultivating a deep and abiding relationship with divine love, I become a channel for that love to flow through me and out into the world. I open myself up to the infinite power of divine compassion, allowing it to heal my heart, inspire my soul, and guide my path. I am worthy of the unconditional love that flows from the Universe, and I choose to honor and nurture that feeling within myself and others. When I choose to focus on the energy of divine love, I will be empowered to transform my life, my relationships, and the world around me.

# Cope with Triggering Situations

**I am strong enough to handle any triggering situations and topics in a healthy way.**

---

When I am uncomfortable, I embrace it as an opportunity for healing and growth. I trust that the Universe is guiding me toward greater understanding and awareness. I see feeling triggered as a call to examine the wounds that still need to be healed within me. I am willing to do the inner work required to release these wounds and step into greater wholeness. When I feel exposed to trauma, I respond from a place of healing rather than reacting from a place of woundedness. Feeling triggered is a reminder to approach myself and others with compassion. I am gentle with myself and others, knowing that we are all on a journey of healing and growth. When I feel triggered, I give myself permission to take a step back, breathe, and process my emotions. I trust that this process is necessary for my growth and well-being. I harness the power of my emotions and acknowledge my trauma, propelling myself forward on my journey of transformation. When dealing with traumatic memories, I can choose to tune into my inner wisdom and listen to the messages that my soul is trying to communicate. I choose to see feeling triggered as an opportunity to release old patterns and beliefs that no longer serve me. Every day, I will do the inner work required to let go of these limitations and step into greater freedom and possibilities.

# Understand the Importance of Loyalty to Yourself and Others

**I am willing to show up for others as a loyal friend, family member, or partner.**

My loyalty inspires hope in others, and I am grateful for the opportunity to be a source of inspiration and support for those around me. The loyalty of my family and friends gives me the courage and support I need to face any challenge that comes my way. I choose to show my gratitude and love for them through my devotion. I am loyal to myself and my values because I deserve this type of commitment. I am worthy of loyal friendships and partnerships. I understand that true loyalty and devotion require bravery and self-sacrifice, but I trust that the rewards of these qualities are worth the effort. I believe that loyalty is a two-way street, and I am committed to building strong and lasting relationships with those around me. I know that my loyalty will be reciprocated and that we will support one another through thick and thin. I am grateful for the opportunity to nurture loyalty in myself, knowing that it's essential for a lifetime of love and connection. I will continue to honor my own needs and desires by staying true to myself and being loyal to my own values and principles.

# Give and Receive Affection to Form Loving Connections

I am grateful for the joy and warmth
that affection brings into my life and know that
affection brings about lasting connections.

---

I choose to give and receive affection freely, trusting that the Universe will guide me toward the people who will love me for who I am. I trust that the Universe will bring into my life those who love and accept me for my authentic self. Affection is the foundation for deep and lasting relationships with others. I know that affection is not a transaction nor a business deal but a genuine expression of love and care for another person. I show affection to those who matter to me, without expectation or condition. I believe that affection is essential for a happy and fulfilling life, and by showing affection to others, I am committed to creating a life filled with warmth, connection, and love. I embrace my natural inclination toward affection and choose to express care freely to those close to me. I trust that my affectionate nature will attract those who appreciate and reciprocate my love. By being affectionate, I am able to create deep and meaningful connections with others. In the future, I will continue to show affection in small and meaningful ways each day, knowing that these small gestures can have a big impact on the people I care about.

# Prioritize Self-Nurturing in Your Work Life

I am a career-focused and goal-crushing machine,
and I'm not afraid to take care of myself
while on my path to success.

Self-care is my secret weapon, and I use it to stay energized and focused on my work goals. I believe in working hard and playing hard too. I'm committed to taking care of my physical, emotional, and spiritual needs while I'm working toward my goals. I know that self-care isn't selfish—it's essential to achieving success and happiness in all areas of my life. I make time for exercise, healthy eating, meditation, and relaxation to keep myself centered and grounded. I know that taking care of myself isn't a luxury; it's a necessity. I don't let stress and feelings of being overwhelmed get the best of me. I take regular breaks, set boundaries, and delegate tasks to maintain a healthy work-life balance. I trust in my ability to handle any challenge that comes my way with grace and ease. I'm grateful for my work goals and the opportunity to grow and learn every day. I know that taking care of myself while pursuing my dreams is the ultimate act of self-love. Each day, I will honor my mind, body, and spirit and choose to make self-care a top priority in my work-life journey.

# Align Your Feelings with What You Want to Manifest

I am now feeling what I want to
manifest before it arrives.

The Universe doesn't respond to what I desire; it responds to my vibrations. I can have anything I want when I am willing to give up the limiting belief that I can't. I am feeling and visualizing my wants and materializing them. I am the creator of my emotions, and I choose to interpret them in a way that empowers me and brings positivity to my life. I am capable of experiencing the best and most beautiful things in the world through the power of my heart and emotions. My thoughts and feelings combined project an energetic blueprint, and the Universe responds to this every single time. I am constantly evolving and changing my identity to align with my life blueprint, allowing me to create a fulfilling and purposeful life. Through acknowledging and embracing my genuine feelings, I am able to gain valuable knowledge and insight into myself and the world around me. By actively listening and seeking to understand others without judgment, I am able to improve my communication with the Universe. I acknowledge and honor my emotions, trusting that they guide me toward personal growth and fulfillment. I will continue to stay connected to my feelings and express them authentically, and this link will allow me to manifest self-awareness, empathy, and connection in my relationships with others and the Universe.

# Remove Debt for Financial Abundance

**I am now changing my thoughts, beliefs, and actions around my finances to manifest more money and pay off my debts.**

I acknowledge my debt and cultivate a mindset of abundance and financial freedom in all areas of my life, knowing that the Universe is abundant and that I am capable of attracting prosperity. I recognize that my relationship with money reflects my thoughts and beliefs, and I commit to transforming my mindset around money to create financial freedom in my life. I take full responsibility for my finances and commit to taking the necessary actions to eliminate debt and create a life of abundance and prosperity. I trust in my ability to create wealth in my life by adopting a prosperous consciousness. I am free from the bondage of debt and financial stress, and I take control of my financial future by making empowered choices that align with my vision of an abundant life. I release any worries about my financial situation and trust in my ability to attract prosperity into my life. I am capable of taking empowered actions to pay off my debts and create a life of financial freedom and security. I am grateful for the lessons that my current financial situation has taught me. I will create a life of financial abundance and security, and I trust that the Universe supports me in my journey.

# Accept the Darkness in Your Inner World to Heal

**I am the light that illuminates my path, and with every day in which I explore myself, I am healing.**

---

I make space to understand my inner world and to then release any fear of the darkness. When I release my fear, I am on my way to my internal healing journey. I embrace the parts of myself that I have kept hidden in the shadows, knowing that by shining a light on my inner darkness, I can cultivate greater self-awareness, self-compassion, and personal growth. I release the fear and shame associated with my inner darkness and allow myself to be vulnerable and authentic in my journey of self-discovery. By acknowledging and integrating my shadows, I deepen my connection to my true self and create space for transformative growth and healing. My inner darkness contains valuable insights and lessons that I can use to strengthen my understanding of myself and the world around me. By facing my shadows with curiosity, I unlock my full potential for transformation. I give myself permission to embrace all aspects of myself, even the parts that I have previously rejected or ignored. By integrating my inner darkness into my consciousness, I cultivate greater self-love, self-acceptance, and inner peace. I choose to view my inner darkness as an opportunity for expansion rather than a source of shame or limitation. Each time I step into the unknown and explore the depths of my psyche, I will open myself up to new levels of understanding, creativity, and empowerment.

# Find Peace in Life's Natural Cycles

I am trusting that life is a journey of
ebbs and flows, and I embrace each season
with openness and acceptance.

By surrendering to the natural rhythms of the Universe, I am able to find peace and meaning in all aspects of my life. I release the need to control or resist the cycles of life, knowing that each experience is an opportunity for growth. By leaning into the highs and lows of the journey, I cultivate resilience, gratitude, and a deeper appreciation for the beauty of life. I honor the cycles of life, knowing that each phase is necessary and valuable. When I am embracing the changing seasons of my life, I am able to tap into my inner strength, wisdom, and creativity. I view the cycles of life as a natural and essential part of my personal evolution. When I am letting go of attachment and embracing the impermanence of all things, I am able to live with greater ease, joy, and purpose. I trust that every season of my life is leading me exactly where I need to go. By relinquishing the need to resist or control the natural cycles of life, I flow with the Universe and tap into my own intuition and inner guidance. Every day, I will allow myself to follow nature's cycles with ease and harmony, and through this practice, I will find joy and purpose in every moment, no matter how challenging or uncertain.

# Live in Harmony with the Universe

*I am in harmony with the Universe, and everything I desire is already within me.*

When I am in tune with the Universe, everything falls perfectly into place. The Universe is not outside of me; I must look within to find everything that I need. I am open to the magic and wonder of the Universe, and I trust that everything is happening for my highest good. The Universe and I are a perfect match that creates a harmonious experience. I trust in the world's perfect timing and alignment with my desires. My thoughts have the power to transform my life, and I choose to align them with the infinite possibilities of the Universe. I trust that this higher power is always working on my behalf, and I am open to the signs and synchronicities that guide me toward my highest purpose. When I let go of resistance and trust the Universe, my life flows with effortless ease and grace. I am a powerful cocreator with my higher power, and I choose to align my thoughts and actions with its infinite wisdom and guidance. I trust that the Universe is always conspiring in my favor, and I am open to receiving its abundant blessings and opportunities. Each day, I will be like a dance partner with the Universe, moving in sync with its rhythm and flow, and together we will create a beautiful masterpiece.

# Honor and Empower Your Heritage

### I am honoring my ancestors by becoming someone they would be proud of.

I fully understand that knowing and accepting where I came from is necessary to getting where I am going. I am soaring through life with the strength of my ancestors. I carry the power and wisdom of my ancestors within me, and their stories inspire me to live my best life. My heritage is not just a story but a legacy that lives forever within me. I am unlocking the power of my cultural identity and discovering the strength of my roots. Ancestral knowledge flows through me, and I am open to discovering the hidden treasures that my ancestors left behind. I am the culmination of my ancestors' wildest dreams, and their resilience and determination live on through me. The foundation of my strength is the hopes and dreams of my ancestors, and I honor their legacy by living with purpose and intention. I am grateful for the powerful foundation my ancestors have provided for me so that I can create a meaningful life. I embrace the ancestral strength within me and use it to overcome any obstacle that comes my way, knowing that my ancestors' resilience lives on within me. The power of my ancestors' knowledge and vitality continually runs through my veins, reminding me that I am capable of achieving anything I set my mind to. I will continue to honor my heritage, ultimately empowering myself.

# DAY 277

## Live a Balanced and Healthy Life from the Inside Out

I am a beacon of health and vitality, in perfect harmony with my body, mind, and spirit.

---

I am not just free from disease but am in a constant state of physical, mental, and social well-being. My health is my greatest wealth, and I treasure it above all else. My body is a temple, and I treat it with the utmost care and respect. Every day, I nourish it with love, wholesome food, and exercise. I radiate positivity and vitality in everything I do, and my thoughts and words reflect my commitment to my health and well-being. I understand the connection between a strong body and a clear mind, and I take responsibility for both. I cultivate purity in my thoughts, allowing joy to follow me like a constant companion. Through diet, prevention, and mindfulness, I prioritize the care of my body and mind, knowing that they are inextricably linked. I am mindful of the thoughts I allow in my mind, understanding that my body hears everything my mind says. I focus on nurturing my inner self, knowing that a healthy outside begins with a healthy inside. My commitment to my health and well-being is unwavering, and it is reflected in the way I live my life. In the future, I will continue to be a shining example of what it means to live in perfect harmony with oneself, and I will be grateful for the joy, vitality, and abundance that flow effortlessly into my life as a result.

# Master the Art of Setting Goals

I am halfway there when I set my goals because
I know who I want to be and where I want to go.

I am excited for all my goals because I truly believe I can achieve
them and bring my dreams to life. My goals are valid and true to
me, and I am thrilled to actualize them. The Universe is conspiring
to help me achieve my intentions. Every step I take toward my
goals brings me closer to my desired outcome. The Universe supports me in my journey and guides me toward manifesting my
goals and highest potential. I am worthy and deserving of all the
good things that come my way as a result of pursuing my goals. I
am grateful for the opportunities that arise as I pursue my goals.
The Universe presents me with everything I need to succeed in my
goals, and I trust in its infinite wisdom. I am fully aligned with the
Universe's infinite possibilities, and I am confident in my ability to
set reasonable and logical intentions in order to achieve my goals.
As the days go on, I will trust in the power of my mind to manifest
my deepest desires, and I will continue to commit to taking intentional action every day toward achieving my goals.

# Break Free from the Fear of Abandonment

### I am breaking free from the fear of being abandoned by others or even by my desires.

---

I must remember that I am always accepted by the Universe and that I have the inner strength to get through all my fears. I am surrounded by friends and loved ones who are starting to heal my fear of abandonment. I acknowledge the damage caused by abandonment, but I am empowered to take control of my life and find healing. I have the courage to trust my instincts, take risks, and develop resilience on my journey of healing from abandonment. As I heal my wounds, I open myself up to deeper connection and intimacy in my relationships. Healing takes time, but I am open to the opportunities for growth and transformation that the Universe presents to me. I release my fear of abandonment and trust that the Universe will guide me toward relationships that are healthy and fulfilling. I am worthy of love and connection, and I am capable of healing from any past abandonment experiences that may have caused me pain or fear. By acknowledging and working through my fear of abandonment, I am able to open myself up to deeper levels of trust, vulnerability, and intimacy in my relationships. I will continue to cultivate a sense of safety and security within myself, regardless of my past experiences of abandonment.

# Build Resilience in the Face of Pain

### I am strong enough to face my pain and embrace what is hurting me.

When I am hurting, I let myself feel my pain fully. I may be hurt, but I am far from broken. I accept my troublesome reality today while working toward manifesting a new reality where I am no longer hurt. I am showing love to myself now, and I also show that love to the sources of my pain. I am resilient and strong, even in the face of pain, fear, and disappointment. I have the power and responsibility to pick myself up and move forward with strength. My struggles and hardships spur me to develop my resilience, making me more capable of overcoming challenges. Like bamboo, I am flexible and adaptable, able to bear the weight of life's burdens and challenges. I accept my new reality, and with the support of the Universe, I am able to build something good and positive out of difficult circumstances. I rise above my darkest moments, and I use my experiences to grow stronger and more empowered. The Universe presents me with opportunities to build resilience, even in difficult times, and I am open to learning and growing from every challenge I encounter. I trust in my own inner being, and I am confident that I can overcome any challenge or adversity that comes my way. Even in the face of pain and disappointment, I will choose to focus on the positive and seek out opportunities for growth, learning, and transformation.

# Use the Mirror As a Tool for Deep Self-Reflection

I am looking at myself in the mirror,
and I see so much beauty and kindness,
even through the pain I have experienced.

---

A mirror is a tool to see myself fully and understand myself completely. As I reflect on my past and see how much I have grown, I am shifting my future. I examine my features, seeing my life plainly and courageously. The person standing in front of me has cultivated deeper levels of self-awareness and personal growth. I recognize that I have the power to transform my attitude and outlook, even in the face of challenging circumstances or emotions. Looking at my reflection, I realize that true wisdom comes not from what I know but from my willingness to embrace the unknown and learn from my experiences. My goals and aspirations are important, but I understand that it is the person I become in pursuit of those goals that truly matters. Every time I look in the mirror, I am committed to looking within myself with honesty and curiosity and using this powerful tool for personal transformation. I embrace the challenges and discomfort that come with self-reflection, knowing that they offer me the opportunity to learn, develop, and become the best version of myself. The Universe will continue to support me on my journey of self-reflection, and I will continue looking to my mirror as a tool for deep self-reflection.

# Revolutionize Your Innate Creativity with Technology

## I am excited to see the world change and to use technology for exciting growth.

As the world changes, I am changing and flowing in a positive way. I know that by combining creativity and technology, people can make the world a better place. Interactive technologies offer endless possibilities for learning, and I am excited to explore them and discover new ways of experiencing the world. While technology can be a distraction, I know that by using it with intention and purpose, I can enhance my creativity and achieve my goals. I believe that creativity is essential to innovation and progress, and I trust that by using technology to make new connections, I can unlock my full potential. I am empowered to shape my own future by embracing creativity and using technology as a tool for positive change. I am open to the infinite possibilities that arise when creativity and technology intersect, and I trust that by exploring this space, I can bring my ideas to life in new and exciting ways. I embrace the challenges and opportunities that come with being at the intersection of creativity and technology, knowing that they offer me the chance to learn, grow, and innovate. Each day, the Universe supports me in my pursuit of creative expression and technological mastery, providing me with the tools, resources, and inspiration I need to make a positive impact on the world. I will tap into my innate creativity with technology to change the reality of those around me.

# Create Work-Life Integration and Balance

**I am balancing my life in a new and wonderful way.
I make time for what truly matters to me.**

---

I am capable of achieving a work-life balance that enables me to pursue my goals and live a fulfilling life. I focus on the quality of my work rather than the quantity of hours I spend working, and I trust that my efforts will be recognized. Boundaries are essential to maintaining a healthy work-life balance, and I am committed to making choices that align with my priorities. I trust my instincts when it comes to managing my time and balancing my responsibilities because only with this trust can I find a sense of harmony and peace. The Universe reminds me to prioritize the things that truly matter in life and to never lose sight of the joy and beauty that surround me. I am committed to creating a healthy balance between my personal and professional lives, knowing that this balance allows me to live a fulfilling and meaningful life. I trust my ability to prioritize my time and energy, set boundaries, and manage my responsibilities. I honor the importance of self-care and relaxation in maintaining a healthy work-life balance, knowing that by taking care of myself, I am better able to serve others and achieve my goals. I will create balance in my career and at home, allowing me to thrive in both environments.

# Make Room to Adopt the New You

*I am like a snake shedding its skin because
as I let go of the old me, I slowly become
the person I always imagined myself to be.*

I am accepted by myself, and others graciously accept the new me as well. I love my new self, and I have time to become more than I ever thought possible. I embrace change and trust that the Universe is guiding me toward my highest good. Each new beginning is an opportunity to let go of the past and create a better future for myself. I release what no longer serves this new, improved version of myself and free myself to soar toward my dreams and aspirations. I am empowered to take the necessary steps toward the life I desire and will not settle for anything less. Transformation is a daily practice that I embrace with open arms, knowing that each step I take is leading me toward my best self. I release all the old patterns and beliefs that no longer serve me, and I embrace the new possibilities that the Universe has in store for me. I am stepping into my new, empowered self, ready to embrace all the positive changes that come my way. As I move forward in life, I will continue to be grateful for the experiences that have shaped me, but I will also let go of the past and create a new, authentic version of myself that aligns with my passions.

# Use Writing As a Tool for Self-Discovery

**I am a powerful manifester, and I can use writing as a way to turn my dreams into my reality.**

When I journal my desires, I see the manifestations of them in my reality. My writing is a tool for healing and growth, and after I have written my manifestations, I get excited for what the Universe has in store for me. It's fun to look back on my writing and see what has come into my life. I honor my stories and experiences and know that sharing them can bring healing and connection to others. Every word I write is a step toward a greater understanding of myself and the world around me. I give myself permission to explore the deepest parts of myself through writing, knowing that this vulnerability can lead to self-discovery. I believe in the power of my voice and unique perspective, and I know that telling my stories can inspire and transform others. I embrace the journey of storytelling and believe that my creativity has the potential to bring greater meaning to my life and the lives of others. My unique voice and experiences are worthy of being expressed through writing and storytelling, and I honor and trust my creative process. Through writing and storytelling, I am able to connect with my authentic self, express my emotions, and bring my thoughts and ideas to life. I will continue to use my writing as a tool for personal growth, healing, and positive change in the world.

# Understand Your True Self

I am constantly learning and growing, discovering new aspects of who I am and who I want to become.

---

I am like an onion, with many layers of personality and valuable insight to pull back. My life is full of ease and balance as I learn more about myself. I am right on track toward discovering all that I am. I trust in the Universe to guide me toward a deeper understanding of my true self, and I am open to the lessons and experiences that come my way. I am worthy of love and acceptance just as I am, and I honor my journey of self-discovery with patience and kindness. I embrace the process of discovering my true self, letting go of old beliefs and patterns that no longer serve me and welcoming in new perspectives and insights. I am committed to living authentically, embracing all parts of myself with compassion and courage, and sharing my unique gifts and talents with the world. The Universe guides me to discover my true self, and I trust the journey. With each passing day, I am gaining clarity about my authentic self and embracing it fully. I am constantly learning more about myself and using this knowledge to live a fulfilling and purposeful life. Each day, I will continue to be excited to see what I discover about myself today and tomorrow.

---- DAY 287 ----

# Master the Art of Tolerating Distressful Situations

**I am emotionally intelligent, and I use the power of my emotions to positively influence my life and to handle distressful situations.**

---

I am riding the wave of life through its ups and downs and regularly embrace laughter and joy to get through the tough times. My adversity keeps me motivated, and I keep on going with an "I can" attitude. I choose to interpret the events in my life in a way that empowers me rather than letting them define me. I embrace the challenges that come my way and use them as opportunities for personal growth and self-improvement. I am unique, and I embrace my true self even when the world tries to make me something else. I am resilient and capable of rising up from any obstacle that comes my way, becoming stronger and wiser with each challenge. I am learning to acknowledge and understand my emotions without letting them take control, and I am proud of my progress. I am grateful for the challenges that come my way because they provide me with opportunities to practice emotional regulation and build my resilience. Each day, I will get better and better at tolerating distress and regulating my emotions, and I will continue to be excited to see where this journey takes me.

# Find a New, Soft Perspective on Manifestation

I am deserving of a soft and easy life.
I live a life that is full of things that I enjoy.

---

The Universe wants me to live in peace, and I do my best to experience this divine mellowness in my everyday existence. I let go of the things that make my life hard and manifest a soft life. By focusing on my own well-being and letting go of the need to control others, I embrace this softness. I have the courage to slow down, simplify, let go of what is unnecessary, and embrace the gentle rhythms of life. As I become softer, I am able to hear more deeply and clearly. My soft life comes from cultivating a sense of ease, balance, and inner peace. By letting go of what is unnecessary, I create space for a meaningful, joyous, and soft life. I am worthy of a life free from stress and struggle. I trust the Universe to guide me toward a soft life filled with abundance and contentment. I honor my need for rest and relaxation, allowing myself to slow down and savor life's simple pleasures, and in doing so, I create tranquility and serenity. Every day, I will release my attachment to the hustle and bustle of daily life and trust that by surrendering to the Universe's flow, I will manifest a soft life of effortless grace and ease.

# Heal Your Brokenness to Become Whole

*I am committed to true healing—
restoring myself to a state of wholeness
by embracing all parts of who I am.*

By embracing my brokenness, I become whole and allow the Universe to guide me toward healing. I accept all parts of myself, even the parts I may not like, and in doing so, I become whole and create space for growth. Each time I rise from a fall, I am moving closer to embodying my full potential. I recognize that my brokenness allows for the light to shine through, and I am grateful for the opportunity to become whole through the Universe's infinite wisdom. I am a whole and complete being, worthy of love and acceptance, and I honor all parts of myself with compassion and understanding. Through embracing my past, present, and future selves, I cultivate a deep sense of wholeness and create a solid foundation for my transformation. I trust that by connecting with my innermost truth and living in alignment with my values, I am able to manifest a complete and fulfilling life. By befriending myself and my experiences, I cultivate a deep sense of wholeness and allow the Universe to guide me toward inner peace and contentment. Through mindfulness, I am able to see clearly what is happening in the present moment and respond with intention and purpose, creating a life of wholeness and meaning. Each moment, I will cultivate a life of wholeness and authenticity.

# Nurture Your Mind, Body, and Spirit with Holistic Healing

**I am healing in a natural way that is true to my values, and I am not forcing or rushing my healing.**

I know that when I heal at a slow and natural pace, I am allowing myself to experience my life in a beautiful way. I trust in nature and the Universe to guide me toward holistic healing modalities that nurture my mind, body, and spirit. Through holistic healing, I embrace the art and science of nurturing all aspects of myself, and I create a life of balance, harmony, and vitality. By healing my mind through holistic practices, I unleash my full potential and create positive change in the world around me. I honor the connection between my soul and my body, and I understand that true healing occurs when I address my being with love, compassion, and respect. By tapping into the power of my mind to heal my body, I embrace the true essence of holistic healing and cultivate a life of wholeness, joy, and well-being. I trust in the infinite healing potential of my mind, body, and spirit, and I journey toward total wellness and vitality. Every cell in my body is constantly regenerating, and I know that I have the power to create a healing environment within myself. As days go by, through self-love, self-care, and a positive attitude, I will open myself up to the healing energy of the Universe, and I will welcome abundance, joy, and vitality into my life.

# Use Words to Shape Your Reality

### I am using my words to build the life that I want.

My words are full of power, and I use them to bless myself and others. I choose my words carefully, for I know that they have the power to create and shape my reality, and I use them to inspire, uplift, and empower myself and others. By focusing my thoughts on positivity, abundance, and growth, I attract the energy of the Universe and manifest my dreams and desires into reality. I take responsibility for the energy and power that my words carry, and I use them to build a life of love, joy, and peace. My words have a direct impact on my destiny, and I speak words of encouragement, hope, and possibility. My mind is a powerful tool, and I use my thoughts to create the reality that I desire. Every word I speak has the power to create and manifest my reality, and I choose to use my words to uplift, inspire, and motivate myself and those around me. By speaking positive and affirming words, I am able to attract abundance, love, and success into my life, and I trust in the power of the Universe to bring my desires into reality. I am continually in control of the energy that I put out into the world through my words, and I will choose to use that power to create a reality of joy, peace, and fulfillment, both for myself and for those around me.

# Use Color to Enhance Reality

I am grateful for the colorful path to
manifesting my dreams, and I trust the
process to guide me toward success.

I use color to vibrationally match my wants and needs. I see color in
everything that I do, and this brings me true happiness. My soul is
deeply touched by the unspoiled beauty of colors, without any pre-
conceived meanings or forms. I allow the power of color to directly
influence and uplift my soul. I am vibrating and beautiful from the
inside out. I love how colorful my life truly is. My life today reflects
where my life is going, just add more amazing and vivid experiences.
With each color I choose to surround myself with, I amplify the
power of my dreams and attract abundance into my life. The Universe speaks to me through the language of colors, and I listen with
an open heart. I intuitively understand the universal language of
colors, and it brings me harmony and fulfillment. By aligning my
intentions with the colors that resonate with my soul, I activate
the Universe's limitless potential to help me achieve my goals. I will
continue to embrace the changes of my emotions and allow the
colors around me to reflect my inner state of being.

# DAY 293
# Cultivate Mindful Awareness

**I am living in the present moment, and I am thankful for my past and present experiences.**

---

There is so much to be grateful for when I focus on the now. I choose to live in the present moment, recognizing that it is the only time that currently exists and that I have control over. I let go of worries about the future and regrets about the past and focus on being fully present in this moment, where I can find peace and joy. I cultivate mindful awareness of the present moment, allowing myself to appreciate the beauty around me and find deeper meaning in my life. I understand that the present moment is a gift and the key to my health, happiness, and success, so I make the most of every opportunity. I start each day anew, with a fresh perspective and a grateful heart, ready to embrace the infinite possibilities of the present moment. I am grounded in the now, where I find strength, clarity, and inspiration to live my best life. I embrace today, recognizing that each moment is an opportunity to create a brighter future. I will practice mindful awareness every day, allowing myself to fully engage with the world around me and cultivate deeper connections with others.

# Examine the Past to Transform the Future

**I am constantly referencing the lessons I have learned in the past to create a brighter future for myself.**

I enjoy reflecting on my life because I always find something to be grateful for. With awareness of my past experiences, I can consciously make choices that align with my true desires and purpose. By understanding patterns I have relied upon, I can consciously create new and positive habits that will lead to a more fulfilling future. Every experience has prepared me for the present moment, and I use each one to shape my future into my own image of success. I release the negative energy of my past and use the lessons learned to move forward with confidence and purpose. When I embrace the power of my wisdom, I can shape a better and more abundant future for myself and those around me. I cannot change my past, but I hold the power to create a bright and promising future. My mistakes create a valuable guide that shapes my present and inspires me to build a better future. I release any prior self-limiting beliefs and acknowledge the valuable lessons that have shaped my current self and will shape my future self. I seek to know myself better each day, and with each realization, I gain greater clarity and understanding of my true purpose. I will continue to use the lessons of my past as a foundation for my present and a launching pad for a brighter future, full of possibility and potential.

# Trust In Yourself and the Universe

### I am worthy and deserving of all the good things that the Universe has to offer.

I have faith in my own intuition and trust that it will guide me toward the right decisions. The world is always providing me with signs to assure me that I'm on the right path. I am confident in my ability to manifest my desires. The Universe is infinitely abundant and always providing me with opportunities to bring my dreams to life. I believe that everything is happening for my highest good, even when it's not obvious. The Universe has a grand plan for me, and I trust that it will all make sense in due time. A higher power is constantly working to bring me joy, abundance, and fulfillment. I am grateful for all the blessings that the Universe has bestowed upon me, and I know that there are even greater blessings yet to come. I believe in the power of the world to guide me toward my highest potential. With each step I take, I am moving closer to the life of my dreams. I am a cocreator of my own reality, and I trust in the Universe to provide me with everything I need to manifest my desires. Each day, I will be open to receiving abundance and prosperity in all areas of my life, and nothing will stop me from achieving my goals.

# Count Your Blessings to Manifest More Abundance

*I am filled with gratitude for the many blessings that have brought me to this moment.*

I am exactly where I need to be, and my blessings are abundant. My gratitude allows me to see the beauty in challenging situations, and I am all the more powerful for it. The Universe responds to my gratitude by providing more gifts and support than I can imagine. I am grateful for every moment, every lesson, and every opportunity that comes my way. Gratitude is my daily practice, and it keeps me grounded, centered, and aligned with my true purpose. When I focus on my blessings, my problems fade away. I live in a state of constant gratitude, knowing that my blessings are abundant and my future is bright. I am grateful for all that has been, all that is, and all that is yet to come. I am grateful for the journey itself, not just the destination. Each step along the way has brought me to where I am today, and for that I am truly thankful. My gratitude is a magnet for abundance. When I focus on the good in my life, I attract even more goodness, prosperity, and joy. Gratitude is my secret weapon for success. I will continue to be grateful for what I have, and I will focus my energy on the abundance I want to create.

# Overcome Self-Betrayal and Embrace Your True Self

I am able to overcome self-betrayal and create a life that aligns with my values when I honor my true self.

---

I release all self-betrayal and embrace my true self with love and acceptance. I trust in my ability to create a life that allows me to follow my passions. My power lies in my authenticity. By embracing my true self, I am able to create a life of purpose and meaning. I choose to live a life of authenticity and self-love. I know that by facing my fears and embracing my vulnerabilities, I am able to utilize my true inner strength. I am in control of my own destiny, and I take responsibility for my thoughts, actions, and beliefs. I trust in my inner wisdom and intuition to guide me on my path to self-discovery and empowerment. By staying true to my values, I am able to unleash my inner power and live a life of abundance and joy. Self-betrayal is no longer a part of my story. Each day, I will choose to honor my true self and live a life of authenticity, abundance, and joy.

# Affirm Love Languages to Manifest Better Communication in Relationships

**I am completely capable of expressing love in many different ways.**

---

I am thankful for the love languages that connect me to others. These love languages guide me to build meaningful relationships with myself and with others. I embrace the diversity of love languages and use them to strengthen my relationships. My words are a gift to those I love (including myself), and I choose them wisely, kindly, and often. I prioritize quality time with my loved ones and cherish every moment. I am present and engaged during the time I spend with my loved ones, or by myself. I am always looking for ways to serve and help those I love. I understand that small acts of service can make a big difference, and I strive to do them every day. I serve myself and others whenever acts of kindness and compassion are needed. I am comfortable with and enjoy physical touch with those I love. I express my love and affection through touch in a respectful and appropriate way. I appreciate the thought and effort behind the gifts I receive. I express my gratitude and love when I receive gifts. I give myself small gifts frequently and freely. I use love languages as a road map to my own heart and the hearts of others, and I navigate this map with care and intention. Each day, I will affirm the value of all love languages, and I will then tap into effective communication in my relationships.

# Celebrate Others

**I am filled with happiness and positivity as I celebrate the successes and accomplishments of those around me.**

---

I am a celebrator of life, and I love to praise the achievements of others! I enjoy seeing others thrive. It makes me so happy to see others smile. I choose to see the successes of others as sources of inspiration and joy rather than feeling jealousy or engaging in competition. I know that when one person succeeds, we all succeed, and there is plenty of success and abundance to go around. I am genuinely happy for the success of others, and I love to shower them with praise and recognition. I know that celebrating others is not only good for them but also good for me, as it increases my own positive energy and success. I choose to spread positivity and love wherever I go, and celebrating the accomplishments of others is a powerful way to do that. I believe that we are all connected, and when I celebrate the success of others, I am also celebrating the success of humanity as a whole. I am grateful for the opportunity to celebrate others, and I know that it brings me joy and happiness. I am committed to lifting others up and spreading positivity in the world. With every successful day, I will celebrate others as a powerful way to create a positive and abundant life for everyone around me.

# Own Your Unique Value to Combat Feelings of Inferiority

I am grateful for my own unique strengths
and talents, and I choose to celebrate them rather
than comparing myself to others.

I rise above feelings of inferiority and recognize my own strength and worth. I am strong enough to be all that I desire to be. I own who I am with power, and I allow myself to shine in my own way. I am on a journey to being myself fully. The only person I am destined to be is the person I decide to become, and I choose to be confident and self-assured. I refuse to stay in the gutter of self-doubt and instead look up at the stars, embracing the endless possibilities that the Universe holds. I know that comparing myself to others only steals my joy and focus, and I choose to celebrate my own unique journey and accomplishments. I believe in myself and all that I am, knowing that the Universe has given me the strength to overcome any obstacle and achieve my dreams. I am worthy and capable of achieving anything I set my mind to, and I refuse to let feelings of inferiority hold me back. Each day, I will remember that the Universe has a unique purpose and path for me, and I will trust in my own journey and abilities.

# Break Generational Curses to Take Control of Your Life

**I am capable of breaking generational curses and shaping the future of my legacy in a powerful way.**

My legacy will be one of character and faith passed down to future generations. I live in harmony with the Universe, trusting in its infinite wisdom and guidance for my journey and knowing that it will break any unwanted mystical powers that have a hold on me. I am changing my relationship with the past to create a new future. I have the power to change my circumstances and break generational cycles. I am the creator of my own future, and I choose to make it a great one. I choose to break free from the patterns of the past and create a new and positive legacy for myself and future generations. The power to break generational curses lies within me, and I am capable of creating positive change in my life and the lives of those around me. I release the limiting beliefs and behaviors that have been passed down through my family line, and I embrace my own unique path and purpose. With each passing moment, I will be ready for the positive changes in my life, knowing I will have put in the work to break any generational curses affecting me.

# Believe In Great Things to Come

I am greater than any obstacle, and my unwavering belief in myself will help me manifest my desires.

I am halfway to my dreams, and I believe that something amazing is about to happen to me. I embrace my inner world with courage and compassion, finding greater understanding and healing in the depths of my being, and I look to the future. I remember all the blessings the Universe has provided for me already, and these memories help me stay confident in what will happen next. My love of life helps me create a reality that reflects my positive outlook. My dreams are not just possibilities—they are a certainty because I believe in them and in myself. I know that I have a unique purpose in this world, and I believe that the Universe supports me in fulfilling it. I gracefully surrender to life's natural cycles, building resilience and finding peace within the ebb and flow of positive change. The Universe is overflowing with incredible opportunities and blessings, and I am ready to receive them with open arms! My positive expectations and excitement create a magnetic force that draws amazing experiences and opportunities into my life right now. I am in control of my reality, and I will continue to focus on the amazing possibilities that surround me, attracting more and more positivity and abundance into my life every day.

# Learn Every Day

**I am on a mission to become a lifelong learner,
fueled by curiosity and a desire for knowledge.**

I hold the most powerful weapon of change within me—my thirst for knowledge and education. I invest in my future by continuously seeking knowledge and expanding my understanding of the world. I love to learn new things about the world. I am committed to daily exploration, and I trust that the Universe will guide me toward knowledge and growth. There are so many great things to discover. Learning is a gift, a skill, and a choice, and I choose to embrace all opportunities for development. I recognize that learning is a lifelong journey, and the more I embrace it, the more beautiful and fulfilling my existence becomes. As I read and learn, I expand my mind and open myself up to new experiences and possibilities in my life. Education is my secret weapon for success, equipping me with the skills and knowledge to conquer any obstacle and achieve my dreams. Learning is the ultimate adventure, and I am eager to embark on new journeys every day. I will approach each day with curiosity and a desire to learn something new, and I will continue to know that every experience holds valuable lessons.

# Put Ideas Into Action

### I am a doer: I act on my ideas and turn them into reality.

My resolve to work toward my goals is only as powerful as the effort I put into executing the work. I am an action-oriented person, ready for whatever it takes to see my desire fulfilled. I take bold steps forward, knowing that success is waiting on the other side. I know that true success comes not just from great ideas but from the discipline and focus required to execute them flawlessly. I embrace the challenge of implementing my ideas, knowing that the journey may be difficult but that the rewards will be worth it. My ideas are valuable and worthy of action, so I actively work to bring my vision to life. I am committed to taking consistent action toward my goals, no matter how small the steps may be. The power to transform my ideas into reality lies within me. I am capable of executing my plans with precision and excellence. I am not afraid to take risks and try new things. With daily persistence and determination, I will turn my ideas into a successful reality.

# Let Go of People and Move On with Trust

*I am grateful for the courage to let go of relationships that no longer serve my journey.*

I trust that the Universe guides me to people who align with my highest good. I release the people from my past who do not celebrate me and my achievements. Forgiveness and letting go are essential to my personal growth and well-being. I embrace this journey of healing and choose to move forward with grace and dignity. The right people will always find their way into my life, and those who are meant to leave will do so with ease and peace. By letting go of what no longer serves me, I create space for something better and more aligned with my highest good. Starting over can be daunting, but it is also an opportunity to learn, grow, and become a better version of myself. I am excited to embrace this new chapter of my life. I let go of the need to hold on tight to people who are no longer meant for me. I release those who no longer serve my growth and make space for those who do. I trust that letting go of certain people is necessary for my personal evolution, and I embrace the positive changes that follow. With each year, I will honor myself by letting go of relationships that no longer align with my highest good and allowing space for better connections to come into my life.

# Manifest Good Communication with Your Partner

**I am open and receptive to my loved one's thoughts and feelings, and I express my own with honesty, respect, and compassion.**

I use the manifestation tool of "acting as if" to fully feel the evidence of my desires. I am living a life full of great communication with those I love. Communication is important to me, and I use it to show love to others. My love and I communicate with ease, clarity, and understanding, strengthening our bond with each exchange. My relationship is fueled by the power of clear communication, and our connection grows deeper and stronger every day. I am willing to put in the effort to improve my communication with my loved one. I am able to speak with love and compassion. I know that my words are powerful, and I use them to uplift. I desire clear communication with the people I have a relationship with. I deserve to feel safe in my communication with others. I listen with my heart as well as my ears, and I understand the unspoken messages. I nourish my relationship by keeping the flames of communication burning bright. I embrace the power of good communication, which energizes and awakens my senses. Each day, I will communicate with love, not just words, by listening, understanding, and responding thoughtfully.

# Utilize a Vision Board to Set Clear and Achievable Goals

**I am the artist of my own life, and my vision board is the canvas that brings my dreams to reality.**

My vision board is a powerful tool that activates the law of attraction and helps me manifest my desires. I use my vision board to see and understand my desires. Whatever I see in my mind, I can hold in my hands. By focusing on my vision board every day, I create a clear picture of what I want. My thoughts create my reality, and by visualizing my dreams, I bring them to life in the Universe. I use the power of visualization to purposefully daydream about my goals, and I take inspired action to make them a reality. I reach for the stars and work hard to achieve my dreams, knowing that the Universe supports me in manifesting all that I desire. My vision board is a colorful collage of my dreams and aspirations, inspiring me to act and manifest my desires. By creating a vision board, I bring clarity to my goals and focus my attention on what truly matters: manifesting abundance and success in all areas of my life. I will take the time to create a vision board that reflects my heart's desires, reminding me every day of the beauty, joy, and infinite possibilities that exist in the Universe.

# Harness Empathy for a Positive Impact

I am an empath, radiating love, kindness, and compassion to all beings and using my sensitivity as a superpower to make a positive impact on the world.

I am sensitive to those who are going through difficult things, regardless of whether I can relate to them. I know how to show compassion and love others through their struggles. As an empath, I find echoes of others within myself, connecting deeply with the hearts and souls of those around me. My empathy is a powerful force for change, inspiring me to create community, act, and make a positive impact on the world. I step outside my own bubble and into the bubbles of others, cultivating understanding, compassion, and love. Through empathy, I listen deeply, hold space without judgment, and connect emotionally, communicating that no one is ever alone. My power as a human being lies in my ability to empathize with others, creating a ripple effect of kindness and love throughout the Universe. I honor my sensitivity and use it as a superpower to connect deeply with others and make a positive impact on the world. Through my empathy, I cultivate a deep understanding of the emotions and experiences of those around me, creating strong, meaningful relationships. My ability to feel deeply and empathize with others is a gift that I will continuously use to spread kindness, compassion, and love throughout the Universe.

# Love Your Enemies

**I am a love warrior, and I choose to love even those who may be my enemies.**

I know that love is the most powerful force in the Universe, and it can transform even the most challenging situations. Loving my enemies is not always easy, but I am up for the challenge. I choose to see them with compassion and empathy, and I recognize that they are struggling with their own challenges and pain. I am strong and courageous, and I choose to respond to my enemies with kindness and understanding. I know that my love and positivity can be beacons of light in their lives, and I am committed to spreading love wherever I go. I am not afraid to stand up for myself when they lash out, and to set healthy boundaries, but I choose to do these things with love and respect. I know that my enemies are also human beings, just like me, and they deserve to be treated with dignity and kindness. I am grateful for the opportunity to love my enemies, and I know that it will bring me peace and happiness. I trust in the power of love to heal and transform even the most challenging relationships. I choose to love my enemies not because it's easy but because it's the most powerful and transformative choice I can make. I will continue to live life as a love warrior, and nothing will stop me from spreading love and positivity to everyone I encounter.

# Celebrate Authenticity with the Universe

**I am an authentic being worth celebrating, and the Universe recognizes my value.**

I belong to myself and the Universe, and my true self is welcomed and celebrated. I am enough just as I am, and the Universe embraces my uniqueness with open arms. My individuality is valued and celebrated, and I am an integral part of the diverse and interconnected tapestry of life. I feel recognized and loved by my higher power, and I celebrate the good fortune of being able to embrace what makes me an individual. I belong wherever I choose to be, and the Universe supports and embraces my journey. There is space for me to make mistakes and learn from them because the learning is part of my authentic journey. I am worthy of love, respect, and acceptance, and the Universe recognizes and honors my worth without question. By embracing my true identity and sharing my gifts with the world, I create a space for myself and others to feel a sense of belonging in and connection to the Universe. Each day, I will remind myself that there is space for me to be exactly who I am, and the Universe will continue to embrace and celebrate my authentic self.

# Measure Progress and Accomplishments on Your Journey

**I am proving that I can accomplish a lot in life with every new and improved choice I make.**

---

I channel my energy into achieving massive success and let my achievements speak for themselves. I trust my instincts and stay true to my vision of success. I create my own future by setting ambitious goals and taking consistent action toward them. My happiness is not tied to external factors but to my own personal growth and fulfillment. I believe in my ability to take action toward my goals, overcome any challenge, and achieve my dreams. When I focus on my own success and work hard to achieve my goals, I rise above the opinions and doubts of others. I use doubt as fuel to propel me forward, and I use my achievements to prove those people who don't believe in me wrong. I trust in my abilities and refuse to let the opinions of others define my potential or limit my success. I embrace challenges as opportunities to prove to myself and others that I am capable of achieving greatness. With each passing day, I will remind myself that success is a journey, not a destination, and that it will continue to be important to measure my accomplishments as I make progress.

# Create a Clear Vision and Become a Trailblazer

### I am a fearless trailblazer, forging my own path toward greatness.

I am a natural-born leader, and I trust in my vision for the future. I embrace what I don't know in order to pave my path forward. I have a clear vision for success, and I am committed to it. I am not afraid to walk alone and explore new opportunities that lead to uncharted territories. I am willing to step outside my comfort zone and embrace discomfort to become a champion in my endeavors. I am both stubborn and flexible, using these qualities to persist in the face of obstacles and find innovative solutions. I lead by example and inspire those around me to embrace their own visions. My unique perspective and creativity allow me to be a trailblazer in my field and beyond. I understand that success is not a final destination and that failure is not the end. I am not afraid to be different, to think outside the box, and to pioneer new ideas and innovations. Each day, I will trust in my ability to lead the way, inspire others with my vision, and make a positive impact on the world.

# Reflect On Your Past Manifestation Successes

**I am choosing to reflect on the past to guide me toward my desired future.**

I remember all the blessings that I have experienced, offer gratitude to the Universe, and humbly ask for more blessings to come. I remember a time when my desires looked impossible to attain. However, I eventually manifested them into my life, which taught me a valuable lesson: I have the power to manifest anything I desire into my reality. I can create and attract greatness in every aspect of my life. With confidence and determination, I can use the law of attraction to make my dreams come true. I am capable of bringing even more positive experiences into my life. I understand that manifestation takes more than just believing in the power of my thoughts. It also requires taking inspired action toward my goals and maintaining a positive mindset. By visualizing and feeling the emotions of already having what I desire, I can align myself with the frequency of abundance and attract it into my life. I know that there may be obstacles and challenges along the way, but I trust that the Universe will guide me toward what is meant for me. Each day, I will be grateful for my ability to reflect on all of my successful manifestations, and I will look forward to seeing what other amazing things I can attract into my life.

# Honor Inner Masculine and Feminine Energies

### I am a beautiful being, worthy and complete just as I am.

I celebrate the feminine and masculine qualities within me, recognizing the power they bring to my life. The creative power of the Universe flows through me, and I embrace both the yin and yang forces within me. By balancing my inner masculine and feminine energies, I attract abundance and creativity into my life. I nurture my soul by connecting with the divine feminine within me and in the world around me, finding peace in the gentle embrace of her nurturing energy. As I honor the bold and soft parts of myself, they bring joy and fulfillment to all that I do. As I embrace the fierce power of the masculine and the gentle grace of the feminine within me, I create balance and harmony in my life. The yin and yang energies within me dance in perfect harmony, weaving a beautiful and powerful expression of my true self. With every step I take, I recognize both the masculine and feminine energies within me, allowing them to guide me toward my highest potential and deepest fulfillment. In this sacred union of the yin and yang, I will continue to be whole, complete, and fully aligned with my authentic self.

# Manage the Loud Negative Thoughts Within

### I am ready to take control and ownership of all of my thoughts.

I am able to think through decisions and the choices I need to make. I am learning how to quiet the negative voices and the voices that do not align with who I truly am. I know how to recognize what is for me and what is not. My thoughts shape my reality, and I choose to focus on positivity, abundance, and success. I have the power to respond to stress in a healthy manner and overcome any challenge that comes my way. Within me lie the strength, courage, and wisdom to handle anything that life brings me. I release the worries and negative self-talk that hold me back, and I embrace a mindset of confidence, self-love, and empowerment. I choose to listen to the voice of my inner wisdom and trust my intuition to guide me toward my true purpose and highest potential. I let go of self-doubt, and I cultivate a mindset of self-love. I will continue to take control of my thoughts and emotions, and I will focus on gratitude and joy in every moment.

# Find Stillness Within

**I am still in the present moment.**

Stillness allows me to work through anything that comes my way. I calm my mind and my heart to open myself to the beauty of what is truly meant for me. In the midst of chaos, I find stillness within me, and I allow it to guide me toward inner peace and clarity. Stillness is the universal language of the soul, and I tune into its whispers to connect with my inner truth and wisdom. I embrace moments of stillness and silence in my life, knowing that they offer a space for reflection, growth, and renewal. Within me lies a sanctuary of calm where I can find refuge from the noise and distractions of the world. I find strength and resilience in the power of silence, and I trust the Universe to guide me toward my highest good in moments of tranquility. In the quiet of stillness, I connect with my deepest truths, find my inner peace, and restore my energy for the journey ahead. Stillness is my superpower, and I use it to cultivate mindfulness, gratitude, and self-awareness and to align with the flow of the Universe. Each day, I will trust in the magic of stillness, knowing that it will help me unlock my creativity, intuition, and spiritual growth.

# Unlock Potential to Receive Your Desires

**I am constantly unlocking the potential
the Universe has in store for me.**

My mindset focuses on how I may unlock my potential to reach my goals. When I see others with the things I want, I remind myself that when I am living up to my potential, those things are within my reach as well. I believe in my power to manifest my aspirations. I trust that my dreams and desires are attainable, and I give myself permission to pursue them with passion and purpose. I choose to release any limiting beliefs and doubts that hold me back from experiencing the fullness of life. I embrace my worthiness and deservingness, knowing that the Universe responds to my vibration and energy. I am open and receptive to all the good things that are coming my way, and I affirm that I am worthy of all the love, joy, and success I desire. My dreams are valid and achievable, and I trust in the Universe to manifest them in my life. As the days go by, I will let go of limiting beliefs and thoughts that hold me back, and I will affirm that I am deserving of all the blessings and opportunities that the Universe has in store for me.

# Turn Your Manifestation Into Reality in Three Days

**I am the architect of my own reality, and in just three days, my manifestations will take shape and shine brightly for all to see.**

I declare that my manifestations will come to fruition in just a few days' time. My positive energy and unwavering belief are attracting abundance and success into my life. My manifestations are knocking on my door, and in just three days, they will burst through with unstoppable force. Every day, I am getting closer to achieving my desired outcomes. In just three days, my hard work and determination will start to pay off and my manifestations will become a reality. The Universe is aligning everything in my favor, and in just three days, my manifestations will come into sharp focus and begin introducing themselves into my reality. I know that in three days, the Universe will conspire to bring me everything that I have been envisioning and more. My thoughts and actions are aligned with the Universe's abundance, and my manifestations are already on their way. In just three days, I will see the evidence of my dreams coming true. The power of my mind and spirit is limitless, and I am in complete control of my manifestations. I declare that in three days, I will experience the joy and fulfillment that come with achieving my heart's desires.

# Start Your Week Off Strong

I am in charge of my week, and I choose
to fill it with joy, gratitude, and abundance.

---

This week, I feel the blessings of my manifestations. I am declaring this week to be the best week I have had in a long time. I am already excited to look back on this week and see all that the Universe did for me. With each passing day, I am creating a life that I love and a future that I believe in. This week is full of opportunities for growth and success. I am excited to see what the Universe has in store for me, and I trust that everything will work out for my highest good. I am capable of accomplishing great things this week. With focus, determination, and perseverance, I know that I will overcome any obstacles and achieve my goals. This week, I am committed to prioritizing my health and well-being. I will nourish my body with healthy food, exercise regularly, and take time for rest and relaxation. I am grateful for the blessings that this week will bring. I will remain open to new experiences, learn from my challenges, and appreciate the abundance that surrounds me. This week is a blank canvas, and I am the artist. I will create a masterpiece by setting clear intentions, taking inspired action, and trusting the process.

# Find Blessings in Random Thoughts

## I am a creative genius, and all my random thoughts are blessings in disguise.

I know that my thoughts are powerful and have the ability to shape my reality. So, I choose to see the blessings in all my thoughts, even the random ones. I understand that my mind is active, and sometimes it produces random thoughts that seem to have no purpose. But I know that every thought has a purpose, and these thoughts can lead me to new ideas and opportunities. I choose to embrace all my thoughts, even the ones that seem silly or insignificant. I know that my mind is constantly working on my behalf, and it's always looking for ways to help me grow and succeed. I trust in the Universe to bring me what I need, and I know that my thoughts are powerful tools for manifestation. So, I choose to think positively and constructively, and I allow my thoughts to help me attract more abundance and joy into my life. I am grateful for all my thoughts because they reflect my creativity and imagination. Every day, I remind myself that my thoughts have the power to change my life, and I will see the blessings in all of them.

# Explore the World and Nurture the Soul

I am a traveler on the journey of life, and
with each adventure, I gain new perspectives
about the world and nurture my inner self.

By exploring the world, I discover the beauty of diversity and appreciate the interconnectedness of all things in the Universe. I use my time to travel and understand all that the world has to offer. By taking in what the world has to offer, I can expand my mind in so many ways. I am feeding my soul with many blessings when I look at the world through my own eyes. I trust in my intuition and follow my heart's desire to investigate new lands and cultures, knowing that every experience enriches my soul. I embrace the unknown and welcome the challenges that come with traveling, for they lead me to the greatest adventure of all—the discovery of my true self. I am a storyteller, enriching my soul by sharing the tales of my travels with the world and inspiring others to embark on their own journeys of self-discovery and growth. The Universe is vast and abundant, and I trust that there is always more to discover and explore, both within myself and in the world around me. Through exploration, I will break free from the limitations of my comfort zone and open myself up to new possibilities, growth, and transformation.

# Explore the Connection Between Wealth and Gratitude

### I am grateful for the abundance of wealth and prosperity in my life.

I am thankful for the abundance that I already have, and I attract more wealth with each passing day. My wealth mindset is fueled by gratitude and positivity, allowing me to achieve great success. Every day, I focus on the things I am grateful for and allow that gratitude to attract abundance into my life. I am a magnet for wealth and prosperity, thanks to my focus on gratitude and abundance. As I express gratitude for what I have, the Universe responds by bringing me even more to be thankful for. When I use gratitude daily, the Universe blesses me with more money than I need, allowing me to live a life of comfort, ease, and joy. With my wealth, I can provide for myself and my loved ones, give generously to those in need, and support causes that align with my values. I know that my wealth reflects my hard work, dedication, and positive mindset. Each day, I will continue to attract financial abundance into my life, and I will use it wisely to create a better world for myself and others.

# Be Enthused about Exciting Future Possibilities

### I am destined to live a wonderful life and enjoy all that life has in store for me.

I am worthy of doing great things, and I feel fulfilled by them. I am ready to receive all the amazing opportunities that the Universe has waiting for me, and I accept them gratefully. I move through life to connect with my desired future. I am excited about future blessings and good fortune. I am grateful for this lifetime and the endless opportunities it holds for me to grow, learn, and achieve my dreams. The future is bright and full of endless possibilities, and I am ready to experience them all. I believe that great things are in store for me in this lifetime. The Universe has a grand plan for me, and I am ready to discover and fulfill my purpose. I understand that there may be challenges and bumps along the way, but I am confident that my positive mindset and unwavering determination will guide me through any obstacle I encounter. Each day, I take inspired action toward my goals and trust that the Universe will align in my favor. I know that by staying enthusiastic about everything coming my way, I will attract all the abundance and greatness that this lifetime has to offer.

# Find a Way Out of Survival Mode

I am strong, resilient, and capable of navigating any seemingly impossible challenges that come my way.

---

I channel my energy into positive actions during times of stress and adversity, and I emerge stronger and more resilient. I am more than just a survivor; I am a thriver. I release the fear of scarcity and open myself up to abundance and prosperity. I am moving beyond survival mode and thriving in every aspect of my life. I am breaking free from limiting beliefs and self-sabotage that hold me back. Even in survival mode, I make time for creativity, fun, and self-care because I deserve to experience joy and pleasure in life. I focus on progress and growth rather than letting negative self-talk rule my inner thoughts. I face my fears head-on, and I am brave and courageous in the face of adversity. Survival mode is not my permanent state of being; I am capable of creating a life full of abundance, peace, and joy. I expand my awareness beyond the present moment and trust in the Universe to guide me toward a brighter future, especially in difficult times. I trust in my ability to find solutions and persevere through trying circumstances. Every obstacle I face is an opportunity for growth, and I am grateful for the lessons and strength that come from surviving and thriving in challenging situations. I will continue to search for ways to leave survival mode, and I will embrace calm.

# Use Your Higher Self to Cleanse Your Lower Vibrations

**I am now calling upon my higher self to descend and guide me toward a state of higher vibrations.**

---

With every passing moment, my higher self is cleansing and purifying my lower vibrational self. I release all negative energy and limiting beliefs, making room for love, light, and positivity to flow into my life. As my higher self descends, I feel a sense of clarity and inner peace. My thoughts become more focused and aligned with my highest vision for my life. I am open and receptive to divine guidance, trusting that my higher self will lead me toward my purpose. With each breath, I feel lifted and am reminded of my higher self's innate power and limitless potential. I am filled with a deep sense of gratitude and appreciation for this moment and the guidance that I am receiving. My higher self is my constant companion, helping me transcend the limitations of my physical form. I trust that my higher self knows what is best for me, and I allow it to guide me toward my goals and desires. As my higher self works its magic, I feel a sense of liberation and expansion. I am no longer bound by my fears and doubts, but rather I am propelled by the confidence and clarity that my higher self brings. Each day, I will be ready to embrace all the blessings that the Universe has in store for me, and I will tap into my highest self to cleanse my lower vibrations.

# Start Self-Improvement Now

I am capable of incredible growth and transformation, and I actively want to pursue positive change.

Today, I commit to starting my journey of self-improvement and growth. Living my best life begins with me making positive changes. I empower myself to reach my full potential, and I take this journey one step at a time. I hold the ability to change and progressively work toward becoming the best version of myself. I am ready to embrace the journey toward becoming my best self right now. I owe it to myself to take the necessary steps to change myself from the inside out. Every time I fall, I use the experience as an opportunity to learn and become even stronger. It's never too late to rewrite the story of my life and continue learning from the chapters I would rather erase. I have the power to make positive changes at the present moment and create the life I truly desire. I honor my true self and trust in my ability to set new goals and pursue new dreams at any age or stage of life. By embracing change and stepping out of my comfort zone, I am creating a life that aligns with my deepest values and desires. Each day, I will affirm that the power to shape my own destiny lies within me, and I will use this power to create a life of joy, purpose, and fulfillment.

# DAY 327
## Manifest Through a Bad Day

**I am resilient and strong, and I have the power to get through the tough moments.**

I remind myself: It's just a bad day, not a bad life. I am still capable of manifesting my desires through this challenging day because there is so much to be grateful for. On tough days, I release negativity and embrace positivity. When things seem to go wrong, the Universe still has a wonderful plan for me, even though it may be hard to see. I choose to manifest joy and happiness. I am not defined by my failures or my bad days but by my perseverance and my willingness to keep striving for my dreams. By aligning my work with my passions and values, I create a life that brings me joy and fulfillment every day. I take full responsibility for my thoughts, feelings, and reactions to the world around me, knowing that my mindset and attitude shape the trajectory of my life. My bad day does not define me; I am capable of bouncing back and turning things around. I choose to focus on the positive aspects of my life and find gratitude in every moment, even on the toughest of days. I will continue to be the creator of my own reality, and even on the days that feel difficult, I will affirm that I have the power to create a happy and fulfilling life.

# Focus On Small or Simple Actions to Change Lives Around You

*I am living a life of purpose and meaning, and I focus on the small gifts I can give to myself and others to improve the lives around me.*

Giving to others brings abundance and richness into my own life, and I am never impoverished by being charitable. When I serve others with love and compassion, I discover new depths of purpose and fulfillment within myself. My hands are meant to reach out to others in need, to lift them up, and to offer hope and healing to those who are struggling. I choose to live a life of service in which I view the needs of others as opportunities to make a positive impact and contribute to a better world. By giving to others with an open heart and a spirit of generosity, I create a ripple effect of kindness and compassion that spreads far beyond myself. Giving to others is not just an act of kindness; it's a way of life that brings purpose, joy, and fulfillment to my own journey. The Universe rewards my kindness and generosity with an abundance of love, joy, and blessings that enrich my life and the lives of those around me. I am creating a legacy of kindness, compassion, and goodwill that will last long after I'm gone. Every day, I will look for opportunities to serve and uplift others, creating a positive feedback loop of generosity and happiness.

# Embrace the Infinite Possibilities of a New Chapter

I am stepping into a new chapter of my life,
and I know it is filled with abundance,
peace, wealth, and success.

---

I believe that everything I desire is already on its way to me as I take my next steps forward. I am confident in my ability to create the life I desire, and I am excited to see my dreams come to fruition. As I step into this new chapter of my life, I feel a sense of excitement and anticipation for what is to come. As I shed my old skin, I make space for new opportunities and experiences to flow into my life. I believe with every fiber of my being that everything good is mine for the taking. As I continue to align my thoughts and beliefs with my desires, I am confident that I am attracting all the good things that life has to offer. I know that I have worked hard to get to this point in my life, and I am grateful for everything that has led me to this new chapter. As I flip to the next pages of my life story, I am filled with a sense of empowerment and purpose. Every day, I will be grateful for this new chapter of my life, and I will be ready to embrace all the infinite possibilities that lie ahead.

# Recognize Your Unique Power

**I am valuable in my own way and have
the power of many unique talents.**

I honor my special qualities, understanding they are part of what makes me exceptional. My individuality is a valuable gift to the world, and I have boundless potential due to the numerous things I can offer. All I need to do is relax and allow what I want to come through, trusting in the Universe's plan. My worth is inherent and cannot be taken away from me. My talents and gifts are incredible and make me so proud of myself. I am specific about my desires, but I always leave room for more or better. I am distinctive and invaluable, with a set of skills, talents, and qualities that no one else possesses. I choose to focus on my strengths and to use them to make a positive impact on the world around me. I embrace my imperfections and failures, knowing that they are opportunities for growth and learning. Each day, I will remind myself that I am constantly evolving and improving, and I will continually recognize the value my unique talents and gifts bring to this world.

# Foster a Sense of Safety and Belonging in the Community

**I am safe to be around, and I strive to create a positive and welcoming environment for those around me.**

I want everyone to accomplish their dreams, and I know that's done most easily in a caring community. I create a safe environment for others, where people understand it's fine to be vulnerable around me. I am always doing my best to allow people to be their true selves when we share space. I believe in treating others with kindness, respect, and empathy, and I understand that everyone has their own unique experiences and perspectives. I seek to understand and learn from those around me, and I am always open to new ideas and viewpoints. I am building a community of people who feel like they belong. I celebrate the successes of others as much as I do my own. I have faith that there is enough success and abundance in the world for everyone, and I do not believe in competing at the expense of others. I trust in the power of collaboration and teamwork, and I know that we can achieve great things when we work together toward a common goal. The more time that passes, the more I will be committed to creating a world where everyone has the opportunity to succeed and where we lift one another up instead of tearing one another down.

# Calm Your Mind and Find Balance in Social Situations

*I am overcoming social anxiety and growing comfortable in the presence of others.*

---

I acknowledge that social anxiety can be challenging, but I choose not to let it define me or hold me back. I listen to my body when I need to be alone, and I also push myself to meet new people and build lasting relationships. I am capable of managing my anxiety and stepping out of my comfort zone to connect with others. I believe in my ability to overcome my fears and take on new challenges, one step at a time. I practice self-care and self-compassion, knowing that it is okay to take breaks when I need them. I am leaning on the Universe to help me handle any social challenges I experience. I know that my anxious thoughts do not reflect what people truly think of me. I am loved, and people want to be around me. I am open to seeking help and support when I need to, and I know that I am not alone in my struggles. I am worthy of love and belonging, and I will not let my anxiety prevent me from forming meaningful relationships. I am brave and resilient, and I will continue to push through my fears and grow stronger in my social interactions every day.

# Prepare Your Heart for Greatness

### I am ready for new levels, new experiences, new challenges, and new blessings.

The Universe is preparing my heart and essence for greatness, and I trust in its plan for my life. I believe that every setback is leading me closer to my ultimate purpose. My heart is open and ready for greatness to enter my life. I am taking intentional steps to prepare myself for the greatness that awaits me. I am preparing my heart to receive the amazing things that are coming my way. I am meant for greatness and am manifesting it every day. I am grateful for the lessons I have learned and the experiences I have had so far, as they have prepared me for the amazing things that are yet to come. I am open to receiving abundance and success, and I know that the Universe will provide me with everything I need to make my heart stronger and more loving. I trust in my intuition and my emotional wisdom. I will continue to be excited for the future and all the possibilities it holds, knowing that the Universe is conspiring in my favor to help my heart achieve greatness.

# Show Up for Yourself in Challenging and Peaceful Times

**I am committed to keep showing up for myself, no matter what I may face.**

I show up for myself before I show up for others, knowing that I cannot help others when my energy has run out. This helps me show myself love. The journey toward my goals may not always be easy, but I am willing to put in the hard work and effort required to achieve them. I believe in myself and my abilities, and I know that I have the strength and resilience to overcome anything when I stay present. With each day that I show up for myself, I take a small step toward my goals, and I know every step will add up over time. I trust myself to make the best decisions for my well-being and happiness, and I prioritize my self-care and self-compassion. I will not let fear and self-doubt hold me back, and I will continue to show up for myself every day, no matter how difficult. I am worth the effort and the investment in myself, and I will never give up on becoming the best version of myself. Even when things aren't looking so great, I am able to show myself grace to get through it. With each new day, I will be so happy to see how this passion for myself shows up in my life.

# Align Values and Passions with Your Lifestyle

### I am choosing to align my values and passions with my lifestyle and purpose.

I know that when I am true to myself and my values, I am in harmony with the Universe and all its abundance. I embrace my unique passions and allow them to lead me toward new and exciting opportunities. I am open to exploring different paths that align with my values to create a meaningful life. I am grateful for my strengths and talents, and I choose to use them in service of my passions and the greater good. I know that by aligning my values and passions, I can make a positive impact on the world and contribute to a better future for all. By facing my fears and stepping out of my comfort zone, I can discover new aspects of myself, uncover new passions to explore, and determine my purpose. I am confident in my ability to navigate the unknown, and I also trust in the Universe to guide me toward my highest good. I am open to receiving guidance and support from others who share my values and passions, and I am grateful for their presence in my life. I celebrate my journey and all the blessings that come with it. I will continue to align my values and passions with my actions and create a life that is authentic, joyful, and fulfilling.

# Feel Good Instantly with High Vibrations

**I am a vibrational being, and I choose to live in a high vibrational state every day.**

---

I know that when I am in alignment with my highest self, I instantly attract positivity into my life. I love feeling good, and I take pleasure in finding ways to raise my vibrations throughout the day. Whether it's through music, laughter, nature, or connecting with loved ones, these moments of joy and gratitude instantly lift me up. I know that there are many other ways (like taking a deep breath or dancing to my favorite song) to instantly feel good and shift my energy toward a positive state. I trust in the power of my thoughts and emotions, and I choose to focus on positivity and love. When I prioritize optimism and care, it instantly contributes to my high vibrations and makes me feel great. I am creating a life that is aligned with my highest vibrations and attracting all that I desire. I know that when I align myself with high vibrations, I am in a state of flow, attracting all that I need to live my best life. I am surrounded by love and positivity, and I instantly radiate that energy outward. By doing so, I am creating a ripple effect that spreads joy and love to those around me. I know that I am worthy of living a life filled with joy and abundance, and I will choose to align with that vibration every day.

# Practice Mindfulness

**I am opening my mind, body, and spirit to the beautiful practice of mindfulness, inviting it to guide me in achieving a greater sense of awareness, clarity, and inner peace.**

I allow myself to experience thoughts, emotions, and events with intention. I am consistently cultivating a deeper sense of self-awareness and emotional intelligence. Connecting with my breath and body is crucial to my mindfulness practice. Mindfulness allows me to be fully present in the moment and grateful for all that it offers. I recognize the importance of gratitude, appreciating the ups and downs of life. As I continue on my journey of mindfulness, I am patient and kind to myself, embracing compassion toward myself and others. Rather than judging or attaching to outcomes, I welcome each moment with a sense of curiosity. I trust that with a continued mindfulness practice, my journey will lead to a fulfilling and meaningful life. I am grateful for the peace and clarity that mindfulness brings into my life. Mindfulness helps me embrace the joy of discovery and learning throughout my life. I give thanks daily to the Universe for its abundance and blessings. By expressing my gratitude, I reaffirm my commitment to mindfulness in each moment. I trust in the Universe's guidance that supports me on my journey of self-discovery and growth. With each day, I will commit to practicing mindfulness for the betterment of myself, others, and the world.

# Treasure Inner Peace

I am at peace with myself, and this
feeling radiates out to those around me.

Peace moves effortlessly through me, calming my mind and soothing my soul. I am a peaceful being, bringing love and harmony to all those around me. In the midst of chaos, I remain centered and grounded in a deep sense of peace. Tranquility is not just an absence of conflict; it is a state of mind that I cultivate every day. I trust in the Universe to guide me toward peace, and I am open to receiving its wisdom. The peace that I cultivate within myself is a gift that I offer to the world. I make room for peace and positivity to flow into my life. I am a beacon of peace, shining my light for all to see and inspiring others to do the same. Peace is my natural state of being, and I return to it effortlessly whenever I need to. I embrace the power of tranquility, knowing that it can transform myself and the world around me. I release all thoughts and emotions that disturb my peace and embrace tranquility in their place. Tranquil energy flows freely through me, rejuvenating my mind, body, and soul. With every moment, I will embrace the power of peace to transform myself and the world around me, one step at a time.

# Take Advantage of the Abundance Cycle

### I am surrounded by love and abundance when I give to others.

As I give from the heart, I am creating a positive ripple effect in the world, spreading love, kindness, and abundance. Giving is an act of love, and I joyfully give myself and my resources to others, knowing that what I give will come back to me via the cycle of abundance. Giving generously is a natural expression of my abundance mindset. The Universe is constantly showering me with blessings and abundance, and I am open to receiving them with gratitude. I release any doubts and face any obstacles that may be preventing me from receiving the abundance that is rightfully mine. I am a powerful manifester, and I attract good vibrations in my life. I am open to receiving gifts and positivity from the cycle of abundance, both expected and unexpected. I am grateful for all the blessings that flow into my life each day. The Universe is conspiring to bring me all the abundance I desire, and I am open to receiving it all. Each day, I will be a magnet for abundance, and I will attract all the resources and support I need to manifest my deepest desires.

# Overcome Insecurities to Find Courage

*I am working on my self-confidence every day, knowing that inner courage will come to me in time.*

Self-love is a mindset I can develop, and I fight off my insecurities so I can experience it. When I develop genuine confidence, I can solve all problems that I am confronted with. As I endeavor to conquer problems, I learn from each struggle and am then more prepared for future obstacles. By enhancing my self-confidence, I feel better in my personal life, professional life, and other aspects of my life. I trust in myself fully, and my courage allows me to be persuasive and open and to act as a role model at work or in the community. I work diligently at developing my self-confidence to reach new potential, step out of my comfort zone, and accomplish mentally taxing goals. I take on the appearance of confidence based on how I carry myself, and that helps me grow more confident. I make eye contact when talking to others, and I stand tall and proud. When I think more positively and confidently, I manifest and attract positivity. Each day, my goal is to focus on the positive things that can and will come my way. Moving forward, I will commit to courageously overcoming my insecurities and becoming the best I can be.

# Prioritize Yourself Every Day

I am devoted to myself and prioritize myself every day.

I choose to give myself the time and attention I need to thrive. I trust that prioritizing myself will lead to a more fulfilling and joyful life. I am deserving of care, and I invest in my own well-being. I am capable of balancing my responsibilities while still making time for myself. I release any guilt and shame around taking care of my needs and embrace the benefits of self-care. I let go of anything that does not serve my well-being and focus on what does. I am my own biggest fan, and I'm always cheering myself on. I'm like a superhero, but instead of saving the world, I'm saving myself. I treat myself like a VIP because I am one. I give myself the love and attention I deserve, and it feels like a spa day for my soul. I create a love bubble around myself through self-devotion, and it's the happiest place on earth. I focus on nurturing my inner child by prioritizing myself. I practice radical self-love by taking time to examine and take care of myself, and it's empowering. I'm putting myself first and living my best life through the power of self-devotion. I am confident in my ability to prioritize myself and make positive changes in my life. Each day, I will remind myself that I am deserving of the time and space I need to recharge and thrive.

# Realize Your True Nature and Live with Purpose

**I am fully conscious of my true nature, and I am committed to living my life with joy and purpose.**

I choose to embody my eternal, indestructible, and pure awareness and live each moment fully. I embrace the infinite potential of my being and trust in my ability to fulfill my purpose. When I bring my attention to the awareness within my spirit and embrace it fully, I can live my life with enthusiasm and real meaning. When I embody my awareness, I am choosing to live in a state of presence and mindfulness. I become conscious of my thoughts, feelings, and actions and can make thoughtful choices that align with my true nature. Any purposeful decisions I make can lead to a more fulfilling and meaningful life, as I am living in alignment with my deepest values and desires. When I recognize the infinite potential of my being, I can trust in my ability to fulfill my goals. I approach challenges and opportunities with a sense of confidence and resilience, knowing that I am capable of overcoming any obstacle. I work to cultivate a positive mindset and a greater sense of self-worth. As I embrace my true nature and live my life with joy and purpose, I will create a life that is rich with fulfillment.

# DAY 343

## Move Beyond the Physical Realm to the Spiritual

*I am more than just my physical body, and my true essence is spiritual in nature.*

I am here on earth to learn, grow, and evolve spiritually, and my physical existence is a temporary state in which I can learn important lessons and gain valuable experiences. I begin to see my challenges and experiences as opportunities for spiritual growth and development rather than annoying obstacles to overcome. I connect with my inner self and access my inner wisdom and intuition. By recognizing my spiritual nature, I can tap into a higher level of consciousness and gain greater clarity and insight into my life. I am encouraged to view my life from a more expansive and meaningful perspective and to recognize the deeper purpose and significance of my experiences on earth. Inner peace and fulfillment flow naturally to me as I embrace my spiritual nature. Each day, I grow wiser and more enlightened on my spiritual journey through this human experience. The Universe is constantly guiding me toward my highest good, and I trust in its infinite wisdom. My physical body is a miraculous vessel that allows me to experience the world and all its wonders. As I deepen my spiritual awareness every day, I will unlock a higher level of consciousness and uncover my true purpose and meaning in life.

359

# Find Solutions Instead of Dwelling On Problems

**I am ready to stop dwelling on negative circumstances and the faults of others.**

I focus on the positive aspects of people and situations. When I constantly look for flaws and shortcomings in people and circumstances, I become critical and judgmental, and this can lead to feelings of frustration, disappointment, and even resentment. Instead, when I adopt a mindset of refusing to find fault, I approach people and situations with a more open and accepting attitude. No one is perfect, and I look for the positive qualities that each person possesses. I also recognize that every situation has its challenges, but I focus on finding solutions rather than dwelling on the problems. When I stop finding fault, I cultivate a more positive and uplifting energy that attracts more positivity into my life. I become more compassionate and understanding toward others, and this helps build stronger, more harmonious relationships. I also become more resilient in the face of challenges, as I learn to focus on what I can control and let go of what I cannot. Ultimately, not looking for fault in others is a call to action that encourages me to shift my focus from what is wrong to what is right. It reminds me that the power of my thoughts and attitudes can shape my experiences and determine my level of happiness and fulfillment. By adopting this simple but profound mindset, I will continue to create a more joyful and rewarding life for myself and those around me.

# DAY 345

# Use the Power of Love to Manifest Your Greatest Desires

I am embracing the limitless power of love, channeling its energy to manifest my heartfelt aspirations.

---

The power of love is an incredible force that has a profound impact on my life. When I focus my energy on love, I am able to manifest my deepest aspirations in a way that is both natural and effortless. Love is not just a word or a feeling; it's a powerful force that can change everything. I know that when I focus on what I truly want from my heart, love supports me and brings special things my way. It's like the Universe is working with me to make it happen. Love is a powerful energy that attracts more of the same positive vibrations into my life. The power of love is a transformative force that can help me achieve my greatest desires. Each day, I will use the power of love to create a life of abundance, joy, and fulfillment.

# Manifest the Power of a Wealth-Consciousness Mindset

**I am excited to receive wealth and put into action many strategies to make money.**

The flow of financial abundance is already directed at me. I am attracting into my life large amounts of wealth that I will manage conscientiously. I am comfortable and at ease with exorbitant amounts of wealth and property. Through my uninhibited accumulation of money, I acquire more wealth than I need. I open my mind and heart to receive a continuous flow of money, and I see myself becoming wealthy. I will have an abundance of financial resources in the next two months. Doors are opening up for me in the financial realm, and no one can shut them. I am worthy and deserving to be financially secure in every area of my life. Money flows to me so that I may manage it with intelligence and skill. I am thankful for the abundance that has come into my life. Money enters into my life effortlessly and without hindrance. I create strong and powerful financial realities for myself that develop abundance. I embrace my financial and material abundance in every area of my life. My philosophy is that the more I give, the more I will receive. My money is protected in all my financial endeavors. Financial prosperity is coming to me in many different ways. Each day, I will receive prosperity through money, property, wealth, health, and happiness.

# Embrace Your Past with Grace

**I am reflecting on my life with grace, and I realize that mistakes have been a part of my journey.**

I see how each of these blunders has contributed to my growth and development, leading me to where I am today. I choose to embrace my past and appreciate the lessons learned from both positive and negative experiences. I now make better choices, feeling grateful for the wisdom and insight gained. By accepting my past with grace, I move forward with confidence and clarity, knowing that I am capable of overcoming any obstacle that may come my way. I let go of any regrets and negative emotions about my past and focus on the lessons I have learned and the tremendous growth I've demonstrated. I give myself permission to make mistakes and learn from them, understanding that they are a natural part of my journey. I trust that everything that has happened in my life has occurred for a reason, leading me to where I am meant to be. I approach my past with an open mind and curiosity, seeking to understand how it has shaped me and how I can use these experiences to create a better future. I will work to love my past self, and I will accept my past actions with forgiveness and understanding.

# Shift Gears to Your Highest Version

### I am shifting into my highest version,
### full of freedom and abundance.

I make a conscious choice to focus on what is going right for me. I release any limiting beliefs and negative thought patterns that hold me back from achieving my highest potential. I choose to embrace a mindset of positivity and abundance, knowing that the Universe is working in my favor. I am no longer held back by fear and doubt, but instead I am guided by my intuition and inner wisdom. I trust that every step I take is leading me closer to my desired outcome. In this moment, I feel I am the highest version of myself, but I know how much more I can still learn and transform. I have shed the old patterns and beliefs that no longer serve me, and I am stepping into a new level of consciousness. My highest self is confident, empowered, and capable of achieving anything I set my mind to. I am open to receiving all forms of abundance, and I trust that everything I need will come to me in perfect timing. As I continue to shift into my highest state, I am becoming more aligned with my true purpose and passion. I am creating a life of freedom, joy, and fulfillment, and I am excited to see what the future holds. Each day, I will wake up grateful for this journey and for the opportunity to grow and evolve into my highest self.

# Become a Magnet for Your Desires

### I am a magnet for all that I desire.

I affirm my ability to attract everything I truly want into my life. My thoughts and beliefs have the power to attract positive experiences. When I believe that I am a magnet for all that I want in this life, I open myself up to receive the Universe's abundance. By focusing my thoughts and energy on my desires, I am aligning myself with the vibrations of those desires, which makes it easier for them to manifest in my reality. I remind myself that being a magnet for my desires does not mean that everything I want will come to me effortlessly. By focusing my mindset on what I want, I am setting myself up for success and attracting opportunities and resources that can help me achieve my goals. To be a magnet for all that I desire, I focus on my desires with intention and clarity, knowing I must be clear on what I want. I believe that I am worthy and deserving of having the tools to achieve my dreams. I am open to receiving, and I act toward my goals when opportunities present themselves. I am aligned to my thoughts, beliefs, and actions. As I embrace the idea that I am a powerful magnetic force, I will attract everything I need to achieve my dreams and create the life I truly desire.

# Achieve Organizational Success Through Presence and Curiosity

I am a born leader, and therefore
I must be thoughtful and genuine about
what is present today in my workplace.

I am aware of all the activities that are transpiring within the organization I am a part of. I am clear on all the goals and plans that are occurring in the department I oversee. I cultivate a curious attitude that is based on open-mindedness and reflects my personal experiences within my business. I remain highly mindful of all aspects of the business in order to help it thrive. I promote aggressive attention to detail and goal-centered intentions. I have an openness and kindness that allows others to approach me. I am a solid leader who is capable of conveying achievement-oriented actions clearly to my subordinates. I understand the concepts of team building, collaboration, and emotional intelligence and their value to developing my team. I am mindful and curious about my working environment every day. My mindfulness goal is to process my environment through the mental, emotional, and physical. My aim is to bring my full attention to the present moment in order to experience the here and now as I lead others to goal achievement. I remember that leading others is a gift I respect and cherish. Each day, I will embrace my leadership role in my organization and support my team with kindness and curiosity.

# Become the Best Version of Yourself to Attract Your Desires

I am ready to embrace my best version
and attract everything I dream of.

---

The Universe gives based on who you are, not what you want. The energy I put out into the world is reflected back to me, making me stronger and better. I will focus on being the type of person who attracts everything they desire. I attract love and healthy relationships into my life by working on becoming a loving and compassionate person. I am kind to others, I practice forgiveness, and I communicate openly and honestly. By embodying positive qualities, I am attracting people who resonate with that positivity and share similar values. I attract abundance and success in my career and finances by working on developing a mindset of abundance and taking actions that align with that mindset. I am grateful for what I have, I focus on the positive aspects of my life, and I take steps toward my goals. I concentrate on becoming the best version of myself and trust that the Universe will provide me with what I need at the right time. Because the Universe gives based on who I am, I will actively choose to focus on becoming the best version of myself.

# Believe In an Easier Life

I am taking control of my beliefs,
as they have power over my experiences.

The way I perceive my experiences can greatly impact how I feel about them. When I believe that life is easy, manageable, and full of opportunities, I experience calm, contentment, and positivity. Believing that life is easier does not mean that I will never face challenges or difficulties, but I approach challenges with a positive attitude and believe in my ability to overcome them. When I believe that life is easier, I look for solutions, seek help when needed, and persevere through tough times. Thanks to my positivity, I am open to the opportunities that come my way. I recognize and take advantage of any positive and exciting possibilities rather than letting them pass me by. When I believe life is easy, many of my worries begin to fade away. By approaching challenges with a positive attitude, seeking solutions, and being open to opportunities, I experience a sense of fulfillment that greatly enhances my overall quality of life. Every day, I will believe that I deserve an easier, fulfilling life, and I will take the steps I need to take to make this happen for myself.

# Realize the Power of Believing In an Amazing Life

### I am meant to have an amazing life.

Believing that I am destined for greatness is a powerful mindset that can lead to positive outcomes and a sense of fulfillment. When I believe that I am destined for greatness, I am more likely to take risks, pursue my passions, and embrace opportunities that come my way. Even when I face challenges, I embrace them as chances to transform myself. I remind myself that setbacks are a normal part of the journey toward an amazing life. I approach obstacles with a positive attitude and a belief that I can overcome them. I regularly focus on my strengths and accomplishments in order to reinforce the idea that I have an amazing life. By recognizing my talents, I build confidence and a sense of self-worth. It's also important to set goals and work toward them, no matter how difficult or easy they may be. Celebrating my successes and learning from my failures helps me stay on track and keep moving forward toward my bright future. I believe that having an amazing life can be a powerful motivator for achieving my goals and living a fulfilling life. By embracing opportunities, facing challenges with a positive attitude, and recognizing my own strengths and accomplishments, I will create the amazing life that I was always meant to have.

# Connect with Your Body and Health Through Exercise

**I am healthy, and I use exercise to connect with my body and call in my desires.**

Maintaining good health is one way I work toward a happy and fulfilling life. When I take care of my body, I not only feel better physically, but I also have more energy, focus, and mental clarity. I promote good health by engaging in regular exercise. Exercise strengthens my muscles, improves my mental health, and promotes my cardiovascular fitness. Exercise helps me connect with my body and my ultimate goals. By tuning into my physical self and being mindful of my movements, I cultivate a deeper sense of appreciation for my body. When exercising, I easily make choices that are in alignment with my goals and values. Incorporating exercises that I find enjoyable and fulfilling is a powerful way to engage with my physical being. Whether it's practicing yoga, dancing, or weight lifting, engaging in activities that bring me joy and satisfaction helps cultivate a positive and abundant mindset. Each day, as I focus on my desires and setting intentions during my workouts, I will tap into the power of manifestation and attract the things I want into my life.

# Unleash Your Creative Inner Power

**I am a powerful creator, and I manifest what I visualize.**

I possess the incredible power to create and shape my own reality. By harnessing the power of my thoughts, creative spirit, and intentions, I can manifest my desires and turn them into physical reality. I easily and creatively visualize a clear mental image of my desired outcome and send that powerful message to the Universe. To become an expert of manifestation through creative visualization, I practice regularly and with intention. I set aside time each day to visualize my desired outcome in detail, using as much clarity and emotion as possible. By engaging my emotions, I create a stronger energetic connection with the Universe and increase the power of my artistic visualization. I approach visualization with a receptive mindset, and I do not become attached to a specific outcome or timeline. I trust in the Universe and my ability to manifest my desires. By consistently practicing visualization, I can manifest incredible things in my life. By believing in myself, trusting in the Universe, and focusing my attention on my desired outcomes, I will continually act as a powerful creator and manifest the life of my dreams.

# Empower Yourself Through Saying No

**I am becoming more and more comfortable with saying no and releasing my identity as a people pleaser.**

Maintaining healthy boundaries is essential for my well-being and happiness. Saying no to requests and obligations that don't align with my values or priorities is an important part of taking care of myself. Although it can be challenging at times, it's important for me to remember that I am not responsible for other people's feelings or needs. While it's important to be considerate of others, I cannot always prioritize their needs over my own. By setting boundaries and saying no when necessary, I am taking control of my life and making choices that align with my goals. Saying no also allows me to create space for the things that truly matter to me. By not overcommitting myself, I can focus on my own self-care and personal growth. This enables me to show up more fully and authentically in my relationships and other areas of my life. As I continue to prioritize my own well-being and practice saying no, I am becoming more confident and empowered. I am learning to trust my own intuition and make choices that honor my own needs and desires. As I let go of the need to constantly please others, I will create a life that feels more aligned and fulfilling.

# Find Gratitude in the Darkest Moments

**I am always able to find ways to show my gratitude even in the darkest of moments.**

Finding gratitude even on my tough days is a practice that I have developed and value deeply. By consciously focusing on the things that I am grateful for, I can shift my perspective during my challenging times and find a sense of peace and contentment. Refocusing my mindset involves actively seeking out moments of gratitude throughout the day, no matter how small they may be. I appreciate a warm cup of coffee in the morning or feel grateful for the support of a loved one. By consciously acknowledging and savoring these moments, I can cultivate a sense of gratitude and joy in my life. Even on the worst days, there is always something to be grateful for—perhaps it's the opportunity to learn from a difficult situation or the kindness of a stranger. By focusing on the positives and finding gratitude no matter the circumstance, I maintain a positive mindset and find a sense of peace. Practicing gratitude is not always easy, but it is a powerful tool for cultivating happiness and well-being. By acknowledging and appreciating the good in my life every day, I will shift my focus away from negativity and cultivate a greater sense of joy, fulfillment, and abundance.

# Overcome Jealousy and Embrace Your Greatness

### I am working deeply on myself in order to be proud of who I am.

I have come to the realization that my own jealousy and insecurities have been holding me back from achieving my full potential. I let go of negative emotions and beliefs and focus on my strengths and unique qualities. It's not always easy to release these deeply ingrained patterns, but I am committed to doing the inner work necessary to overcome them. I learn to identify when insecurity arises within me, and I approach my emotions with curiosity and self-compassion rather than judgment. Through this process of self-exploration and growth, I discover my confidence and self-assurance. My greatness is not determined by external factors, such as others' opinions or accomplishments, but rather by my own inner qualities and values. As I continue to let go of jealousy and insecurities, I create space for positivity, abundance, and joy in my life. I am embracing my own unique path and trusting that I have everything within me to achieve my goals and live a fulfilling life. I celebrate and support others' achievements rather than feeling threatened. I am choosing to approach life with a growth mindset, seeing challenges and obstacles as opportunities for learning. Each day, I will no longer hold myself back from my greatness, but instead I will step into my power and create the life I desire.

# Celebrate Your Journey

**I am now celebrating my journey, every step of the way, knowing that the sum of all its parts makes it uniquely mine.**

I honor and embrace every experience, whether it brought me joy or challenged me to grow. I am grateful for every moment, every setback, every triumph that has led me to where I am today. I let go of the need to compare my journey to the journeys of others, understanding that it's not a competition but a personal path. I appreciate the beauty of my own journey, with all its twists and turns, and I trust that it's leading me exactly where I need to be. Challenges empower me, and I embrace them as valuable lessons to be learned. Obstacles are a natural part of life, and they ultimately help me become a stronger, more resilient person. I celebrate the good times and allow myself to bask in the joy and positivity they bring. I acknowledge and appreciate the hard work and dedication that I've put in to get to where I am today. I recognize that every milestone, no matter how small, is a cause for celebration. Above all, I celebrate my journey by living in the present moment and enjoying the ride. I trust that the Universe has a plan for me, and I let go of the need to control every aspect of my journey. Every day, I will embrace the unknown, knowing that it's all part of the adventure.

# Trust Your Instincts about Other People

**I am learning that when someone tells me who they are, I do not simply have to believe them.**

It is important to trust my instincts and not dismiss red flags and warning signs. I do not hold grudges or cut people out of my life at the first sign of trouble, but rather I evaluate their meaning in my life. I pay attention to patterns of behavior and listen to my intuition. If someone consistently shows me that they are untrustworthy or toxic, I make the conscious decision to distance myself from them and prioritize my own well-being. By recognizing and accepting someone's behavior for what it is, I make informed decisions about how to interact with them. In the past, I may have made excuses for someone's behavior or given them the benefit of the doubt, but now I know to set boundaries and protect myself from potential harm. I believe in people's actions, not their words, so that I can make better decisions about who to let into my life. When I trust my own judgment and listen to my intuition, I create healthier and more fulfilling relationships with those around me. Whether it's in my personal or professional life, I am empowered to make choices that serve my best interests and help me to thrive. I will continue to trust my inner voice and not take the words of others at face value.

# Understand Your Calling Through Your Passions

*I am passionate about my calling because it fuels me and gives me the motivation to wake up every day and work toward my goals.*

---

Knowing that I am on the right path and doing what I am meant to do brings me a sense of fulfillment and joy. I believe that everyone has a unique purpose, and it's up to me to discover mine and pursue it with dedication and enthusiasm. I am dedicated to making a meaningful impact on the world and leaving a positive legacy. When I am aligned with my calling and purpose, everything falls into place. I am able to overcome obstacles and setbacks with resilience because I know that I am working toward something greater than myself. I also recognize that my purpose may evolve and change over time, and that's okay. As I continue to grow and learn, I remain open and receptive to new opportunities that align with my passion and purpose. Every day that I am passionate about my calling and purpose, I will receive a sense of purpose and fulfillment, and I will continue striving toward my goals with enthusiasm and dedication.

# Release the Shackles of Overthinking and Find Peace

**I am learning to release the hold that overthinking has on me.**

I recognize that overanalyzing only leads to confusion and anxiety, and it does not serve my highest good. Instead, I focus on the present moment and trust that everything will work out in due time. I acknowledge that overthinking is fueled by fear and self-doubt, and I am working to combat those feelings by building my confidence and trusting my intuition. I let go of the need for control and allow life to unfold as it is meant to. Through mindfulness practices, such as meditation and deep breathing, I am training my mind to stay present. I am also practicing self-compassion and reminding myself that it is okay to make mistakes and that I do not have all the answers. This process of releasing overthinking requires a willingness to let go of old patterns and beliefs that may be holding me back. My journey requires me to trust in myself and the Universe and know that everything will work out for my highest good. As I continue to release the shackles of overthinking, I am finding more peace and clarity in my life. I will be able to make decisions more confidently and trust in the journey ahead.

# DAY 363

# Break Free from the Belief of Being a Burden

*I am not a burden but a blessing. I am worthy of love, acceptance, and support, and I do not need to apologize for who I am or what I need.*

I recognize my value and the unique contributions I bring to the world. It's essential to acknowledge that everyone has their own strengths and weaknesses, and it's okay to ask for help when I am struggling. I am not weak for seeking support; it takes courage and vulnerability to admit when I need assistance. I will never let anyone make me feel ashamed or guilty for asking for help. I surround myself with people who see me as a blessing and appreciate the positive impact I have on their lives. I am mindful of my energy and make sure to focus on relationships that uplift, inspire, and encourage me to be my best self. Practicing self-compassion is crucial in embracing my value. I need to treat myself with kindness and understanding, acknowledging that I am not perfect and that is perfectly okay. When I am gentle with myself and take care of my needs, I can develop a sense of self-love and genuine appreciation for who I am. I know that I have a purpose in this world, and my special talents and abilities make me an asset, not a liability. Each day, I will continue to be proud of who I am and the person I am becoming.

# Find Satisfaction in the Now

### I am the creator of my own satisfaction and contentment in life.

In the present moment, I find immense joy and fulfillment by appreciating what I have and the experiences I am currently living. I embrace the present with open arms, cherishing the relationships, activities, and moments that bring me happiness and fulfillment, and I also maintain an optimistic outlook toward the future. I am eager to explore new possibilities, set ambitious goals, and pursue my dreams. I am confident in my ability to shape my own destiny and create a future that aligns with my aspirations. Being satisfied with my current life does not mean settling or becoming stagnant, but it serves as a foundation for growth and progress. I strive for personal and professional development, knowing that there are endless opportunities for learning, expansion, and self-improvement. Every day, I will be grateful for what I have achieved, but I will also be driven by a sense of purpose and the anticipation of what lies ahead. This mindset will allow me to find fulfillment, gratitude, and excitement in both the present and the future, creating a truly enriching and meaningful life journey.

# Create the Blueprints of an Ideal Life

*I am the designer of my destiny and can use the blueprints of my ideal future to build a great life.*

I have the power to create the life I want to live. I am the architect of my future, and I am capable of building a new one if I am not happy with my current path. I believe that the life I want is possible, and I am committed to changing the blueprints of my destiny until I find the future I want. I am willing to learn from my mistakes, grow, and evolve. I decorate my life with vibrant colors, and I am filled with joy, happiness, and abundance. I am empowered to design my life and make choices that align with my values and goals. I am confident in my ability to create the life I want to live, and I am determined to succeed. I have everything within me to deal with whatever the world throws at me, and I know the Universe approves of all the drafts of my future life. I am focused on my goals, and I do not let the opinions of others alter my plans. I understand that my destiny is not determined by external factors but by my own actions and decisions as well as my connection to the Universe. I will continue to be in control of my life, and I will choose to create a bright future for myself.

# Index